D0041188

THE WORST OF TIMES

PATRICIA G. MILLER

HarperPerennial
A Division of HarperCollinsPublishers

First HarperPerennial edition published 1994.

Designed by Alma Hochhauser Orenstein

The Library of Congress has catalogued the hardcover edition as follows:

Miller, Patricia G., 1933–
    The worst of times / Patricia G. Miller. — 1st ed.
      p.   cm.
    "Aaron Asher books."
    ISBN 0–06–019034–5 (cloth)
    1. Abortion—United States—Case studies. 2. Abortion—Moral and ethical aspects. I. Title.
HQ767.5.U5M54   1993

363.4'6'0722—dc20   92–53351
ISBN 0-06-099512-2 (pbk.)

94 95 96 97 98 ❖/CW 10 9 8 7 6 5 4 3 2 1

To MARY DAVIES
and all our other daughters, sisters, and mothers
who didn't survive the worst of times

CONTENTS

AUTHOR'S NOTE

Names and identifying details have been changed to protect the privacy of the individuals whose stories are told in this book. Real names are used when accounts have already been disclosed in public records, and for District Attorney Colville, an elected public official.

PREFACE TO THE PAPERBACK EDITION

When I wrote this book, *Roe v. Wade* was under siege. The Supreme Court, in its *Webster* and *Casey* decisions, had countenanced restrictions on women's right to seek an abortion. Chief Justice Rehnquist and Justices White, Scalia, and Thomas had announced their belief that *Roe* should be overturned, a prospect that seemed imminent if Justice Blackmun, eighty-three years old and a staunch defender of *Roe*, should decide to step down.

Since then, legal abortion has won an apparent reprieve. In early 1993, following President Clinton's election, it was not Justice Blackmun who announced his resignation but Justice White, one of the original *Roe* dissenters and an avowed advocate of its reversal. His replacement, Ruth Bader Ginsberg, has left no doubt that she believes women have a constitutionally protected right to abortion, though she thinks it is more properly grounded in the constitutional guarantee of equal protection than in the right-to-privacy rationale of the *Roe* ruling.

Justice Ginsberg's appointment to the Court suggests that the immediate danger of an outright reversal of *Roe* has abated, if not vanished. However, the "undue burden" test enunciated in the *Casey* decision remains to be fleshed out—a fertile field of endeavor for abortion foes. Such obstacles as twenty-four-hour waiting periods may not be considered undue burdens by abortion foes or by the courts, but they can have a severe effect on the availability of abortion—for example, to a poor woman from a rural area who is forced to travel to a distant location and make two trips if she cannot afford to stay overnight.

The fundamental right enshrined in *Roe* may also be of little practical benefit to American women if abortion providers continue to be harassed, intimidated, and even murdered in retaliation for their commitment to choice—that is, if abortions are legal but effectively unavailable because there is no one to perform them.

In August 1993, Dr. George Tiller was wounded in both arms outside his Women's Health Care Services clinic in Wichita, Kansas, a city previously targeted by Operation Rescue. Several months earlier, in March, Dr. David Gunn, a forty-seven-year-old gynecologist, was shot in the back by a protester outside an abortion clinic in Pensacola, Florida. When Dr. Gunn first began doing abortions—not because he wanted to but because every other doctor in the area was too frightened to perform a service he believed women were entitled to—he spent one day a week at it. By the time of his death, he was driving a thousand miles a week to six different abortion clinics because his colleagues were not willing to expose themselves to the intimidating tactics employed by some opponents of abortion, including death threats and stalking, not only of the doctors themselves but sometimes of their families as well.

The impact of anti-abortion harassment on the medical profession is also reflected in other ways. In response to pressure from certain segments of their communities, more and more teaching hospitals have abandoned abortion training. Over the last decade, the number of medical residency programs that require abortion training has dropped by 50 percent. The National Abortion Federation reports that 38 percent of all obstetrics-gynecology residencies do not currently offer any abortion training and only 12 percent require it. Because young doctors are not learning abortion techniques, the average age of doctors performing abortions is now about sixty. These older doctors are the very ones who witnessed firsthand,

and still remember, the horrors of the pre-*Roe* days. Their younger counterparts, who never saw the abortion wards and the mangled women, often display the same naiveté as many post-*Roe* policymakers.

The scarcity of doctors trained to perform abortions has an easily measured and ominous impact on the quality and accessibility of abortion care: in 1988, 83 percent of counties in the United States had no abortion providers, and that number is unlikely to have decreased in the intervening years. For women in those counties, the dishwasher or a well-meaning friend may be the only real alternative.

In the year since *The Worst of Times* was first published, on the twentieth anniversary of *Roe v. Wade,* I have spoken with a great many people about the topic of abortion. Some told me of their firsthand experiences with abortion, and many of their stories, like those of the people I interviewed for this book, were heart-wrenching: the old woman whose mother died after an illegal abortion in 1936; the woman whose sister had an illegal abortion in 1952 and bled to death; the many retired doctors who described the septic abortion wards in their hospitals before 1973.

Other people told me about their awareness of what abortion was like in the pre-*Roe* days, and in this group, not surprisingly, I noticed a pronounced age-based difference. Those under forty, and particularly under thirty-five, typically made such comments as, "Motorcycle mechanics! I had no idea!" When I asked them what they thought the term "back-alley abortion" meant, they said that if they thought about it at all, they assumed that illegal abortions were done by dedicated and highly skilled physicians, in medically appropriate facilities with antibiotics and suction machines, but that these facilities might be located in a back alley or back room. Dishwashers, dairy farmers, attics, basements, and the back seats of cars were new and upsetting bits of knowledge for them.

Perhaps most important to me were the people who spoke of the effect my book had on their attitudes toward abortion.

The most memorable was a well-educated man in his fifties, a practicing Catholic, former altar boy, and product of a Catholic education. He said that he had always believed abortion to be morally reprehensible, a practice engaged in only by shallow, desperate women who lacked any kind of moral training. Although he was aware that other, seemingly moral people felt differently, he did not know why they felt as they did, and he didn't even wonder. Nor did he have any interest in hearing about anyone's personal experiences with abortion. Nonetheless, he read *The Worst of Times*, and his conclusion was that he would never again have the arrogance to tell a pregnant woman that he knew better than she what was best or right for her. He too said, "I never knew," but for him it had a deeper meaning: "I never understood. Now I do, and the abortion debate is forever changed for me," he told me.

I have learned as much from my readers as I have from the people who related their experiences to me while I was researching *The Worst of Times*. Thank you—all of you. We must use this collective knowledge to forge a better and more tolerant world, and to insure that our daughters and granddaughters never experience the worst of times.

ACKNOWLEDGMENTS

D URING THE TWO YEARS I SPENT writing this book, it became my all-consuming passion. In my enthusiasm, I assumed that everyone around me shared my passion for the topic and the task. Thus, I unhesitatingly asked for help whenever and wherever I needed it.

I am indebted to Mary Litman, Dr. Tom Allen, Commander Gwen Elliott, retired police chief William Moore, and Claire Capristo for helping me to gain access to interviewees who might otherwise have been unavailable. Dr. Bill Robinson graciously reviewed the medical portions of the manuscript for accuracy, although any remaining errors are my own. Margie Peterson in Pottsville, Pennsylvania, whom I have never met, responded to my request for help in locating newspaper stories about the death of Mary Davies and Dr. Spencer's trial. Librarians Maggie Moffett and Louise Weimer got me obsure books, microfilms of newspapers, and most important, the answer to any question I ever asked—such as whether abortion was legal in Cuba in 1958 and what Dr. Spencer's Lubeck's paste might have been all about.

I want to thank my two researchers, Ellen Godkins and John Miller, who always seemed to put my urgent demands for priority treatment at the top of their own busy agendas. My secretary, Pat Anderson, who thinks I am a lousy typist, was unfailingly helpful in many ways during the two years of my great obsession. I am indebted to Carol McCarthy for taking time out from her busy law practice to drive me to Ashland, Pennsylvania, because she knows I don't like highway driving, and to Don Friend not only for the computer on which I wrote the book, but even more for being instantly accessible every time I was unable to figure out some computer-related task. I am sure that my urgent telephone calls came at inconvient times.

I am deeply indebted to James C. Mohr, whose 1977 landmark book *Abortion in America* was my primary source for the history of U.S. abortion policies from 1800 to 1900.

I am particularly indebted to three people: Mary Ellen Tunney and Joseph Michenfelder, who believed in me and in the book before it was a book, and who helped guide me through what was to me the unknown and mysterious world of literary agents and publishers; and my former husband, Richard Miller, a journalist who spent hundreds of hours over a two-year period editing the manuscript and giving me the benefit of his critical review.

But it is a long trip from manuscript to book, and the support of loyal friends, while invaluable, is not enough for that journey. The skillful guidance and gifted editing of my literary agent, Sydelle Kramer, and my editor, Joy Johannessen, were indispensable. Thank you for your confidence, your criticisms, and your patience. Every author should be so blessed.

First and last, of course, I thank all the people who allowed me to interview them. For some, it was uncomfortable and even frightening. Those were painful times to remember, but without your willingness to let me intrude on your lives, and in many cases to ask the most personal and probing questions, this book would not have been possible. Thank you for helping to shed light on times that must not be forgotten.

THE WORST
OF TIMES

INTRODUCTION

L EGAL ABORTION IS UNDER THREAT. As a nation, we are being asked to deny women the fundamental right to control their own bodies. We are being asked to reformulate a major policy that has broad social consequences. We are being asked to return to a time when women got abortions from motorcycle mechanics and dishwashers.

The purpose of this book is to convey what life was like for women in this country in the days before *Roe v. Wade*—to remind Americans old enough to remember, and to explain to the many more young enough never to have known.

There has been a major change in the composition of the American public in the twenty years since *Roe v. Wade* became the law of the land. Before *Roe*, only a fraction of American women had had any firsthand experience with legal abortion, because abortion was permitted only under highly restrictive conditions, if at all. However, millions of women had had direct experience with illegal abortion. Dr. Kinsey found that in 1955, when abortion was almost entirely illegal, almost one in four American women had had an abortion by the time she was forty-five. By 1992, nineteen years after *Roe*, more than twenty-four million American women had had legal abortions, in their own country and often in their own hometowns. An even greater number of women have come of age, in a biological sense, since 1973. For the most part, they have no knowledge of what abortion was like when it was against the law.

Many of today's legislators and policymakers were not old enough to hold office or perhaps even to vote in the years before *Roe*. When these newcomers formulate abortion policy, they often have no idea what abortion was like in the United States before 1973. How many of them know the barbaric and dangerous techniques of the abortion underground? How many know about the untold millions of women who terminated their pregnancies by whatever means available for reasons known only to them? How many know about the sheer numbers of women who died from illegal abortions? How many know anything at all about the public health consequences of recriminalizing abortion? Indeed, how many understand that the real public policy question is not *whether* we will have abortions but *what kind* of abortions we will have.

If it is true, as George Santayana wrote, that "those who cannot remember the past are condemned to repeat it," policymakers would do well to learn something of this part of our history, of the time when abortion in America was driven underground. Who got abortions? Why? Who did the abortions? How did women go about finding abortionists? What abortion techniques were used? What were the medical risks? The legal risks?

My first task when I began this book was to find the people who could answer these questions. I started by thinking about who had actually participated in or observed underground abortions. Several "groups" quickly became apparent: women who had abortions; "orphans" (children whose mothers died from the consequences of illegal abortions); observers, medical or otherwise; and abortionists themselves.

Initially, I placed ads in newspapers and newsletters seeking interviews with such people. The ads produced many responses from women who had had illegal abortions, a few from doctors and orphans, and one from an abortionist. After I had interviewed a substantial number of subjects, word of mouth began to lead me to others like Clifford, Dr. Edith, Jane, and Estelle. Then I simply contacted retired doctors, more or less randomly, and inquired about their abortion-related observations and experiences during their medical training and after. I tracked down police officers and other observers from old court records and newspaper accounts. Inquiries among retired police officers helped me to find others.

The abortionists were much more difficult to locate, and often much less willing to talk to me. Sometimes the women remembered their abortionists or gave me information that helped me to identify them. Others were identified by the policemen who arrested them, or from old news stories and arrest records. Occasionally, through simple luck, I got a phone call about someone who used to do illegal abortions and would agree to an interview. In those cases, it might be only a few days from discovery to interview. More often it took me months to locate the abortionists, and more months to convince them to talk to me.

Altogether I interviewed about fifty people, mainly from the Pittsburgh area, and pored over countless pages of microfilm in a process that took almost two years. The interviews with Barry Graham Page, Helene, Detective Jack, and Marilyn were conducted by telephone because they lived so far away that it was not practical to visit them, or because they were otherwise physically inaccessible. All the other interviews were face to face and tape-recorded, usually in the subject's home. Some of the orphans showed me pictures of their mothers. Some of the women took me to the neighborhoods where they had their illegal abortions. I went to Ashland, Pennsylvania, to see the town and the people who remembered Dr. Spencer. His widow showed me the now vacant building that had been his office.

With the exception of the opening testimony from Coroner Fred, the interviews are arranged in rough chronological order—necessarily rough because many of the subjects' experiences and memories span decades. All their stories are told in their own voices, except for my accounts of Dr. Spencer and his trial; Campbell, Ensor, and Lang; and the trial of Barry Graham Page. Though my interviewees are in no sense a scientific, statistically representative sample, it is instructive to look at some of the similarities and differences among the individuals in each group.

THE WOMEN

The women whose stories follow are among the thousands upon thousands of American women who had illegal abortions and survived. They are not celebrities but ordinary people leading ordinary, otherwise law-abiding lives. They are not unlike the "typical women" Dr. Kinsey wrote about in 1955. Their experiences with illegal abortion cover a period of some thirty years, from 1939 to 1970. Bridging the generations, one woman describes her own 1963 underground abortion and her daughter's quite different legal abortion in 1991.

There are many differences among these women. One of them had to leave the country to get an abortion; others were able to obtain help right in their own neighborhoods. Some were teenagers; others were approaching menopause. Some were married; more were not. A few had emotional or financial support from their families; more did not. One of the major differences involves the medical qualifications of their abortionists. A few found medical doctors willing to treat them; most found abortionists with no real medical training to speak of.

Although it is not as evident in the women's stories as in the interviews with the abortionists themselves, there was an apparent difference between black women and white women in terms of access to information about abortion, especially in racially segregated communities. In black communities, information appears to have been more openly available. A black woman might talk to her neighbor, her sister, or her friend, and find out about established practitioners right there in the community, prepared to meet the needs of the people.

White women had no comparable system, and often no idea how to go about getting abortion information. Their women friends were likely to produce the response Janet received: no one knew anything. As far as many white women were concerned, they were the first in their families, their circle of friends, their entire universe, to be unwillingly pregnant and to seek an abortion. For them, there was no one to ask except total strangers—cab drivers, salesmen, bartenders. But even though black women may have had better information networks, that is not to say that they received better care. Black or white, women were turning to the same unqualified people. Black women were simply having an easier time locating them.

The similarities among the women who speak here are more striking than the differences, especially considering their diversity in age, race, religion, and class. A number of them had been taught that abortion was morally wrong, but that appears not to have mattered when they were confronted with what they considered impossible pregnancies. Indeed, for most of them, there wasn't even a conflict, a moral dilemma to be wrestled with. Their lack of ambivalence is striking.

Also striking is that none of them, regardless of the attendant circumstances, seems to have been deterred in the slightest by the inadequate or wholly lacking qualifications of their abortionists. Virtually all of these women were dealing with people they didn't know, and most of them recall being terrified, but they didn't even inquire about the background of the stranger who was about to perform a medical procedure on their bodies. Why? Because it simply was not relevant to their decisions, there being no better-qualified people available.

Almost as if they were part of a giant choral group reading from the same sheet music, most of the women had heard of and tried the same folk remedies for causing abortions. Before giving up and seeking the help of a third party, almost all resorted to one or more of such popular home remedies as violent exercise, hot baths, quinine, and ergot. And later, since the catheter was clearly the method of choice for illegal abortionists, infection appears to have been a constant companion for most of the women. Further, the high incidence of infection seems to have had little correlation to the competence of the operator, perhaps because the abortionist's skill was more than offset by the clandestine and furtive medical conditions.

Another similarity is the women's lack of access to birth

control. For some, like Estelle, there truly was no birth control to be had. Others may have had opportunities to obtain it, but they simply could not overcome the psychological and societal barriers that said, "Nice girls do not have sex when they are not married, so they have no need for birth control." That indoctrination made it almost impossible for an unmarried woman to consult a doctor about birth control. The few who did were turned away precisely because they were unmarried.

Perhaps the most striking similarity of all is the nearly universal sense of isolation these women describe as they had their underground abortions in frightening and inappropriate places, at the hands of strangers with unknown qualifications. Every woman was alone and terrified, but determined to do whatever was necessary to terminate her pregnancy.

If so many women were having illegal abortions, how could that sense of isolation have been so pervasive? It is the price of silence, of things hidden. This was abortion underground.

THE ORPHANS

It is impossible to understand "the worst of times" fully without looking at another group of people who were profoundly affected by the abortion policies of the underground period—the orphans who lost their mothers to illegal abortions.

The people who tell their stories here were children when this traumatic event occurred in their lives. The oldest was twelve; the youngest, four. Their experiences differ widely in terms of the year their mothers died, their ages at the time, the character of their fathers, the presence or absence of other supportive and nurturing caregivers. The one characteristic they all share, unlike most of the other people in this book, is the raw pain they still feel. When interviewed, each seemed to experience the loss again, as if it had happened the previous week. The anguish had not abated with time, even though decades had gone by—in one case, more than sixty years.

Some of these orphans have led relatively happy and productive lives. Others experienced an impairment that lasted into adulthood. Clearly, for all of them, their mother's death was a searing loss with incalculable consequences.

THE DOCTOR-OBSERVERS

Women who had underground abortions had a sense of aloneness, of something hidden. The orphans had that same experience of something hidden. Indeed, they didn't even know until much later that underground abortions had killed their mothers. This secrecy—even among the people whose lives were most directly touched by illegal abortion—helped make it possible for society to ignore what anti-abortion laws were doing to American women.

But there is one group that had a unique opportunity to observe the magnitude and the horrors of illegal abortion—doctors. Not those unusual doctors who broke the law and did abortions, but the far greater number who, by virtue of their profession, had abundant opportunities to observe the medical consequences of illegal abortion. Those who practiced medicine before the advent of antibiotics tended to see the severest consequences. However, Dr. Francis, who spent one wrenching year at D.C. General Hospital in 1968 and was the most recent graduate among the doctor-observers I interviewed, may have seen the largest number of critically ill women, in spite of sophisticated antibiotic therapy and better emergency medical care.

In hindsight, the doctors were as strangely silent as the women and the orphans. They were viewing an enormous public health problem—wards filled with desperately ill women whose names and faces changed, but whose medical histories were identical from one hospital to another and one decade to another—yet they accepted the problem as "inevitable," despite some alarm at its extent and severity. The doctors I spoke with seemed almost startled as they looked back and reflected on the sheer volume of septic abortion patients and the attitude of the medical community as a whole: "That's how things are. It is just a fact of life."

Some of their stories are funny. Most are painful. All said they were shocked and dismayed when they first encountered the medical consequences of illegal abortion. No matter when they went to medical school or what training they received, they were not adequately prepared for what they saw and uniformly described it as both "tragic" and "unnecessary."

Most important, perhaps, is what the doctor-observers didn't see—and when. After January 1973, the septic abortion wards and the hospital abortion committees simply disappeared. After that date, doctors no longer saw the sick and dying women they had become accustomed to treating in earlier years.

These doctors all had the training and ability to perform abortions—and vastly safer ones than their mangled patients were receiving. Several of them had the uncomfortable experience of having their own desperate patients ask or even beg them for help. Yet they said no. Why?

It is important that we understand why doctors are unwilling to perform abortions when it is illegal to do so. No matter how strongly they are committed to choice—and the doctors in this book all are—a jail term or loss of license is simply a greater price than they are prepared to pay. And why should they? As women look to doctors to make sure that abortion is safe, doctors are entitled to expect women to fight to keep it legal.

POLICE AND OTHER OBSERVERS

Members of the medical community are not the only observers who have something to tell us about illegal abortion in America. Any widespread illegal activity inevitably involves many police officers. They can tell us about the medical qualifications of the people they arrested, as well as how they went about finding them, given the women's usual reluctance or inability to reveal the identity of their underground abortionists. They can tell us how important a police priority abortion was compared with other crimes, and what triggered police involvement. Sometimes it was a dead woman, but sometimes it was just politics.

Illegal activity also tends to lead to the involvement of lawyers specializing in criminal law. Depending on who hired them, they saw underground abortion from a different perspective. So, too—grimly so—did coroners.

Not because of his occupation but because of his advanced age, Clifford, who was born in the last century, remembers the herb peddlers with their guaranteed cure-alls for a host of human conditions, including unwanted pregnancy. He tells us about bluing and other abortion home remedies in the rural South of his childhood, and about some illegal abortionists who operated in Pittsburgh in the twenties, thirties, and forties.

A district attorney gives us his memories of arresting illegal abortionists in the sixties, when he was a young police officer, as well as the memories of his father and friends who were on the force in the forties and fifties. He discusses the changing role of police in the control of underground abortion as police departments became more professional and less political.

We should heed what we learn from all these observers, since the events and conditions they describe will in all probability be with us again if abortion is recriminalized.

THE ABORTIONISTS

The former abortionists in this book are as varied as the women who once used their services. They are now gray-haired grandparents with ordinary lives and ordinary problems, though almost all of them had at least one brush with the law. Many have children and grandchildren who know nothing about their pasts, which are safely hidden and never discussed. Though their days as abortionists seem remote, they, no less than the women and the orphans, have vivid memories of what abortion was like twenty-five or thirty years ago.

I have included the stories of several abortionists who are now dead. In those cases, I consulted newspaper stories and trial transcripts, and interviewed people who knew them in some capacity. Not surprisingly, the interviewees' relationship to the abortionist—spouse, neighbor, arresting officer—greatly influenced their perceptions of the abortionist's skills and motivations.

Dr. Spencer, Barry Graham Page, and Campbell, Ensor, and Lang appear under their real names because they all had trials and were publicly identified as abortionists—and in Dr. Spencer's case, because he made no secret of his willingness to perform abortions. Otherwise, as with the other interviewees, the names and identifying data of the abortionists have been changed to protect their privacy.

The abortionists whose stories follow are black and white, male and female. However, those who were doctors are all male—probably a reflection of the larger medical community. Most of the female abortionists appear to have had no occupation other than as abortionists. The male non-doctor abortionists, on the other hand, all had regular occupations—dairy farmer, motorcycle mechanic—and did abortions on the side, as a source of extra income. Although illegal abortion is reported to have been the third-largest moneymaker for organized crime, none of these abortionists were connected to organized crime. Except for their abortion activities, most seem to have been law-abiding citizens.

There is a marked difference in their skill levels. Some were competent, well-respected physicians. Some were in related medical fields like nursing. Others had no formal medical training of any kind. Individually, they performed anywhere from two or three to one hundred thousand abortions. Ironically, the only known fatalities reported here involved abortions done by doctors, which is not what we might expect to find in a larger, statistically significant sample.

Some of the lay abortionists routinely used antibiotics, while the doctors, for the most part, did not. The physical environments where they performed abortions varied from a multiroom clinic to the back seat of a car. Most used a catheter or similar foreign object and then sent the women away to abort elsewhere, hours or days later. Most kept their abortion activities clandestine.

Many of these abortionists appear to have been motivated by a desire to help desperate women. Others candidly admit that they did it for the money. Perhaps, for most, the motives were mixed. The money was good and tax-free, at least for the non-doctor abortionists.

I found the abortionists I interviewed surprisingly likable as they earnestly described their experiences in the underground. Like the women who sought them out, these people became involved in underground abortion out of necessity—sometimes their own, but more often that of people around them. Just as the doctor-observers help us understand why doctors won't do abortions if it means breaking the law, the abortionists help us understand why ordinary people will do abortions illegally. Those I spoke with all expressed the belief that they were meeting a need, but that it is much better to have abortions done legally by doctors under safe medical conditions. None longed for a return to the old days.

The people you will meet in the pages that follow shed a bright, painful light on a period in our history that for American women was truly "the worst of times." As we have seen, they are not politicians, policymakers, or legal scholars. They are ordinary people, black and white, blue-collar and white-collar, rich and poor. Their stories do not directly address the political and legal issues that comprise the abortion debate today. They simply talk about how they experienced abortion before it was legalized.

By looking at our past, perhaps we can more wisely choose our future. But we must look at that past unflinchingly. We cannot pretend it didn't happen. We must understand what illegal abortion means to the women of this country and to our national soul.

CORONER FRED

I WORKED AT A HOSPITAL in a large Pennsylvania city from the middle fifties until 1966. I was an autopsy technician, or a "diener," as we were called. I'm a funeral director by trade, but I was also deputy assistant chief coroner in that same metropolitan area.

In the coroner's office we would see three or four deaths a year from illegal abortions. I know that very few of the abortionists were ever arrested. Generally they were only arrested if someone died. When we discovered that a woman had died from an illegal abortion, we notified the police. Now, what they did about it I don't really know. I think they tried to find out who had done it, but we were never in on the follow-up, so I really don't know. I don't recall any big hue and cry in the newspapers when a woman died from an abortion. There might be a story, but it was just a fact of life. These things happened.

The dead women we saw had either bled to death or they had died from overwhelming infections. Some had tears along the vaginal tract where they had used coat hangers to get up into the uterus and break things up—like rupture the amniotic sac.

Mostly, of course, I only saw the women after they were dead, but once I saw someone before she died. That was in the early sixties. It was a woman who worked in the hospital lab with me. She was a very nice person. I don't know anything about her personal situation or why she wanted an abortion, but she had one, and she bled and bled. I remember she called in sick and told us that she had a bad cold. Finally she did come to the hospital, but it was really too late. She died just a few hours after she came in.

Probably the death rate wouldn't have been as high if people had come to the hospital earlier, but the way it was, with the shame and the secrecy, they tended to stay at home as long as they could—sometimes too long, as it turned out.

In the coroner's office or at the hospital, the death certificate always listed abortion as the cause of death. I think you got a diagnosis like tetanus, uremia, or pelvic infection—something other than abortion—from private doctors where no autopsy was done and the coroner was not involved. Now, if there were three or four a year that I knew about because there was an autopsy, you can be sure that there were three times that number that no one knew about—and that is just in one county in Pennsylvania. But those were only the women who died. The number of abortions was much greater than that because it included everyone who didn't die and everyone who died being cared for by a private doctor who put something other than abortion on the death certificate. We just saw a few—the tip of the iceberg, you could call it.

Most of the dead women I saw were in their teens or twenties. I don't recall too many older than that. I don't know if they got smarter as they got older or they found better abortionists or what.

The deaths stopped overnight in 1973, and I never saw another abortion death in all the eighteen years after that until I retired. That ought to tell people something about keeping abortion legal.

ELEANOR

I WAS BORN IN 1920. My family set great store by education and had great hopes and expectations for me. I was the baby of the family. In 1939 I was eighteen years old. I had just graduated from high school but had not yet gone on to college. I fell in love with a very dashing, totally inappropriate "older" man (twenty-four, as I remember it). It was my first sexual experience, and I promptly got pregnant. You know, I never really understood that. I had an older sister who could never have children. I never knew why. But with me, all I had to do was think about it and I got pregnant.

When I realized I was pregnant, I knew immediately that I wanted an abortion. I knew even less about how to find an abortionist than I knew about birth control. However, my gentleman friend, who had been married before and had connections with people who would know things like that, was able to find someone. His former wife came from Pittsburgh's Northside. That was a tightly knit blue-collar, low-income, hardworking, but poorly educated community. There was a saying, and I think it is true, that on Pittsburgh's Northside in the late thirties you could "find anyone to do anything."

I think he got the name from his first wife. All I ever knew about the abortionist was her first name. I suppose no one ever used last names in that business. This woman was somewhere on James or Foreland Streets on the Northside. My friend made the appointment. We went on a Saturday. I was living at home and working, so I could only do this on a Saturday. We went to the woman's home. A friend of his—a man—drove us there. I don't know if he knew what we were doing, or if he did, whether he cared. We just went up and knocked on the door. She was very nice. She was expecting us. Her husband was there. I don't know if he knew or cared what we were doing. No one mentioned it, and I was too frightened to care what he might have thought.

She took me into her bathroom. It was neat and clean, but it was just an ordinary bathroom in an ordinary row house on the Northside. She talked to me for a few minutes, no more than five or ten. She asked me a few basic health questions—did I have diabetes, when was my last period, how old was I?—and then she told me to remove my underpants and squat down. She filled the sink with water and added some Lysol. She washed her hands in this and dipped a long rubber tubing, which I later learned was called a catheter, into the same sink water.

I was terrified. I had never seen this woman before. I had heard horror stories about back-alley abortions, and I really had no idea what to expect. If she had brought out a knife, it would not have surprised me. I knew absolutely nothing about her qualifications to be doing this, and I didn't care. I was only grateful that she was going to help me and that she was kind.

I could never have gone to my mother. It isn't that she was anti-abortion. She wasn't. She very much admired Margaret Sanger. But in the late thirties young ladies simply did not have sex—and they particularly did not have sex if they were going to the seminary.

Let me tell you what my abortion cost. You will probably think it's funny, but in 1939 it was a great deal of money: thirty-five dollars.

But back to the procedure. I squatted down, and she inserted this red tubing into my vagina. I don't know how she knew it was going where it was supposed to go, because it all happened so fast. She inserted it, handed me a pad and a belt, and told me to keep the catheter in until "something happened." That was not easy to do, because every time I urinated I almost lost the catheter, or at least I thought I almost lost it. I suppose my knowledge of anatomy was not much better than my knowledge of birth control. She told me something would happen within twenty-four hours.

My gentleman friend and I left. I couldn't go home, so we went to a cheap hotel on the Northside and waited for something to happen. Nothing did. When it got to be dinnertime, I had to go home because my parents were expecting me. That night I felt really sick. I had a blinding headache. I've never had anything like it before or since. It was excruciating—far more painful than the actual abortion. My mother asked what was wrong. I said I had no idea. I really thought it was the beginning of an infection. She called the family doctor, who came to our house to see me. Now, remember, I still have the catheter in place and nothing has happened. He examined me very perfunctorily, although he did feel my belly and gave me some medicine. I have no idea what the medicine was, but antibiotics didn't exist in 1939.

Remember, I was only eighteen and I was terrified, but I had to conceal my true condition from these two people. Nothing had yet happened, and as far as I knew, I was still pregnant. I was still waiting for something to happen, and I didn't know what they might do if they knew the true facts. Could they stop it? Was this abortion thing a reversible process? Could I be arrested?

The next day, with the catheter still in place, I pretended that I felt better, because I had to get out of the house before anything began to happen. I went to my girlfriend's house because she knew what was going on. I just waited. Finally, about forty-eight hours after the catheter was inserted, I did abort. As soon as that happened, I felt psychologically fine although I was physically ill. There was a lot of bleeding and other drainage, which I think must have been due to infection.

About ten days later, I went to a doctor. This was not the

family doctor. This was someone I picked out of the phone book and had never seen before. He was pretty sure he knew what had happened, and he insisted I go to the hospital. He threatened that if I didn't go, he would tell my mother. I was certainly not going to go to a hospital, because then my mother would know for sure. Besides, I didn't know what they would do to me. Maybe they would put me in jail. I left without any medical treatment because he gave me what I considered to be a no-win choice: Don't go to the hospital and have the doctor tell my mother, or go to the hospital and have her find out anyway.

I toughed it out, and the bleeding finally stopped. I was fine. But then, I was young and healthy.

Over the years, I actually took two other women to the same woman who did my abortion, because she was good and kind and seemed competent. It is hard for people today to understand that, but in those days there wasn't such an openness about sex and pregnancy. I never forgot how desperate I was and how grateful I felt when I found someone who could help me. I wasn't going to refuse to do what I knew meant so much to another desperate woman.

In 1939 I had no real access to birth control, but nothing existed then anyway, except condoms. He used a condom. That is all we had. There weren't pills or foam or creams or any of that. He was my first sexual experience (we did get married afterward), and I really didn't know anything about anything. I never had any knowledge of or access to birth control. It wasn't until after my son was born that I went to Planned Parenthood and got birth control of my own that I could control.

This was my first experience with abortion. To my knowledge, no one in my family and none of my friends had ever had this problem. But remember, "nice girls" didn't talk about things like that, so I had no real way of knowing about anyone else. When I look back on it, I find it interesting that it was not really difficult to find someone. That suggests to me that back in 1939, although no one talked about it, a lot of women had the same problem.

I don't think the woman who did my abortion had any links

to organized crime. She was just a housewife who either needed more money or cared about women. I think she was a "loner," which is sort of ironic, because that's what most women are when they're looking for an abortion. I know I never felt so alone as when I was going through all of that.

I had a second abortion in 1962 or 1963. I was forty-two. The man I was involved with was older than I was. He was "successful." He was also married and intended to stay that way. That was fine with me, because I never intended to get married again. We began the relationship in 1962, and it lasted until he died in 1981. It was a good relationship, more loving and more long-lasting than my marriage. By 1962, I had very good access to contraception. It was very different than it had been in 1939. I had a diaphragm, and I always used it. I never forgot it and never took a chance. It only failed me once, and that led to my second abortion.

When I got pregnant in 1962 or 1963, I didn't know what to do. My friend didn't know either. Being desperate, I called a friend of my first husband's. He said he didn't know, but he promised me he would "look into it." A week after we first talked about it—a week he had presumably spent looking for contacts, while I just worried and looked for that bright red spot that could tell me my life was mine again—he called to report that he had found a doctor who would "help" me. In my naiveté, I believed that the word "help" meant to actually do the abortion. Unfortunately, in the early sixties that was not really a possibility in Pittsburgh.

I went alone. I know this is a theme I keep coming back to, but it is so characteristic of the experience of the unwillingly pregnant woman. People talk about how very commonplace abortion was and always has been, whether it was legal or not. But you see it from a very different perspective when you are the pregnant woman. You are all alone. A supportive man may provide financial or even emotional help, but it is your problem.

The doctor was a very competent, very caring, and very successful physician with an office in Pittsburgh's East End. When

I arrived at his office, I was surprised because the waiting room was very crowded, and not with pregnant women. It was filled with patients who seemed to have a variety of medical problems. He was apparently a real doctor with a real practice. There was no nurse and no receptionist. You just sat there with lots of other people and waited your turn.

When I finally got in to see the doctor, it took me a fair amount of time to get up my nerve to even mention the purpose of my visit. First he had to do a pregnancy test to see if I was even pregnant. He doubted it. I didn't.

In the thirties, they had no pregnancy tests. In the sixties, they had tests, but they weren't very reliable and seemed to take forever. In those days, a pregnancy test involved injecting the woman's urine into the ear vein of a rabbit and waiting a week or more to get the result.

He took the urine for the test and sent me home, telling me not to worry. In a week, he called and told me the test was negative and that I had nothing to worry about. I knew better because I had felt this way before, and I insisted that the test be repeated. He had me come in the next week, and we had to wait another week or more for the result. This time, of course, it was positive.

He told me to come out to the office and we would "see what can be done." He asked me a lot of questions about why I wanted an abortion. I didn't tell him the man was married, but he knew I was forty-two years old and trying to put two children through college without any help. He was not a moralist. He respected my assessment of my life, my priorities, and my decision. He said he knew someone who could help me. I was disappointed because he wasn't going to help me himself, but I said, "Great. Whatever it takes."

He told me someone would call me on a certain night. A few days later, this woman called. She named a price—five hundred dollars—and told me where she was located. We made an appointment. My friend gave me the money, but I had to go alone. Bertha was her name, and she was located in one of the little mill towns on the river outside of Pittsburgh. She said,

"Jerry asked me to call." I didn't know anything about that part of town, but she said she was on Main Street and anyone could direct me if I had trouble finding it. I wondered later whether that meant Main Street was easy to find or whether Bertha was so well known that anyone would know how to find her. I never really got the answer to that question.

My children were away at college, so this was quite unlike 1939. It wasn't going to matter if I didn't come home at night. I didn't have a car, so I didn't have that to worry about. I had had to sell it to send the boys to college. In a way, not having a car didn't matter, since I didn't know my way around anyway. I took a bus into downtown Pittsburgh and then a cab to Bertha's neighborhood.

The weather was really awful. It had been raining, and the rain had turned to sleet. By the time the cab driver got there, it was getting dark and the sleet had turned to snow. Neither of us could find Main Street. There was one dark and lonely-looking street. I'll never forget it. It was very steep—just straight down. I said, "It has to be this street. There aren't any other streets. It must be down there." Well, he just wasn't about to go down there. He kept saying, "It can't be down there, lady. There's nothing down there but the railroad tracks. I'm not going down there on a night like this. I'll never get back up." As determined as he was not to go down there, I was more determined to get to my destination. "Then just let me out here. I'll walk down," I said.

Well, then the cab driver got all chivalrous. "This is no part of town for a woman to be in alone at night. You can't walk down there!" he said. "I must get down there, and I must get down there tonight!" I insisted. I don't know if I sounded as desperate as I felt, but he seemed to realize I was determined, and he drove me down the steep, dark, and by now very icy hill. We slipped and slid, and I could hear him swearing under his breath. But we made it. We got to the bottom, and I wiped the steam off the window and peered out into the darkness. It seemed like he really was right. There was nothing there. I could see two or three small, tacky, run-down row houses, but they were all dark and looked almost abandoned. Then I saw a faint light—nothing as bright as a porch light, you understand. It was more like a dim lamp in a back bedroom. I almost wasn't sure it was really there. But I hopped out of the cab, smiling a lot more confidently than I really felt, paid the driver, and started off into the darkness. He yelled after me that he would wait so he could take me back to town.

"No. You can't do that! Go away! I'll be fine," I said, and he replied, "I'll just wait a while and make sure you're all right." Well, I couldn't let him do that! I was afraid that if I didn't come out in fifteen minutes, he would call the police. Maybe, if he didn't go away, Bertha would never answer the door—if the dim light was even Bertha.

He finally left, and I knocked at the door of the house with the dim light. A big husky man in shirtsleeves came to the door. I said, "Is Bertha here?" He muttered, "Who are you?" I told him, and he grudgingly let me into the seedy little house. I noticed that the living room had a great big crucifix over the mantel.

A woman appeared from somewhere in the back of the little house. This was Bertha and I'll tell you, she didn't do much to inspire confidence. She didn't look real. She had dyed red hair teased and sprayed to a stiff, towering beehive on her head. She had too much makeup and long bright-red fingernails. She had on a gaudy print kimono-type thing and high-heeled floppy mules, which were decorated with what looked like ostrich feathers. She clattered when she walked. I gave her the money—cash, of course. She counted it carefully and stuffed it somewhere inside the kimono.

Now, she had a real setup. She was in business and was a lot more organized than the woman in 1939. When I say she was organized, I don't mean she was part of an organization. She seemed to be a loner like the woman in 1939, but she seemed organized in the sense that I thought she had a much bigger referral system and did many more abortions than the 1939 woman. The doctor probably got a kickback of some sort from her, although I always wondered why he would do that. He seemed to be a very nice person, and very busy and successful. Every time I ever went to see him—and he became my regular gynecologist after the abortion—his waiting room was always filled with patients.

But back to Bertha. She had a room she obviously used for this. It was an ordinary, somewhat shabby bedroom. There wasn't a sterilizer, and I don't think the things she used were sterilized or boiled or anything like that. She just reached into a cupboard and took things out with her bare hands. I guess she used a catheter, but she didn't really let me see what she was doing. Maybe she wanted to keep it mysterious. Anyway, she told me to take off my underwear and lie down on the bed. She sat on a stool at the foot of the bed. She inserted something, and I felt a bad cramp. That was all. It only lasted a minute or two. I'm pretty sure she didn't leave the catheter inside. She told me she was finished but that I had to stay overnight until something happened. She asked me if I wanted some supper. I didn't, but I did go out and sit at her kitchen table and have a cup of tea.

She talked a lot, mostly about her hair-raising experiences. They sure didn't inspire much confidence, and I was glad she waited until after the abortion to tell me. She told me about a girl with collapsed veins. I don't know quite what that meant, but it sounded serious, because they rushed her to the hospital. I'm sure they didn't go in with her, but I didn't press her for details. I didn't really want anything new to worry about, in case I had to be rushed to the hospital. She told me other stories of "nearly losing a patient," usually from a hemorrhage. She told me stories of women coming in who were dirty or had diseases. Now, remember, she hadn't sterilized anything as far as I could tell. What diseases might my immediate predecessor have had? Think about it. In 1962 we wouldn't have considered doing any other surgical procedure under those conditions, even on a battlefield. When I look back on it, it is hard to imagine.

After the tea and "war stories," she told me to go to bed and that she would see me for breakfast in the morning. She gave me what we called a slop jar. She told me that if I had to get up in the night, I was to use the jar. She said, "If you get up in the night and it's dark, *don't* turn the light on! If the hall light is on, that's enough light for you to see by. If the hall light is out, it means there are police in the area and we've pulled the fuses and left so the house will look abandoned. You won't be able to turn the light on. But don't be frightened. We'll be back in the morning and give you breakfast." Now, think about that for a minute. Imagine any other surgical procedure where the "doctor" says, "I'll be back tomorrow," leaving you absolutely alone.

I went to bed hoping I wouldn't wake up in the night to find it all dark. My cramps got worse and finally I aborted. I had bleeding but no infection. Everything was fine. Bertha was skillful, and that's probably why the doctor referred me to her.

The next day the weather was clear, and I went home. It's funny, but I have no recollection about getting out of there. I was so paralyzed with fear during the pregnancy and the abortion, but when it was over, I had my life back, and nothing was scary after that. The sky was blue, and Bertha's neighborhood was nowhere near as scary and abandoned as it had seemed the night before. I took a bus home from town and stayed home from work for one day, but I was fine. I remember that Bertha called the doctor while I was there to tell him it was over and I was okay. The business relationship between them seemed close. If there had been a problem, he probably would have met me at the hospital. I don't know that. I'm guessing.

Bertha looked like a Kewpie doll. She claimed she had been a nurse, but I really doubt it. I never saw a nurse who looked or acted like that. For example, when I first went in, she threw some white pills at me and said, "These are penicillin. Take two a day." I said I couldn't because I was allergic to penicillin. She said, "You should have thought of that before!"

In my experience, these people who perform illegal abortions don't want you to know anything about themselves, particularly their "medical qualifications." But you know what? I didn't really care. I just wanted to get it over with. I didn't care who she was, what she did, or where she came from. I didn't care about her "qualifications." Bertha was maybe fifty-five. In spite of the way she lived and looked, she talked like she lived well. She told me about what seemed to me a lot of frequent and fancy vacations. I had the sense that abortion was more than "pin money" for her. It was the major income stream.

I never saw Bertha again. I never referred any women to her. But in spite of the dyed hair, floppy mules, and long finger-nails, I would have referred women to her. You know why? Because she was reasonably competent and she was kind. That counted for a lot in those days, when the Berthas of this world were all we had. It's hard for people to imagine, I suppose, but Bertha was, quite literally, the best there was.

THE DAY TRIP

*After describing her own abortion experiences, Eleanor
wanted to talk about a friend of hers.*

LET ME TELL YOU ABOUT DOLORES, because she isn't here
to tell her story, and I'm probably the only one who
knows it.

I worked with Dolores in the mid-fifties. In 1955 she was an
attractive woman, probably in her early forties. We were both
divorced, and both of us were struggling to raise our children
alone. It was not easy, and Dolores had some special burdens I
didn't have. She was solely responsible not only for her sixteen-
year-old son but also for her two elderly parents, who lived with
her. The parents were in poor health. As I remember, each of
them had some kind of cancer. They required special care, and
Dolores never—but *never*—went anywhere on the weekend,
because she was always caring for the old people or for her son.
She worked hard at her job, and it was a job with a lot of
responsibility. I kept telling her she needed to get away for a
weekend, but she always said she couldn't. Then I tried to urge
her to at least take a day trip on the weekend, but she insisted
she couldn't do that either.

She had a gentleman friend. I never met him. I think he was
older than she was. He was Jewish, I remember that. I was glad
when she met him, because I could see that she seemed happier.

One Thursday at work, she told me she was going to take a

day trip that upcoming Saturday. She was going to Ligonier with her gentleman friend. I was surprised and asked what made her change her mind about being able to get away. She tersely told me she had no choice and abruptly changed the topic.

On Sunday night I received a telephone call from Dolores's sister, who told me that Dolores was sick and would not be going to work on Monday. I asked what was wrong. "I don't know," she replied. "It has something to do with her period." Well, I was pretty sure I knew. I felt certain that the "day trip" was a trip to a Ligonier abortionist. I asked to speak to Dolores, but her sister said she was much too ill to come to the phone. In fact, the sister admitted, she was in the hospital. I asked a few more questions about what was wrong. The answers I got left me reasonably sure that the sister didn't really know about the abortion. Dolores was so responsible and hardworking that what I suspected was probably unimaginable to her family.

I hung up and wondered what to do. I knew her doctor because he went to my church. What if it never occurred to him either? But what if I was wrong? What if the day trip wasn't for an abortion? I decided to go and see Dolores in the hospital. Maybe then I would know what to do.

Dolores was in an oxygen tent and seemed to be unconscious. She was not going to be able to tell me what to do. Her parents weren't there. Her son wasn't there. The gentleman friend wasn't there. Just the sister, who didn't seem to know what was happening. The doctor had told her that there seemed to be little hope of recovery. How could this be when two days earlier she had been fine? I decided that if Dolores were to have any chance of surviving, I had to tell the doctor what I suspected. I called him repeatedly on Monday night and Tuesday morning, but he never returned my calls, even though I said it was an emergency.

Dolores died on Tuesday. She never regained consciousness, and I never knew whether the doctor or anyone else knew what had happened. I went to the funeral home because I wanted to talk to the man she had been involved with. I figured he knew what really happened and would tell me. It was too late to help Dolores, but somehow it might help someone else. You know what? He wasn't there. He didn't even show up. I don't think he even sent flowers.

Her son was there. I never knew his name because Dolores always called him Sonny. He was dazed and tearful and seemed stunned by the sudden loss of his mother. He looked much younger than his sixteen years. Her parents were there, looking old and frail and as dazed as the boy. The sister and her husband had to come and live with the parents and care for them and the boy. I don't know what ever happened to Dolores's family. I never saw them again. And I always wondered. I wondered what really happened on the "day trip." And I wondered if it would have made a difference if I had been able to talk to her doctor.

DR. EDITH

I'M EIGHTY-THREE. I graduated from medical school in 1935. I spent my first two years at the University of Wisconsin and my last two years at Cornell in New York City. There were only four women in my class of sixty.

In my senior year of medical school we had electives, and I elected to work with Margaret Sanger in the birth control clinic she had established on New York's Lower East Side. I had heard about Margaret Sanger and her clinic. I knew that she had been in jail. Of course, that had nothing to do with abortion. She went to jail over contraception because that's how it was in those days.

We had been taught nothing about contraception in medical school. No gynecology course even mentioned it. I had heard of diaphragms but knew nothing about them. Of course they weren't mentioned in medical school, but I did know Margaret Sanger was handing them out at her clinic. I thought people in the real world were probably interested in things like that and if I was going to be a "real doctor" in the "real world," I had best learn about them. Besides, as a woman doctor I would surely have women patients, and they would want to know. So I signed on at Margaret Sanger's clinic.

Working under Mrs. Sanger's supervision, I learned all about diaphragms and how to fit them. Sometimes I would actually hand them out too. I guess I was also breaking the law, but I never got into any trouble. I was only there for three months, but in that three months I learned a lot, and I am sure it affected the way I practiced medicine and related to patients after I got out of medical school.

After I graduated, I did a two-year rotating internship at Philadelphia General Hospital. Then I opened my own general practice in Philadelphia. I did that for four years. Then, in 1941, I decided to do a residency in obstetrics and gynecology at the Women's Hospital in New York City. After I completed that, I established my own private ob-gyn practice in Baltimore. During my training I had experiences with women who had had illegal abortions, but the ones I remember most vividly are the ones after I started my own ob-gyn practice.

Once, after I was established in my practice in Baltimore, I got a telephone call from the family doctor of a woman I later came to call my "pen lady." He called me and said that she had taken the metal innards out of a ballpoint pen. Then she had taken that plastic outer sleeve and inserted it into her cervix in an effort to abort herself. It was her idea that if she took out the metal parts, it would somehow be less likely to cause an infection. She was about four months pregnant, and she was determined not to have a baby.

Well, she told her doctor that she inserted this pen and then lay down to take a nap. When she woke up, she felt to see if it was there and she couldn't feel it. She decided that it had fallen out when she was asleep, so she looked under the bed and in the covers, but she couldn't find it. Her doctor didn't know what to make of this or what to do, so he sent her to me.

We first had to decide whether or not to believe her. You see, it was always a problem for a doctor to know whether or not to believe women when they told you a story like that, because they told those stories precisely to get you to do something! If they could trick you into doing a D and C, they would be getting a safe abortion. So that was always something you had to be careful of.

I examined her. She didn't have any symptoms. She wasn't

bleeding. No pain. No pen either. We put her in Johns Hopkins Hospital for observation for a few days. We had X-rayed her, and absolutely nothing showed up on the X-ray, but I tended to believe her story. Bizarre as it seemed, it had a ring of truth to it.

At Johns Hopkins we had medical conferences where all the doctors would get together to review and discuss the most interesting or challenging cases. Well, my pen lady was deemed interesting enough to be brought up in conference for all the doctors to review. At conference, everyone except one other woman doctor and me thought that this woman could not have done what she said she did. The majority view was that she was just trying to get someone to open up her uterus to look for the pen. All the big experts said, "Don't do anything. It can't be true," so I sent her home. She went through the whole rest of her pregnancy, and I delivered her baby. Right after she delivered, I put my hand up inside her uterus and felt all around. There simply was no pen anywhere in that woman's uterus, and she hadn't birthed a pen either!

Five days later, when she was getting ready to be discharged from the hospital, she said, "I have a pain down here," pointing to her lower abdomen. Well, women who have just had a baby do have pain in their abdomens, because as the uterus contracts, it causes cramping. So I didn't think too much of it. I put my hand on her belly to see what I could feel. I could feel her uterus. It was about the size it was supposed to be and was where it was supposed to be. But over to the side I could feel this long, hard object. Might this be the missing pen?

We took her down to X-ray, and this time we X-rayed right on top of where all of us could feel this object. The doctor in the X-ray department insisted that something should show since there would at least have been a column of fluid where she had taken the works of the pen out. Again the X-rays were negative. Absolutely nothing showed!

We operated on her, and I saw something I had never seen before—or since, for that matter. Here was this pen, and it had gone through the wall of her uterus, but it had moved so slowly that it was entirely covered by fibrous tissue. It was totally encapsulated, so that in spite of the fact that it had gone through three loops of bowel—that is, in and out six times—it was completely encased, and she had no peritonitis.

That woman was very lucky, because things like that just didn't happen. And of course she had been telling the truth all along when she described her efforts at self-abortion. She had indeed inserted the pen through the cervix, which had then closed behind it. But when we examined her, it just seemed so farfetched that we couldn't believe it.

I never forgot the pen lady, and she was to stand me in good stead, as it turned out. Later I was the chief of ob-gyn at Church Home and Hospital in Baltimore. That is a very old hospital; Edgar Allan Poe died there. A woman came in with the tip of a metal catheter sticking out of her cervix. She told us that approximately one year earlier she had had an illegal abortion. It had all gone very smoothly, and she had not had a bit of trouble. Now, a full year later, here was this thing. The interns wanted to just pull it out. I said, "Wait a minute, because a year is a long time, and if the catheter has punctured the bowel and we just pull the catheter out, we are going to release the contents of her bowel into her uterus, her peritoneum, and who knows what all."

We X-rayed her, and sure enough, on X-ray you could see that the metal catheter was not entirely in her uterus. We could see one end of the catheter, which was sticking out through the neck of her cervix, and the other end had gone through the wall of her uterus and was in the abdominal cavity. We called the general surgeon, who operated and safely removed it. But if it hadn't been for my earlier experience with the pen lady, I too would have just gone ahead and pulled this thing out, inadvertently giving this woman some serious medical problems. You know, this thing in her uterus probably functioned as a primitive but pretty effective IUD, because she hadn't gotten pregnant for an entire year.

When abortion was illegal and I was in private practice, I certainly had women ask me to help them end their pregnancies. It bothered me greatly when I knew I had the technical skills to help a woman like that, but I was not going to do it because the personal risk to me was too great. There was no way in the world I was going to jeopardize my entire family and risk going to jail and all of that—just simply no way in the world.

In the mid-forties, when I first started doing ob-gyn after I finished my residency, this woman came to me. She was Catholic and unhappily married. She and her husband would have gotten a divorce, but their son was studying for the priesthood and they thought a divorce might disgrace him. So they were handling it by living in the same house, but on totally separate floors and with totally separate lives. As she relayed it to me, one night she went to a party, got drunk, and got pregnant. Just like that. This was a bit of a problem, because she had long ago ceased to have sex with her husband. He would surely know it wasn't his doing, and he would throw her out and that would be awful—awful for her and awful for the student priest, probably even more awful than getting a divorce.

Well, she begged me either to do an abortion or to help her find someone who would. In those days, in any large city, there was an assortment of illegal abortionists, and some of them were quite good—people you could safely send your patients to. The trick was in knowing who was good and who wasn't. But if you could find a good one, it was great. They did clean, safe abortions, and it was good money for them. Some told me that they came out of medical school during the Great Depression and couldn't get a job, so they turned to this.

We had two good abortionists in Baltimore. One was Dr. Timanus. The other was a doctor too, but I just can't recall his name. He has been dead for fifty years, I'm sure, so probably no one else can recall his name either. These two doctors had a very clever system for figuring out who referred patients—and doctors from all over referred patients to them. We referring doctors didn't want the abortionist-doctors to know who we were, because we didn't want our names appearing in some file or little black book of an abortionist who got arrested. So we would all instruct the women to answer the question "Who referred you?" by saying, "No one." Well, we learned later that these doctors were really smart. Instead of that question, for which we had all rehearsed our patients, they would ask, "Who diagnosed your pregnancy?" The woman would just answer the question truthfully, and then, if it was my patient, my name would get added to the big list of referring doctors. I didn't realize until much later that these two doctors knew about every single referral I ever made. I might not have made the referrals if I had known, although I might have, because these two doctors were really good.

Well, as it turned out, when my new patient came in—I'll call her Alice, but that is not her real name—one of those two good abortionists had just died and the other one was in jail, so there was no one I knew of in the city that I could send her to. Of course, there were people in New York and just about every major city. I could have also sent her to Paris or Mexico or Puerto Rico. Some women did that on a package deal, with a week's sightseeing thrown in after the abortion. But that wasn't possible for Alice for two reasons. For one thing, her husband would know. Even though they lived in separate parts of the house, he would know if she was away. Besides, her financial resources were very limited, and she simply didn't have the money to travel to another city. And I would not have known exactly who to send her to in any city but Baltimore. I would not have been as confident of the skill levels of the abortionists in other cities. I would not refer to someone who was not a physician, no matter how good they were supposed to be, because I just didn't think it was safe.

This woman was my first direct, personal experience with abortion, and it was heart-wrenching for me to have to tell her that I couldn't—should I say "wouldn't"? No, I will not say "wouldn't." I *couldn't* help her because in those days the law wouldn't let me. Anyway, it was heart-wrenching for me to tell her that I couldn't help her. This was new for me. I had certainly seen women with unwanted pregnancies during my residency and even earlier. But this wasn't a clinic or a hospital, some bigger entity where responsibility was more diffuse. This was just me and my patient, one on one. I was all there was, and I had to tell her that I couldn't help her.

So Alice asked around, and one of her friends referred her to a man named Al. She called Al, and he was only too glad to help her out for four hundred dollars. He took her, blind-folded, up the back stairs, through some halls, and then almost all the way down the front stairs of an old run-down hotel. When he was pretty sure she wouldn't be able to tell where she had been, he led her into one of the rooms in the hotel and introduced her to this woman, who my patient assumed—prob-ably wishful thinking on her part—was a doctor.

The woman took Alice's four hundred dollars from her and then had her undress and climb up on this makeshift table. I don't know whether they observed the amenities and had Al leave or not. Alice didn't ever tell me. She was probably too numb or too frightened to notice. Then the woman reached over to the washbasin in the hotel room, picked up a catheter, and started to insert it with her bare hand. Well, that scared my patient, and she cried out, "Aren't you going to sterilize that first?" The woman stopped and looked at her and said, "Look, do you want this abortion or not? Decide." Alice thought about her son and this impossible and improbable pregnancy, decided that she had no choice, and shut up about the catheter.

The woman inserted the catheter and told Alice she was done, but that when she started bleeding, which would happen in a day or two, she was to go to the hospital and tell them she fell down the stairs. Al then redid the blindfold and led Alice out of the maze. That was certainly effective, because she could not figure out where she had been or who the abortionist was.

I had no idea that all of this was going on. That particular evening, I had stayed late at the office to work on the books. After Alice got home, she began to panic about what she had done and what was going to happen to her. The unsterilized catheter really did frighten her, so in the same impulsive style that created this pregnancy, she just called a cab and came to my office. Unfortunately for me, but I suppose luckily for Alice, I was still there.

She walked in with the catheter still in place and said, "What do I do now?" There was a law then that if you treated an infected abortion patient without reporting it, you could get into serious trouble. To protect yourself, you had to report anyone you treated for a septic abortion.

I put the books aside, looked at her, and decided that at a minimum, I had to pull the catheter out, because that seemed like the appropriate thing to do. But I did tell her that I couldn't treat her unless I reported it. At that point she was so frightened that she didn't care. She said, "Go ahead and report it." I didn't know who I was supposed to report it to. After all, she was the first patient I had ever had like this. All I could think of, from watching *Perry Mason,* was the medical examiner's office. So I called the medical examiner and said, "I want to report an abortion." Their response was, "Okay. Where do we send the wagon?" I said, "Oh no, she's not dead—at least not yet." They told me that in that case I should call the detective bureau. So I did.

They sent over a male and a female detective who asked Alice questions. She could tell them Al's name and telephone number but not much else. The two detectives got marked money and then called Al, asking for an abortion. Well, they did the whole thing just like my patient had—the back stairs, the front stairs, and all of that. Of course they got the same woman and the same unsterilized catheter. The female detective actually climbed up on the table, but right before the woman started to insert the catheter, the female detective yelled, the male detective ran in, and they arrested Al and the "doctor."

As it turned out, Al was a worker at the Bethlehem Steel plant and the woman who was doing the abortions was a chorus girl from the Block. That's a place in Baltimore where all the striptease joints and places like that were. It was not a high-class part of town. She split the money with Al, whose job it was to arrange the appointments and bring the women to the chorus girl. I don't think he had to work at finding "clients." I think that just happened. He functioned more as an "appointment secretary."

My patient did get a bad infection from the abortion. I treated her with antibiotics, but I had to hospitalize her because she was very sick. Not only did she have to go to the hospital, but there was a trial and she was called as a witness. The whole thing was really quite dreadful, and it was all so unnecessary. I felt very sorry for my patient. Just think—she was afraid to even get a divorce because people would find out and it might hurt her son. This was about a thousand times worse, I'd say!

Then there was the woman who had been a classmate of mine at Vassar almost fifteen years earlier. When she was pregnant with her second child, she was the patient of a doctor for whom I was working as an associate. I hadn't seen her in all those years, and we sort of renewed our college friendship and told each other what we had been doing. We had lunch a few times when she would come to the office for her checkups. She had her baby, and then I didn't see her anymore because our paths just didn't cross.

A few years passed, and one day the doctor I was working for asked me to go out and visit one of his patients. It seemed she was pregnant, didn't want to be, and had tried to abort herself. I went, and there she was—my Vassar friend, with a catheter sticking out of her cervix. She insisted she had done it herself, and maybe she had, but that would be hard to do. She told me that she had two children and she absolutely wasn't going to have any more. Her mind was made up.

I pulled the catheter out and gave her antibiotics. Nothing happened. She didn't have any bleeding or anything. Now, this was a well-educated and determined woman. She had called the doctor because she believed that if she started it, he could legally finish it. And she had called him almost immediately after she did it because she figured the sooner the better—less chance of infection and all that.

We gave her antibiotics and watched her. She didn't abort,

and she didn't get an infection. She was fine. When a week or two had passed and she realized that she wasn't going to abort, she announced that she was going to an illegal abortionist because she was simply not willing to have any more babies. Her regular doctor and I both told her that she mustn't do that, that it was very dangerous. Well, she didn't care. She was determined. As it turned out, she got an illegal abortion and she was fine—probably because at that point she was so well laced with antibiotics that she couldn't possibly get an infection. She was one of the lucky ones!

I saw her about ten years later. By then she was at least forty-five. She still had only two children, so I guess she was managing to control what happened to her body, even though abortion was still illegal.

Later in my career, the Baltimore hospitals began to establish abortion committees and to permit a doctor to do the abortion if the committee thought it was necessary to save the life of the woman. Her mental functioning could also affect her life, so sometimes psychiatrists were involved in the work of the committee. Because I was the chief of ob-gyn, I was on the abortion committee at my hospital.

Well, all these women would come and say, "If I don't end this pregnancy, I'll kill myself." As a result, that statement very quickly became one to be ignored by the committee in deciding who was entitled to an abortion. So here came this pregnant teenager. Thank goodness she wasn't my patient, but she did come before the committee. She said that she was going to kill herself. Of course that wasn't good enough, so the committee turned her down. When she discovered that she couldn't get an abortion, she tried to kill herself by taking an overdose of pills. She was in a coma for three days. When she came out of the coma and discovered that she wasn't dead, she was more determined than ever to have an abortion, so she began acting "crazy." She would scream and carry on, talk to herself, say irrational things.

The committee considered her case again. The committee's decision was that because she had tried to kill herself, she might do it again if she got the opportunity. Therefore, the committee reasoned, the best way to "save her life" was to keep her confined in a psychiatric hospital until her pregnancy was over so that she could be prevented from killing herself. And that is what they did! So if you were a fake suicide threat, you didn't get an abortion, and if you were a real suicide threat, you didn't get an abortion. Something wrong with that thinking, I'd say!

Actually, this teenager did beat the committee and get her abortion, as it turned out. She spent every waking minute in the psychiatric hospital trying to jump out windows, cut her wrists, bang her head against the wall, hit herself—anything and everything. When she wasn't doing that, she was screaming and yelling. She just made it impossible for the hospital to function! After she had screamed and carried on for a week or two, making everyone else really crazy, the committee considered her case for the third time. This time the committee approved her abortion. Guess what. As soon as she had the abortion, her mental condition improved dramatically. Then, about two weeks later, she shot herself. I guess some of her "crazy stuff" was real. What happened to this young girl was tragic, and the committee didn't help any.

Of course, after 1973 the committee stopped, and so did the illegal abortions. As a doctor and as a woman, I think that the way it was before was awful. How could anyone who has seen even part of what I have seen in my eighty-three years possibly want to bring that back? That would be just plain irresponsible. No excuse for that.

MARILYN

LET ME TELL YOU about my pretty, wonderful, talented mother. She died in March of 1929 from peritonitis, which resulted from an illegal abortion she had.

I had just turned six when we lost her. She left her parents, my father, and five children. My brother Gerald, the oldest, was twelve. Next was my sister Eileen, who was ten. Rose was next at eight. After me came Constance, who was only eighteen months old when our mother died. My mother was born in 1895, so she was only thirty-four when she died. She was too young! We were all too young, but I guess you are never really old enough for something like that.

At the time, we were living in Pittsburgh, in a big house owned by my mother's parents. My father was a newspaperman, and he also worked in public relations. He worked as an editor for two of Pittsburgh's daily newspapers. He also did freelance public relations for sporting events around the area.

My mother, whose name was Claudia, was a very talented musician, but with five children she didn't work outside the home. She was a full-time mother and a wonderful one. She had a lovely voice and was the first woman to sing on the radio in Pittsburgh. The song she sang was "The Prisoner's Song," and the first words were "If I had the wings of an angel, over these prison walls I would fly." It turned out to be horribly prophetic. She was also a pianist, and she sang light opera in the Pittsburgh area, Victor Herbert and that sort of thing. She also made bread, was active in the PTA, and sang in the church choir. She gave of herself to her community and to her family. She was a good person, and what happened to her was wrong.

I didn't learn until I was sixteen what Mother died of. The official word at the time, and what I was brought up to believe, was that she died of pneumonia. My brother didn't learn of the true cause of her death until about ten years ago, when he was in his late sixties. I never found out why she wanted an abortion or where she got it. No one ever talked about that, not my father or her parents or anyone.

She was pregnant eight times, and it was that eighth one that killed her. I derived this kind of information by asking probing questions in my later years, after I was a parent myself. Her first pregnancy ended in a spontaneous abortion. Then my brother was born the next year. Between me and my youngest sister, unlike the rest of the siblings, is almost a four-year span. In that interval, she had a successful abortion. Then my baby sister was born, and then the next year was the abortion that took Mother's life.

She had a woman friend who was the wife of one of Pittsburgh's best-known industrialists. They were close friends, and that woman helped her in the abortion process, with both the successful one after my birth and the fatal one after Constance's birth. I guess women did a lot of that kind of help for each other in those days, since information about who did abortions was not easily available. But even though this woman had lots of money, and so, presumably, had access to the best and told my mother about the best, it wasn't good enough. My mother died anyway.

I don't have any idea where my mother went to have that last abortion. I don't know if it was done in our house or somewhere else. I don't know if she did it or whether the industrialist's wife or even some stranger did it. I don't think my father or her parents knew either.

I did learn from my sister Eileen that Mother used a knitting needle. Eileen was the oldest girl, so she may have had conversations with our mother before she died. Mother lay dying at home for several days before she went to the hospital. Eileen lay on a cot right by her bed and was with her all the time during those several days. My mother knew she was dying, and she said to Eileen, "You are going to be the mother now."

The knitting needle perforated Mother's uterus, and she developed peritonitis and then gangrene. The doctor who was treating her was just our family doctor. He was not a skilled gynecologist or anything. He didn't know what he was doing, and I don't think he knew what he was dealing with either. He doctored her at home for several days. Then one day he said that she was just too sick and he would have to take her to the hospital. She was in the hospital for three days before she died.

We were all there when my mother died—my grandparents, my father, and all five of us kids, even my baby sister. Mother died at seven-thirty in the evening. We children were kept downstairs in a little waiting room, and I remember my father coming down and saying that Mother was gone. Mother's death notice in the paper said that she died of pneumonia, and that is what we all always believed. That was a lie.

Then we had what I would call an Irish wake. My grandfather had been born in Ireland, so that is how he would have wanted to do things for his daughter's death. My mother's body lay for three days in an open casket in our living room. The casket was of beautifully polished mahogany. It was a magnificent casket, and the inside was lined with tufted satin, as if to say, "This is a beautiful place to be." Although dead, my mother looked very alive to me. We children all just stood and stared at the casket. My next-older sister, Rose, said to my baby sister, Constance, "Go give Mother a kiss," and my eighteen-month-old sister crawled into the casket to do so. These are things one doesn't forget. Those images are imprinted on the mind forever. When one's mother is laid out dead like this, no matter how young you are, you know that death has occurred. This made a huge impression on me and on all of us children. I will simply never ever forget my lovely, young, dead mother laid out in the parlor in her best clothes.

I lost my mother under tragic and unnecessary circumstances. Then what remained of the family was also torn asunder. My father's own family all came up from Baltimore for the funeral. After my mother's death, my father just packed us all up and moved us to Baltimore. Here he was with a full-time job and five children, the youngest of whom was just a toddler. He was lucky to have a job, because it was the beginning of the Depression and a lot of people didn't. So he stayed in Pittsburgh and worked, and we all went to different places in Baltimore.

That move to a strange place, so soon after our mother's death, was a very significant and a very traumatic event for all of us. My brother Gerald went to live with my paternal grandparents. My sisters Rose and Eileen went to live in the Episcopal School for Girls, and Constance and I were sent to live with my father's eldest sister, who was a widow from World War I.

My aunt had two boys who were a lot older than we were. They were ten and twelve, and we were just little. They had never seen us before, and suddenly here we were in their home. They didn't like it, and they didn't much like us. Also, they were pretty poor, and when you added two more mouths to feed, it became really bad. For example, you couldn't just put butter on a piece of bread and eat it. You put the butter on and then scraped it all off and passed the butter on to the next person, so that all five of us could get the benefit of one serving of butter. My father and my maternal grandparents weren't rich, but I had never seen anything like that before. It was a very desperate situation. Very unpleasant.

My aunt was a desperate woman, and it showed in the way she responded to us. She simply couldn't handle two more children. She tried, but it was bad. I missed my mother so much. I was also suddenly deprived of my father, whom I adored, and my maternal grandparents, with whom I was very close. It also seemed like I had suddenly lost my brother and sisters as well. In Baltimore we saw each other once in a while, but probably no more often than once a month during this period.

We stayed in Baltimore until at least October or November of 1929, maybe a little longer. I know that they enrolled me in school in Baltimore. Then my father brought us all back, and we lived with him in Library, Pennsylvania. He had a housekeeper for us. By that time he had started keeping company with a newspaperwoman in Pittsburgh. Ultimately they married, and we moved to a small thirty-two-acre farm in Ingomar, not far from Pittsburgh.

That farm probably did more toward saving our lives than anything. We had horses to ride and all that wonderful land to roam around in. We felt safe, and we had each other again. We didn't have much money—the Depression was worse by then—but my father had hired a man to help him work the farm, so at least we ate well. Clothes and shoes were often a problem, but food was plentiful.

This stepmother was to be the first of two. She had absolutely no interest at all in five children. She was a career woman. Her only interest, other than herself and her career, was my father. She just left us pretty much to ourselves, which was all right with us, I must admit. She was not a warm person, and we were just as glad to escape unnoticed. After about two years, they were divorced.

My father married again in 1936. She had been married and divorced a couple of times, and then she married my father. He was really floundering. He didn't know which way to turn. He needed comforting himself. Let's face it—five children are a burden, especially when you're broke.

My second stepmother's name was Catherine. She was a very beautiful woman who had done modeling when she was younger. She was also a talented woman with many skills. For example, she was a wonderful cook and an accomplished seamstress. But coping with what she called my father's "willful ways" was not something she did well. Dad would go off with some of his newspaper cronies and gamble all night. Sometimes he would come home from one of those sessions and have no paycheck. She would be extremely upset, and they would fight about it.

Her way of dealing with us, if we did something she disapproved of, was to say, "Apples don't fall far from the tree!" She could be affectionate, but in matters of childrearing her style was to castigate rather than to instruct. I was about twelve when Catherine came into my life. She never paid much attention to the three older kids, and as between me and Constance, Constance was her favorite, possibly because she was younger. However, she did do nice things for me, like she made clothes for me and she did interest me in sewing.

By the time I was to be graduated from high school, I had met my future husband and was planning on getting married. That caused a lot of dissension in the family. My father never said a word, but my stepmother was very disapproving and interfering. It was extremely unpleasant, and things became very strained. My father and stepmother didn't even come to my high school graduation, even though I graduated with honors. No one from my family was there. That hurt a lot.

Finally, my father, my younger sister, and I actually moved out of the house and into an apartment in Pittsburgh. I got married in 1942. My stepmother didn't come to the wedding either, and she stopped speaking to me. My father did come to the wedding though, so that was better than my high school graduation. I don't know what my stepmother's objection was. My husband and I have been married for fifty years, and we have really had a wonderful marriage. I would say that I had a far better marriage than she did. But whatever her reasons, she did not speak to me for years. As she got older, she mellowed somewhat—never so much as to be a grandmother to my children, but the vituperativeness of the earlier years was gone. She also came to admit, some ten years after my marriage, that I had made a good choice and my husband was a good person.

After my husband and I were married, my stepmother divorced my father and she married a steelworker. She was married to him for only one year when she divorced him and remarried my father! I think that these in-and-out marriages of my father's were just symptoms of his own emotional disturbance following my mother's death. He had adored her. This stepmother had a really nasty temper and a sharp tongue which could be very biting. She didn't bother to control it either. But after I got married, I moved away, which effectively solved the problem. As I say, she and I didn't speak for years, but I did maintain contact by mail with my father over those years.

Once, in 1950, after I had become a mother, my father and I had a rare and unusually intimate conversation. I had never had such a conversation with him before, and I don't think I ever had another one afterward. I was trying to find the reasons for what I saw as my mother's tragic and unnecessary death, and I said, "Dad, why didn't you and Mother use birth control? You know, it was available then." His immediate response was, "Honey, we never talked about those things." Think about that. My mother had to die because certain things couldn't be discussed! I'm sorry, but that makes me very angry. That was when I drew the broad conclusion, which I still hold, that when we don't talk about things, women die.

My grandmother Sarah was the one who first told me how my mother died. We were standing in her kitchen—a particularly warm and comforting place, I always thought—and I said, "Nanny, how did Mother die?" She looked at me and said, so softly I could barely hear her, "She died from an abortion." I was stunned. I had no idea.

My grandparents had three sons, but my mother was their only daughter, and they took her death very hard, especially my grandmother. And the fact that she died from an abortion was something that my grandmother could never forgive my father for. That was simply too much to ask. As a result, there was vitriol and constant emotional attack between the two of them. My father usually called my grandmother "the bitch of Beechview" because he felt that she made unnecessary trouble for him and his children. My grandmother had no words for him. He was, quite simply, the man who killed her only daughter.

Once my grandmother told me why my mother died, it was like a light bulb suddenly went on in my head and I understood all the antagonism between my father and my grandmother. Now it all made sense to me.

We were so beautifully cared for before my mother's death and such bedraggled ragamuffins after. "Before" and "after" pictures show a very telling contrast, and they are still painful for me to look at. My parents met on a riverboat ride. They both loved that, and we children loved it too. It was one of our favorite family outings. One spring evening my mother and father were going to take us all to ride on the riverboat. My younger sister was just an infant and too young to be dressed up, but the three older little girls were all dressed in matching navy blue coats with red satin linings. My brother was wearing a navy blue jacket and a tie. We were properly dressed and properly cared for. Our hair was neatly trimmed, shiny and clean, and well groomed. Dad took a picture of all of us on the front porch on a white wicker swing. We are all smiling and looking into the camera. It's true that we were happy because we were going on a boat ride, but it was more than that. We were happy, loved, well-cared-for children, and it showed.

In pictures taken after Mother's death, we all looked markedly different. For one thing, there were many less pictures being taken. And all of a sudden it seemed like we had no clothes. I think my father didn't understand that children's clothes are outgrown before they ever wear out. He didn't realize how fast children grow, and in some of the "after" pictures you see each of us wearing clothes with sleeves that are too short. Everything is mismatched, unironed, and generally uncared for. Buttons are missing and shoelaces are broken. Our hair looks wild and uncombed. I guess my father didn't understand that the way we looked before didn't just happen automatically and naturally. It took a lot of effort by Mother. I don't mean to seem too critical of him. He did his best, but in many ways he was as bedraggled as we were.

All of us siblings married and had children. In one sense, we are all functional, productive adults. However, there is a lingering visible trauma, or maybe a sort of emotional fallout, that we all still carry around. That mahogany coffin is part of each of us.

We four girls each had a different response to our mother's death. Eileen absorbed a very major responsibility of caring for her three younger siblings. Too much responsibility for a ten-year-old girl, but she took the responsibility my dying mother had placed on her: "You will be the mother now." She was the nurturer and the emotional caretaker that the stepmothers never were. She didn't see that we were fed. It wasn't that kind of nurturing. What she gave us was affection, and we needed that at least as much as food.

My response was that I felt that I was almost outside the family looking in, like a disinterested observer of the conduct of these people. I became somewhat detached from everything. I have never been to the cemetery where my mother is buried. At the wake and after the funeral, my father decided that my younger sister and I would not go to the cemetery because we were too little. I am not sure why, but I have never gone. That is probably significant, because I could have gone many times after I was older. Maybe it is part of the emotional distancing.

Rose spent her entire life being angry at the world. She was one of the angriest people I knew—at anything and anybody. She had a hard life, though. Her children had a lot of troubles, and she is the only one of us who ended up being divorced. It happened to her after twenty-seven years of marriage, and that was awfully hard on her.

I think Constance suffered the most from our mother's death. Eighteen months is pretty young to lose your mother. And she spent her whole childhood in the emotional turmoil that the rest of us only experienced after several years of normal childhood. She had seven children. She kept saying that her diaphragm failed, but I'm not sure that was it. She was angry at our mother for having an abortion. Maybe all the babies were Constance's way of showing her mother what Constance wished she had done. Maybe she was saying, "See, it can be done, Mother. You didn't have to do what you did and make me lose my mother."

It is one thing to have a loved one die. That happens to everybody. But how and why a person dies also matters. A tragic and unnecessary death is somehow worse, I think. Rose summed it up best when she said, "The child in me weeps still for her, and the woman in me grieves the loss of another woman who died as she did."

JANE

MY MOTHER WAS BORN IN 1899 and passed away in 1932, just a few days before her thirty-third birthday. She bled to death after an illegal abortion, leaving six motherless children who needed her desperately. I was the oldest, twelve, and the youngest was only two.

There aren't words to describe the impact illegal abortion has had on my life, or if there are, I don't know them. I'm seventy-one years old now, and the pain I still feel hasn't faded in over half a century. I lost my mother, but that's not all. I lost my brothers and sisters as well. The world as we knew it was destroyed overnight, and things were never the same for any of us. Some of my brothers and sisters suffered more than I did. I think I did better because I was older.

Some of us were reunited well over fifty years after we lost our mother, and in fact, more than fifty years after we lost contact with each other. But some of us have never been found. Like my mother, they too were lost to me forever as a result of illegal abortion. Even those of us children who finally found each other as adults lost the precious childhood memories of growing up together that brothers and sisters usually have. I feel so incomplete somehow, like part of me passed away on that same blood-soaked mattress with my poor mother.

We lived in Nebraska. My dad worked in a factory. I don't

know what he did, but he made pretty good money. The problem was that a lot of that money went into drink. My mother was a housewife. There were so many children that she could never have worked an outside job. I was the oldest, born in 1919. Next was my brother David, born in 1920. Anna came along in 1922, Ray in 1923, Martha in 1927, and James in 1929. From my very earliest memories my mother always had a baby on her hip or in her arms. I remember that by the time I was nine I was cooking meals, changing diapers, and giving bottles to help her out. When she was in the hospital having another baby, I did all the cooking and taking care of the little ones, even though I was still pretty little myself, because we didn't have the money to hire housekeepers.

My mother was a very sweet, gentle woman. She worked hard and didn't have a lot of time or energy to play with us, but she cooked and cleaned and washed and ironed and took good care of us. We were Methodists, and I don't remember anything about birth control being wrong. Big families weren't a religious thing. That's just how things were in her world. She came from a big family—one of thirteen children. She married when she was about sixteen.

My mother had had several abortions before the one that ended her life. My aunt, her sister, told me about this man in our town who did abortions. My aunt said that my mother went to him when she had a "problem." I think she must have gone to him several times between 1923 and 1927, because my mother didn't have any babies in that four-year period, and that was very unusual for her. I never knew about this man and the other abortions until about fifteen years ago, when my aunt made some remark about my mother going there so many times.

I remember the 1932 abortion like it was yesterday. That evening I had gone out to babysit for a family who lived about two blocks from our house. My mother had gone to bed early, saying she didn't feel well. I don't know what I thought was wrong, but I certainly didn't think it was anything serious. She had cooked our supper and put the little ones to bed, just like she always did. It was early in January and very cold. I thought she might be coming down with flu or something. My dad was working the night shift, so he wasn't going to get home until six the next morning. Not giving it much thought, I went off to babysit. I was to stay overnight, because the people were going to be out until late.

The next morning my dad came to the neighbors' to get me. He was cold sober and looked scared. I couldn't ever remember seeing him frightened before, and that made me frightened, although I didn't exactly know why. He told me my mother was sick and was going to the hospital. He didn't tell me what was wrong, just that I had to be home to take care of the littler children. I wasn't terribly alarmed about my mother going to the hospital, because she was always in the hospital having babies and she always came home. Besides, she had seemed basically all right the night before, so I wasn't sure why he seemed so frightened.

When we got home—as I said, only two blocks away—an ambulance was there and they were carrying my mother out on a stretcher. But it was too late. She was gone.

The night before my mother passed away, she promised the little ones that they would have a party. This was the night I was babysitting, and I didn't even know she was sick. While I was babysitting and my dad was working, she talked to the little children and told them—she must have known how sick she was—that she was going to the hospital but when she came home they would have a party, with ice cream. Ice cream! Can you even imagine what a treat ice cream was in a family which was often so strapped for money that beans, bread, and milk were luxuries? Ice cream! They all knew that whatever was happening at the hospital must be really special to produce this miracle.

It was many years later before I found out she had died from an illegal abortion. I found out about my mother's abortion from my aunt Violet, my mother's sister. Aunt Vi said that my other aunt—Constance, my mother's older sister—had gone to this man and had abortions, and that she was the one who told my mother about him. As I say, my mother had several abortions before the one that killed her.

The day my mother passed on, I didn't know what had happened to her, and no one told me anything. Although I was the oldest, I was only twelve, so I guess they figured we were all too young to be told anything. I just couldn't or wouldn't believe she was gone. I was pacing back and forth in our living room, and I kept saying to my dad, "What are we going to do now? What will happen to us?" And he just kept saying, "I don't know, I don't know."

My aunts on my dad's side came over and stayed with us that first night. I slept in the middle of my parents' double bed, between my two aunts. When I got up in the morning, I could see there was a lot of blood on the bed. It was her blood! They had changed the sheets and everything, but they couldn't do anything about the mattress. I was lying in the same spot where my mother had bled to death less than twenty-four hours earlier! Oh, God! I never told anyone this before, and I think I never will again, because it hurts so much to remember. I can't say it, or even think about it, without crying. I see it and feel it like I'm twelve again, instead of seventy-one.

When my mother passed away, we kids didn't have decent shoes, and I remember we had to put cardboard in our shoes to go to the funeral. My teacher felt bad for us and bought us shoes. I remember that, and how embarrassed I felt.

One aunt stayed with us for about a week. We children were all so scared. We didn't know what was going to happen to us. My dad was drinking heavily, but he was staying out all night, so he wasn't around to be mean to us. Besides, his sister was there, and he was never mean around his sister.

Life was hard in our family even before my mother died, but I have wonderful memories of her. There was a hotdog stand not far from our house. She would give me ten cents, and I'd go down to the hotdog stand while she put the babies to bed, and I'd come back with hotdogs for the two of us. In those days you could buy them on a bun, with mustard and wonderful homemade relish, for a nickel each. We could relax because the little ones were in bed, and that was our special time. She never played with me or read to me or had birthday parties or such like that, because she never had time. Taking care of the babies and the house took all of her time. But those precious moments when we ate hotdogs and talked—those special times and quiet times when I could have her all to myself—were among the most wonderful moments of my childhood. We didn't talk about anything special, we were just together. I loved her so much!

The only thing my mother ever told me about sex or anything like that was when I got my first period. She just looked at me and said, "Don't ever let a man touch you!" That was all she ever said to me. She might have told me more if she had lived longer, but I doubt it. She was a very private person and never talked about things like that.

Sometimes, after we ate the hotdogs, we would listen to the radio, and using the radio music as accompaniment, she would sing to me. She sang "Baby Feet Go Pitter-Patter Across My Floor." She loved that song, and I loved having her sing it to me. None of the other children had those special times.

After my mother passed away, we all went to live with my Grandmother White—that would be my mother's mother. She had a big house, and all six of us lived there for six months, from January until the summer. My dad lived there, sort of, but he was either at work or staying somewhere else at night. We didn't see much of him. Several of my mother's sisters lived there too. They were young women in their late teens or early twenties. It was a big house, so there was room for all of us. My grandmother was good to all of us. She was jolly and hugged us a lot. I liked being with my mother's family because it made me feel closer to my mother.

I had always gone to my dad's parents for two weeks during the summer, so I did that again in that first summer of 1932. At the end of the two weeks I was ready to go back to my mother's people, but then something happened. I don't know why, but my dad appeared on the doorstep with the two youngest children—

Martha, who was five, and Jimmy, who was three—and told me that we were going to live with his parents from then on.

That was the beginning of the loss of my brothers and sisters, because after that I never lived with the other three— David, Anna and Ray—again. Over the next two years I saw David and Anna, maybe two or three times, but it wasn't the same. They were living different lives, and it never felt like we were family after that.

As it happened, after the summer of 1932 I only saw Ray once more in my whole life. The first time we all got together— the three of us went back to Grandma White's house to visit— Ray was there. That was probably around Christmas in 1932. The next time, the summer of 1933, Ray was gone. It was just David and Anna in one house and Jimmy, Martha, and me in the other. We were told, and I guess it was true, that Ray had gone to live with a relative in Montana or Michigan. I don't even remember where, but it was a long way away from our home in Nebraska. I tried to find him after I was grown up, but I have never been able to, and I have never seen him again.

Anna died about a year after Ray left. She must have been about twelve by then. They said she had something wrong with her kidneys.

Martha, Jimmy, and I stayed at my dad's parents' home for the next two years. My grandparents Parker were nice enough, but I hated having us all split up. As I say, we probably saw the other children two or three times in that two-year period. I never understood what happened in the summer of 1932 or why we had to be split up like that. Maybe six children was just too many for one family to take on, or maybe there was trouble or bad feelings between my mother's people and my dad.

My dad's people wanted to put all six of us in the Methodist Home that first year. I don't know whether that would have been better or not. Maybe we would have stayed together longer. Maybe Anna wouldn't have gotten sick and died. I don't really know why we didn't go to the home, but we didn't.

Martha, Jimmy, and I were really very close, because we

each felt that the other two were all we had left. I was the oldest and had taken care of them since they were babies. I suppose that's why they kept looking to me to take care of them in all the different places we found ourselves. People were nice to us, but no one loved us like we loved each other. I felt bad that I couldn't take care of the other three children, but I couldn't.

Grandmother Parker had heart problems, and I guess three children were just too much for her, so in 1934, when I was fourteen, they told me I was being sent to a boarding school. After I got there, I discovered that it wasn't a boarding school at all. It was a correctional school for bad girls. Do you know, there was only one other girl besides me who hadn't been sent there by the courts. When I realized that, I knew it wasn't a regular boarding school, but there was nothing I could do about it then. I was in it and couldn't get out.

It was so unfair. I had always had very grown-up responsibilities, which I tried to live up to. I had been cooking meals and taking care of children since I was only nine. I tried very hard to be good, grown-up, and responsible. I went to church on Sunday. I *was* a good girl, and here I was in an institution for bad girls. I never could understand why my grandparents did that to me. Did they think I was bad, or did they just need to do something with the children? If they needed to get rid of us, why couldn't they send us back to Grandma White? Ray was already gone from Grandma White's house, so it may be that Grandma White was having trouble too.

I found out several years later that my mother's family never knew what had happened to me. After I had been at the correctional home for three years, one of my mother's sisters did some snooping around and learned what had happened. She came to the home to visit me and asked if I wanted to come live with her and her husband. My father had remarried and he didn't care, so he agreed and I went to live with my aunt and uncle. I was seventeen by then, and I stayed with them until I graduated from high school and got married.

I told you that I thought I might have had an easier time than some of the other children because I was older. Well, very soon after I was sent to the correctional institution, Martha and Jimmy were sent to an orphanage. I didn't know that was happening, and even if I had known, I probably couldn't have done anything to stop it because I was still underage.

Martha was only seven and Jimmy was five when they went to the orphanage. In 1936, while I was still at the correctional institution, they were adopted and their names were changed. When I got out of the correctional school and found out what had happened, I tried to find them, but I never knew what their new last names were, so I never could. I knew they had left the state, but I didn't know where they had gone. Like Ray a few years earlier, they just vanished.

By the time they were adopted, Martha was nine and Jimmy was seven. Maybe they were lucky to be adopted, since they were older. What I was told later was that the new people wanted to adopt Jimmy but they really didn't want Martha. By then the two children were so close they were inseparable, and I don't wonder, since all they had was each other. The orphanage had separated the two of them before. They put Jimmy out in a new home and left Martha in the orphanage, but it just didn't work out because Jimmy was so unhappy without his sister. So this time the orphanage just told the new people they couldn't have Jimmy without taking Martha. They took her, but they didn't want her, and I guess they always treated her differently than they did Jimmy.

I hear that she had a hard life. I never saw her again either, because she died before the rest of us found each other in 1986. I guess she always felt rejected and abandoned. She got married, and then her husband abandoned her. It made her kind of strange, and she was never right after that. She died in a car accident in 1981 when she was only fifty-four.

After Martha died, Jimmy felt all alone again, I guess, and he wanted to find his original family. He was living in California. By that time he was married and had children and grandchildren—all with his new last name, of course—but he remembered his original last name and what part of Nebraska he had lived in. He also remembered one of my mother's brothers who had been a railroad conductor. When Jimmy was little, he loved Uncle Fred's blue uniform and shiny buttons and badge, and he loved it when Uncle Fred would take him to the roundhouse or let him sit in the caboose.

James—I think of him as "Jimmy" because he was a little boy when I had last seen him in 1934, but "James" sounds better on a gray-haired grandfather—took his wife and one of his grandsons and came to Nebraska to look for Uncle Fred. Well, Uncle Fred had been dead for at least ten years when James began his search, but James made contact with a retired conductor who remembered Uncle Fred. He told him that Fred's two sisters—Jimmy's aunts—were still alive, although they were in their eighties and in poor health. Aunt Martha had never married, so she had the same last name as Uncle Fred. Jimmy found her address by just looking her up in the telephone book of our small town in Nebraska.

I will never forget that day. It was July 9, 1986, and I had done some grocery shopping for Aunt Martha. I was standing in the kitchen putting the food away when the doorbell rang. I went to the door, and here stood this gray-haired man with a woman and a teenage boy. The man didn't know who I was, but I knew who he was. It was Jimmy! I would have known him anywhere, even though it had been fifty-two years and he had only been five when I last saw him. As I say, he didn't know who I was—and didn't even remember his oldest sister. Uncle Fred and the roundhouse were more vivid than I was. I guess that's because he had so many older sisters and aunts that we just all blurred together in his mind.

I told him who I was, screamed for Aunt Martha to come, and we all began to cry and hug each other. His wife was wonderful, and I loved her right away. She told me how long it took Jimmy to find us—and how, before he even began the search, it took him a long time to be willing to even try to find us. He had felt very abandoned by the adoption and was hurt because no one came looking for him. He thought he was "given away" and no one wanted him. He was angry at what he saw as abandonment by his original family.

Dear God, I wanted to find him so much, but I didn't know how. Because he was my mother's last baby, he was so special to me! He felt rejected. I didn't feel rejected. I just felt like another part of me died when I lost another person I loved.

Anyway, after I found Jimmy—or I should say, after Jimmy found me—we had a wonderful weekend. We laughed and talked and hugged and cried. I don't think we slept at all. Then Jimmy had to go back to California. But you know, a weekend just wasn't enough after fifty years.

After Jimmy left, I called David. He hadn't been home that weekend, so he didn't know about Jimmy. David was the only other sibling left, and I didn't see him very often, but I just picked up the telephone and told him I had someone special I wanted him to meet. I said there was just one catch. We would have to travel to California for this special introduction. It was funny. David didn't ask any questions. He just said okay, like he knew.

He and I flew to California. We stayed for a week and we really had a ball with Jimmy. We all got to know each other. It was great fun, but in a way it was really kind of sad, because the three of us were all that was left and our reunion had taken half a century to happen.

That is what illegal abortion cost my family. Too much. Why did it have to happen? I have never gotten over it and I never will.

HELENE

I WAS BORN IN 1927 and grew up in New York City. My father
was an illegal abortionist of sorts, although I don't know
how many he did. Probably not a lot. He was a doctor. He
was also a womanizer and a woman hater. I don't know quite
how all those things fit together, but I think they did.

He was a general practitioner. Although a general practitioner in those days did everything, my father didn't do much
gynecology, because he worked in conjunction with another
doctor who was a gynecologist. Like my father, he was rather
heavily lacking in character.

My father was a very competent doctor. His ethics were
questionable, but not his ability. In 1945 the *New York Times* ran
a story about some unethical medical practices. One involved a
fee-splitting case. Doctors were referring patients to a certain
roentgenologist [radiologist] and then splitting fees, a practice
considered unethical. My father was one of the doctors named
in the paper as being involved in this fee splitting. He was also
involved in an insurance compensation scam. He got some sort
of suspension for that. He didn't lose his medical license, but
for a year he was not permitted to do any kind of insurance
work. Since that was at least fifty percent of his practice, it was a
fairly stiff economic penalty.

The combination of those two things was more than he felt

like dealing with, so he decided to just go into the army until it all blew over. Everyone thought he was going in because he was so patriotic, and he let them think that.

My father admitted only one of the abortions to me, but I'm certain that there were others. I would bet money on it! The one he told me about happened in 1928. He was a ship's doctor, and the patient was one of the women on the cruise. Now we think of a cruise lasting five days, but in those days they might have lasted two months. He told me that this woman asked him to do an abortion on her and that he agreed, provided she would have sex with him first. She didn't have a lot of choices, so she agreed and he did the abortion. I was in my twenties when he told me about this. He didn't tell me anything about how he did the abortion—just that he did it and the payment he extracted.

He was certainly not all bad or devoid of human feelings, however. For example, he told me about a time when he was a very young doctor. A seventeen-year-old patient asked him to do an abortion. He refused, and she committed suicide shortly thereafter. He said that he felt horrendously guilty. I suspect that if he hadn't been so neurotic, his response to each of these abortion-seeking women might have been different, probably less extreme.

My father once refused to do an abortion on my mother. Then, with a later pregnancy, he did do one. My parents were both very unhappy in their marriage. It was like an armed camp at home because they bickered with each other constantly. At first there were economic difficulties that prevented them from getting a divorce. In those days, in New York State, someone would have had to go to Reno for six weeks to establish residency in Nevada. That just wasn't possible. He had to take care of the practice, and she had to take care of the children. Later, when we were older, I think they stayed together out of habit. Finally, after twenty-three years and after New York changed its divorce laws, they did get a divorce.

My father really had very little use for women. He had nothing good to say about them, and he used derogatory language.

For example, he called any woman who was sexually active a "pig" and worse.

When I was a child, my father adored me and I him. But when I became an adolescent—when I began to look like a woman—then everything was different, and I too was the recipient of the same hostility. A complex and neurotic man. I'm a psychologist now, and he has become much more understandable to me, although not any more likable, I must say. But he had a viewpoint that unfortunately is not so uncommon. To him, all women were either the Virgin Mary or sluts. He couldn't categorize them any other way. He had great respect for his mother—she could do no wrong. But other women were something else again.

What motivated my father to do abortions was money and sex and anything else he got out of it, like maybe a sense of power. With the one woman he told me about, he had another obvious motive—to humiliate her. Put yourself in that woman's place. She was obviously desperate, and the only way she could buy what she needed was to meet his price.

SANDRA

I WAS BORN IN 1927. In 1945 I was an eighteen-year-old college student living in Boston. I lived in a rooming house on Beacon Hill. I had a boyfriend, Bob, also a college student. He wasn't the best thing that ever happened to me, but I didn't know that then. I got pregnant. I really can't remember much about what, if any, birth control was available to me back then. Intellectually I had a lot of knowledge about birth control, but on a practical level I don't think I really had much actual access.

When I found out I was pregnant, I went to Ralph, a pharmacist friend of mine. He gave me pills. I took lots of different kinds of pills because Ralph tried one kind after another. None of them worked. It's not that they did nothing. Some made me sick. One kind gave me terrible diarrhea. But none of them had any effect at all on the pregnancy.

Finally there were no more pills to try, and I began looking for a doctor or someone who could do an abortion. I had a friend named Leslie. She was ten years older than I was, and she had had an abortion herself, so she took me to that person. The pharmacist gave me the money. It cost two hundred dollars. The money wasn't a loan, it was a gift. Maybe he felt bad because none of the pills worked. I don't know.

Leslie went with me to the abortionist. She called him a doctor, but I'm pretty sure he wasn't a real doctor. He didn't even wash his hands! He was filthy. I mean, he even looked dirty. He stunk of booze. His hands shook. Maybe he had been a doctor at one time, but I doubt it. This man was the local abortionist. I don't know if he specialized in college students or that particular part of Boston, but I found out later that everyone seemed to have heard of him.

I can't remember how I got to his place. I didn't have a car. Leslie didn't have a car. The abortionist was several blocks from my rooming house. Maybe I walked. We might have. I didn't really have any money except what I had been given to pay for the abortion.

The abortionist's place looked like something out of a bad movie. As horrible as you can imagine, it was worse! It was a hovel—dirty, like he was. There was a kitchen table. I was literally aborted on the kitchen table. I don't know what he did, because I couldn't really see. He had something that looked like a funnel. He inserted the narrow end of the funnel into me and did something that sort of felt like grinding. I don't know what he was doing. Then it just sort of came out in a bucket—right then. I've heard stories about it taking hours, or even days, but this wasn't like that. It happened right away and was all over right away. It was quick and relatively painless. I didn't stay when it was over. He wanted me out of there right away, so I left.

Leslie and I went back to my rooming house. Again, I don't remember how I got there, but I do remember I had to walk up five flights of steps to get to my room. My boyfriend was there. He hadn't gone with me to the abortionist, and he hadn't come up with any of the money I needed. He just came around when it was all over. I remember going to bed in my rooming house and being real sick for several days. I had chills, and my temperature was a hundred and four. There was some bleeding and pain, and I knew I had a bad infection. I didn't go to a hospital and I didn't go to a doctor. I just waited it out. How could I go to a hospital in those days in Boston? They would have arrested me!

No one in my rooming house paid much attention to me. It was sort of a bohemian place. There were lots of odd or unusual people, and I suppose people either didn't notice unusual things or maybe they just left people alone. Not all the tenants were college students. Next door to me was a man who was a writer for the *Boston Herald*. I wonder if in those days someone getting an abortion was a news story. Probably not. If I had died, that would have been a news story. I wonder if the credentials of the "doctor" who did my abortion would have been a news story. Probably not. I'm sure that he was fairly typical. If it had been a news story, he would just have been driven out of business, and then we would have had no one.

I got through the whole experience without my parents knowing anything about it. About a year later, I married my boyfriend. It wasn't a very good marriage, and later we got divorced. Remember how he wasn't around for the abortion? Well, he wasn't around for the tough times in the marriage either. I should have realized what kind of person he was, but I was young and headstrong. After I got married, I had two more abortions. My husband didn't want to have children, and neither did I.

The next abortion was in 1952. I was twenty-five. That time I know I was using a diaphragm. I lived in Pittsburgh then. My husband and I tried to find a doctor in Pittsburgh—like my gynecologist or other doctors—but no one would help us. We were told that I would have to go to Puerto Rico. Finally someone gave us the name of a doctor in New York City. He was a fancy, expensive, successful Park Avenue doctor. He made me have sex with him before he would do the abortion. My husband never knew that. He would have been wild if he had known. This abortion was expensive in lots of ways. First, the cost. It was one thousand dollars. Then there was the cost of the travel to New York, and Bob and I had to stay overnight in a hotel. By the time I got to the sex part of the "price tag," what was I going to do? We had already spent all of the other money. Besides, I wanted an abortion and I'd have done whatever it took, at that point, to make it happen. The doctor probably knew that.

The sex occurred in his office. Then he picked up the telephone and arranged to have me admitted, that day, to a New York hospital. I'm not going to tell you the name of the hospital, but it was very well known, a fancy place where all the movie stars went. Bob went with me. In the hospital, the doctor gave me a shot, and about an hour or so later I began to get bad cramps. Then the doctor did a regular D and C and discharged me from the hospital. He was really a very good, very skillful doctor. I felt fine afterwards—no chills, no fever, no complications.

The third abortion was in Pittsburgh between 1964 and 1967, but I can't remember exactly when. It was done in a hospital by a competent and skillful doctor who was my regular gynecologist. This time I didn't have to have sex with the doctor, but I had to have letters from three psychiatrists stating I don't know what. That I was "unbalanced"? "Insane"? "Disturbed"? I just don't know. I also had to consent to be sterilized. I guess that went with the mental thing. My gynecologist and the three psychiatrists had to protect themselves, and the message in the psychiatrists' letters was that I would become insane if I were pregnant, or maybe that pregnancy somehow triggered insanity—not just this pregnancy but any future pregnancy.

Anyway, I had my tubes tied. It was really not unlike the situation in New York fifteen years earlier. I just did whatever it took to get the abortion. I guess some things just don't change.

MIRIAM

I WAS BORN IN 1925. In 1946, when I became pregnant, I was living with my mother in Pittsburgh. I wasn't married. I had graduated from college about a year earlier and had been working. I still lived at home because that is what girls did in those days—at least that is what "nice girls" did. It goes without saying that nice girls weren't supposed to have sex, but a lot of us did. Of course I got pregnant, which was something else nice girls didn't do.

As soon as I realized I was pregnant, I started looking for a solution to my problem. I knew I wanted an abortion. There really weren't any other choices for me. It was very hard to find someone, and it seemed to take forever. I went from place to place. The whole process was word of mouth. I didn't know anyone and I had no connections. I was just out there looking. First I went to my own doctor. He confirmed that I was pregnant but told me he had no help to offer. He suggested that I go out of town. I'm not exactly sure what he had in mind. Maybe he thought I should go away for several months and give birth. Maybe he thought I should go away and look for an out-of-town abortionist. No matter—neither was possible. I had a job and a mother. My job meant I had to be at work every day. My mother meant I had to be at home every night. For many reasons too complicated to explain, I could not possibly discuss with her the fact that I was involved in a sexual relationship, let alone that I was pregnant.

My sources of information were usually men, not women. I worked in advertising, and there were lots of salesmen around. Salesmen always seemed to know everything, or at least they acted like they did. They gave me names and telephone numbers. One of the names was of a black doctor in Pittsburgh's Hill District. Although it was a scary part of town for a white woman alone, I went by myself. I went alone to all of the places I tried. I remember walking up rickety stairs in a very bad part of town and feeling very weird, scared, and out of place. All he would do was confirm that I was pregnant, which I knew anyway, but he wasn't willing to offer anything more. He wouldn't even give me a name. Why should he? He had never seen me before. He owed me nothing. I don't know if he was really a doctor or not. He wore a white coat and was in a sort of office-like place, but he didn't have a nurse or anything. I just don't know.

It was really hard to try to find someone when you didn't know who to go to. You just had to keep asking around. I couldn't talk to too many people, because I didn't want too many people to know about it. I always said I had a friend who had this problem and did they know anyone or any way. They would tell me things they had heard. I tried anything anyone recommended. Actually, "recommended" is too strong a word. I tried everything I heard of, whether it was recommended or not. I tried diet pills, jumping jacks and other vigorous exercises, and lying over a barrel. I took different kinds of pills. I don't remember what they all were or where I got them. I saw several different "real doctors" during my search for an abortionist. Again, I only think they were real doctors. They looked real, but I had no way of knowing. The second doctor gave me an injection that was supposed to bring on my period. It didn't do anything.

I was getting really panicky as time was going by and I was going nowhere. Mostly, it was difficult to even be lucky enough to hear about places to go or people to contact. Being success-ful was another issue.

Eventually I got to a nurse in East Liberty. I had been given only her first name and her phone number, so I just called and made an appointment. I was sort of coy but fairly blunt. On the phone I said, "I understand that you help women who don't want to be pregnant." She said, "Why don't you come over and we'll talk about it."

I went to her house. She didn't have an office or anything like that. I think she was a white woman, but I really remember almost nothing about what she looked like. I know she told me that the cost would be four hundred dollars and that I had to have the money in cash. Now, that was a lot of money in 1946. I had been out of school for a year and had been working, so I'd had a chance to accumulate some savings. I went to my bank and cashed in my savings bonds, my savings account, and every-thing else I had. I got absolutely no financial help from the man. He knew I was pregnant, but he had been in the service and had just gotten out and gone back to college. He told me he didn't have any money, and I had no basis to doubt him, although in hindsight he probably was no worse off financially than I was.

The day of my abortion, I went by myself. I remember a very small room with a couch. I was told to lie on the couch. That is where the abortion was done. There was no bed. Nothing was sterile. The couch was covered with one of those things you used to see on pianos, like a cloth with fringe hanging down on all four sides. I lay down on the couch, and she put something up my vagina. I never saw what it was. It sort of hurt. Then she put some sort of packing in and gave me some medicine in a small container. They were dark brown pills. She never told me what the medicine was; she just said that I should take it when I got home. I didn't get any kind of "aftercare" or instructions or anything like that. I was just given the pills and told to take them. I think she didn't want me to be there any longer than was necessary, and I don't think I was there more than thirty minutes. I left the same way I had come—alone and on foot. At that point, I didn't have a feeling of fear. It was more like disgust: "This is an awful thing to have to go through." But my overwhelming emotion was one of relief.

I had taken the day off from work to get the abortion. I went home and took the medicine. I thought everything might be okay, but then I got terribly sick. I don't know if it was the abortion or the medicine, but I suddenly got terrible cramps. She had told me, I think, to take the medicine whether or not I had cramps, so I took it anyway. My cramps became very severe, and I felt like I was going to throw up. Now, my mother knows nothing, right? I tell her I have eaten something bad. She believes I have a stomach virus. In the middle of the night I went to the bathroom and suddenly began hemorrhaging. I had a miscarriage right there. Then I started screaming. My mother comes, takes one look, and puts me to bed and calls the doctor. You know, I'm talking about this in the present tense even though it happened almost half a century ago. Okay, so it's only forty-four years, but that's a long time ago, and sitting here on my porch on a late summer evening in the twilight, I remember it all, almost as vividly as if it were yesterday.

Anyway, where was I? In the bathroom, I start screaming. My mother rushes in. I tell her what really happened. No time now for "stomach viruses" or the fact that I really have a lousy relationship with my mother and couldn't talk to her during any of the traumatic periods that have gone before.

You know what she did? She called a doctor, and it was the same doctor I had originally gone to. As soon as she told him I was bleeding, he knew immediately what was going on and sent an ambulance to pick me up and take me to the hospital. When I got to the hospital, they did a D and C, and someone, either from the police department or the hospital, came in and interrogated me about "who did this." I refused to answer. I said I didn't know. They told me they didn't want to punish me but they really wanted to get the abortionist. I said, "It wasn't a doctor. It was a nurse, and I don't know her name." I don't know that I ever knew her last name. I just knew her first name and her phone number. When they finally were convinced that I wasn't going to tell them who she was, they left me alone. I was in the hospital for quite a while because I had peritonitis. Even after I got out, it took me weeks to really recover.

My boss fired me when he found out that I had had an abortion. I think he found out while I was in the hospital. Maybe one of the salesmen told him. He said he didn't want someone of my "character" working for him. But speaking of character, he didn't have the nerve to tell *me*. He called my mother and told her to tell me not to come back.

I continued going to the same doctor after the abortion, although I'm not sure why. He didn't treat me very well when he was treating me for the peritonitis, and it didn't get any better later. I suppose I stayed because I didn't know anyone else to go to. Several years later, when I got engaged, I went to him to be fitted for a diaphragm. He refused to do it! He refused, as he put it, because of the kind of person I was. He made me feel like dirt, slime—a despicable person. Needless to say, I was very upset.

The doctor had told my mother that he didn't know if I would ever be able to have children. He said I was really lucky to be alive, and what he implied was that a person like me didn't deserve more. I had no right to complain about being sterile, if that was what ended up happening to me. As it turned out, I wasn't sterile. I got married and had two children.

My relationship with my mother was really complex, and it got more complex after the abortion. The problem was that I had let her know I "needed" her when I was hemorrhaging in the bathroom. She was "there for me" when I was dying, or thought I was. Well, let me tell you, she never let me forget it. She felt that it gave her more power over me. I was more "imperfect" in her eyes and more of a failure. Now I really "owed her." I owed her, and I spent the rest of my life paying her.

I was never really scared or even concerned with the medical qualifications of the people I dealt with. I never dwelled on what could happen—that I could die. I just kept trying to find someone who would help me. I am sure it took me at least a month, or more, before I finally found someone. I don't remember how much money I paid to all of the different people. I think I paid four hundred dollars to the woman who did my abortion and twenty-five dollars to each of three different doctors I saw before I found her. When I found the "nurse," I really knew I had stepped out of the traditional medical world, which had been my only experience before that time. I didn't ask her about her medical qualifications, and frankly, I didn't care. This woman *could* and *would* help me. She had no competition! I had no other choices. Her qualifications didn't matter. It's interesting that as soon as I left the traditional medical world, I found someone who would help me. Maybe I should have given up on the medical people sooner.

At the time of my abortion, 1946, there wasn't much in the way of birth control, and I didn't have much knowledge. We had health classes in high school, but they didn't focus on birth control. That topic wasn't even discussed. Instead, we learned about the basic food groups and things like that. When I got pregnant, we were using a condom. That was all we had access to. Diaphragms existed, but you had to have a prescription to get one, and in 1946 you had to be married to get a prescription. Remember how the doctor wouldn't give me a prescription even when I was engaged? I guess that because of the abortion, whether I was married or not, I was still not "worthy" of having access to birth control. When he turned me down, I went to Planned Parenthood and got fitted with a diaphragm. They were very nice to me.

I never regretted having the abortion. I only regretted that it was so difficult to obtain. I never had an unwanted pregnancy again either. I didn't die and I wasn't left sterile. Considering what happened to a lot of women in those days, I guess I have been very lucky.

DR. TED

I GREW UP ON A FARM in western Pennsylvania. Growing up, I never heard anything about abortion. I never had any contact with anyone who had this problem. In medical school there certainly was no training about how to do an abortion. I don't even remember what I would call "attitudinal indoctrination" about abortion in medical school. It simply wasn't discussed. I graduated from medical school in 1943. After my internship I went into the army, and when I got out, I did a residency in ob-gyn. In the residency we were taught that abortion was wrong unless it was done to save the woman's life.

In my third year of medical school—that's when the clinical training begins and you go out onto the wards and see real patients—I spent time on an ob-gyn ward. That was the first time I had any patient contact. It wasn't "caring contact," and by that I mean actual patient care, but it was "knowledgeable contact,"where I got a look at real people with real medical problems and heard real doctors talking about them.

During that year, in 1942, I first saw women with septic abortions. In 1942 antibiotics existed, but they were very scarce. We had sulfa. Penicillin was around, but most of it was going into the war effort.

In those days the only available abortion treatment was the same as the treatment for a woman with puerperal sepsis, which is an infection after delivery, except that the puerperal sepsis patient was easier to treat. What we did there was to try to irrigate the uterus—which in a postpartum patient is much larger and more open—with antiseptic solutions in an attempt to wash out or clean out the infection.

With the abortion patient, you couldn't really do that as well, because you couldn't get tubes far enough up into the uterus to do an effective job of irrigating it. The result was that the septic abortion patient tended to be a lot sicker and was more likely to die. There really wasn't any effective treatment for the septic abortion patient. What she usually had was twin problems—blood loss and infection. Even today these two things, without blood replacement and massive doses of antibiotics, can be bad news and are often fatal.

A perforation isn't the only way you bleed to death. The woman could bleed to death from an incomplete abortion. She has the catheter inserted, goes home, and two days later she spontaneously aborts, but she doesn't pass everything. She would be bleeding fairly heavily as her body tries to rid itself of remaining tissue. If left untreated, she will just keep bleeding until she exanguinates—dies from blood loss.

With infection, it usually took the woman several days to die. It would be a death from septicemia, which is blood poisoning. Her symptoms were usually severe pain and ultimately renal shutdown—her kidneys failed. It is what we call "septic shock." The body is just overwhelmed by the infection. The death rate was high, but a lot of the ones who didn't die became "gynecological cripples"—sterile or with other chronic gynecological problems.

The hospital had a twelve-bed ward where these women were treated. It was called the septic floor. It was reserved for any patient with severe blood poisoning, but more than half of these beds were occupied by abortion patients. They were pretty representative of the general population in terms of white or black or rich or poor. The abortion patients were just average women—wives, mothers, young girls, mature women. They didn't seem different than the non-abortion patients, except they were often sicker. The only medically safe abortion technique at that time, for the extremely rare hospital-performed abortion, was a hysterotomy, because it was least likely to result in an infection. However, it was abdominal surgery, which required a general anesthetic, so that added an element of risk. You wouldn't get any training about how to do a hysterotomy until you were an intern or a resident, and then you would assist the gynecologist who was performing the surgery. The only time a hospital did what it considered a "therapeutic abortion" in those days was for a woman with severe renal disease or maybe heart disease, where she might die if she continued the pregnancy. In those days, no one thought that a woman should have any choice about these things.

The illegal abortionist didn't do anything fancy like a hysterotomy. Instead, he—or often she—inserted a catheter into the uterus. That wasn't a D and C. The purpose of the catheter was to introduce an infection, because the body's way of dealing with an infection, or with any foreign material in the uterus, would be to expel the contents, including the embryo or fetus. Sometimes the abortionist would puncture or rupture the amniotic sac, which would lead to an immediate expulsion of the fetus.

The problem for the woman was that this pretty primitive technique could also puncture the uterus itself, which could lead to a fatal hemorrhage or to the type of bad infection we talked about earlier. No one learned that technique in medical school, because it was not a medically approved or medically safe method, even in that rare instance when an abortion might be done for medical reasons. A medical student or intern wouldn't learn to do a D and C either. That didn't happen until we were residents. A first-year medical student—or really, a dishwasher or anybody at all—could do the catheter bit. Probably all you needed was to get your hands on an anatomy book and a piece of tubing or wire or anything like that.

Slippery elm was also used. That is a hydrophil, which means it absorbs water. It could be inserted into the cervix—

the opening of the uterus—and the slippery elm would expand because it was absorbing moisture. When it expanded, it forced the cervix to open up, and that would cause an abortion. Slippery elm is like laminaria, which is used today to do abortions. Laminaria is a reed which grows in a swamp. It expands when it gets wet and can be used to dilate the cervix. Things like laminaria and catheters are not too hard for lay people to get. Of course, knitting needles and wire coat hangers are even easier to get.

Sometimes the abortion patients at the hospital would tell you what happened, but sometimes they totally denied it all. But even the ones who would talk never told *who* had done the abortion. Often they really didn't know exactly what had been done. They might describe it as some sort of "manipulation" and would candidly admit their intention of getting rid of the pregnancy. I don't recall the hospital involving the police or anything like that in an effort to make a woman "confess."

During the forties and fifties I don't remember any concern by the hospital or the medical community about the wards being full of septic abortion patients and whether that was a public health problem. I first recall learning in the mid-fifties about how abortions were done in Japan. It was legal there, and they were done under sterile conditions. It was kind of an eye-opener for me, and other doctors, to discover how safe abortions could be when they were done under proper conditions. Nothing in my medical school or postgraduate training had taught me that, and it was a surprise.

But it was at least another ten years before the medical community began to talk about abortion as a public health problem. In the mid-sixties our hospital set up a committee to review and act on requests for abortion and sterilization. There were five doctors on the committee. I was one of them. Sure, we were all men, but women doctors were rare in those days. The committee members were by and large sympathetic, and I thought we did a pretty good job. The committee system was really set up in response to pressure from patients, who were becoming more insistent and more demanding about receiving good, safe abortion care.

The committee system was cumbersome for the woman, and it was probably degrading. She had to go to two psychiatrists and build a medical record that her mental health, if not her physical health, was threatened by the pregnancy. It was a charade, and we all knew it, but doctors and hospitals had to have a lot of protection, since abortion still wasn't legal. Involvement of gynecologists and psychiatrists, combined with a hospital stay, added a great deal to the cost of the abortion and probably put it out of sight of any woman who didn't have health insurance. I know that the committee system was not great. In fact, it seems really bizarre when you look back on it now after all these years, but the woman had a much better— and by that I mean safer—chance than she would have had ten years earlier.

Before legalization, and even before the committee system, I had patients who told me they wanted abortions, but I never knew any doctor who did them. I felt bad when I had to tell a patient that I couldn't help her and had no idea who could. It made you feel incompetent or inadequate, because you were supposedly trained to have solutions and to solve problems.

We always heard rumors about doctors who did abortions, but it wasn't the kind of thing you wanted to come right out and ask a colleague. I heard about one doctor who was rumored to do abortions in his office, and the next thing I knew, he was in jail because a woman had died. That was a double tragedy. She was dead, but his career was over, and he wasn't a bad person or even a bad doctor. It was the conditions that were bad. The problem was that even if you were a competent doctor, the whole illegality thing meant that you were doing it in your office under dangerous conditions. Those were bad times for everyone.

FRANCINE

I'M A WHITE MIDDLE-CLASS WOMAN. I had an illegal abortion in 1948. I guess I'm the exception that proves the rule, or maybe I'm the stereotype that people always have about white middle-class women and illegal abortions. Except for the fact that it was expensive—and that is more of the same stereotype—it was very easy for me to find a real doctor to do my abortion. He did a good job, and I had no problems with it afterward.

I was living in New York City then. I was on my own, having graduated from high school four years earlier, and I had a fairly good job, especially considering my youth and my educational background. I was doing public relations work for a big company. I got to travel all over the United States. It was really a fun job, and New York City was an exciting place to be. Best of all, I had managed to save a modest nest egg, which gave me the financial ability to take advantage of the solution that came my way.

Of course I wasn't married. I met this man, had sex with him exactly once, and promptly got pregnant. Now, the problem wasn't so much that I couldn't get good birth control as that I had bad information. On the day of this isolated moment of passion, I was having my menstrual period. I had always heard that you couldn't get pregnant unless you had sex when you were ovulating, and that you only ovulated between periods and never during periods. That made perfect sense to me. So, convinced that I could not possibly get pregnant, I gave in to my youthful desires and had unprotected sex. I had no idea that I was taking a chance. It was the one and only time I had sex with him, but that was all it took.

Surprise! The next month I didn't get a period. I went to a doctor in the neighborhood to get a pregnancy test. I lied about being married but forgot to get a dime-store wedding band. I really wasn't very good at the necessary intrigue. He examined me and did a test. Sure enough, I was pregnant. He recommended a gynecologist in the neighborhood. I smiled and took the name, but I had absolutely no intention of continuing the pregnancy. I certainly didn't mention abortion to him. I was afraid to. But I knew immediately that I would find a way to get an abortion. It was either that or jump off a bridge.

I knew that I needed to have this abortion done by a doctor if at all possible. In New York I was part of a group of young people who ran around together. One of the young men, who was from Manhattan, was the son of a dentist—Dr. Carter, his name was—and one of the young women in the group worked for him. Dr. Carter was sort of a father figure to all of us, since the rest of us were from out of town and had no family in the area. I went to Donna, the woman who worked for Dr. Carter, and told her my problem. She said, "I'll ask Dr. Carter if he knows any good doctors." So she did, and she got back to me the next day to report that yes, Dr. Carter did know a good doctor. Even better, Dr. Carter was willing to call for me and arrange the appointment. Best of all, this doctor was not just an ordinary doctor. He was a gynecologist.

But it was going to cost three hundred dollars, up front, which was a lot of money, particularly in 1948. Meanwhile, I was a little nervous about whether or not this was really a good doctor. You know, I was so lucky that I was even able to check *that* out fairly easily. Donna gave me the name of another friend of hers who had gone to him. She cautioned me that the woman might not be willing to talk to me, perhaps being reluctant to admit that she had done something illegal. My luck held. She was willing to talk to me, and more important, she assured me that he was a good doctor, that there had been nothing to it, and that she was fine afterward. That certainly dispelled any nagging worries, and I pressed ahead.

My instructions were very specific. I was to go to a certain downtown office building at a certain date and time. It was a nice building in a respectable part of town. Then my instructions were to look on the directory in the lobby for the doctor's name and office number. I had been told that his name was Dr. Cypher. I can't believe that was real! It's so phony-sounding, it's corny. I looked on the directory board, and there he was—Dr. Cypher, with a suite or office number. I don't remember the office number, but I will never forget that name! My instructions were to go up to his office. The door would be unlocked. I was to go in, put my money on the table, sit down, and wait.

I went up, and sure enough, the door was unlocked. I walked in, put my money on the table, and sat down. The room was empty. There were no nurses or other patients. There wasn't much furniture either. To me it seemed to have only about half as much furniture as it needed.

I waited. Pretty soon this man came out. He seemed young, maybe in his mid-thirties. He picked up the money and ushered me into another room. It was clean and professional-looking, with a regular gynecological examining table and all that. It looked just like any other doctor's examining room. I was instructed to partially undress and get up on the table, which I did. Then he did the abortion. I have no idea what he did, but it was quick and painless. It was also eerily quiet. He didn't talk, and I didn't either. There was no radio, no piped-in music—not a sound.

When it was over—and I doubt that it took more than five or ten minutes—he gave me the briefest of instructions. I could sit in the waiting room if I wanted to, but for no more than ten minutes. Then I was to leave. He asked if I had anyone waiting for me. On learning that I didn't, he suggested that I take a cab. If I had excessive bleeding, I was to go to a hospital, but I was not to mention his name. He disappeared. I sat there by myself for about five minutes, and then I left. I went down to the lobby, and that's when something really weird happened.

The whole experience upstairs had seemed almost surrealistic, with the silence, the half-empty rooms, and no people. As I stood there in the lobby, I felt I needed to pinch myself or something to see if I was dreaming. Had that experience upstairs really happened? I turned and looked at the lobby directory. You know what was there in the slot where Dr. Cypher's name had been only thirty minutes earlier? Nothing! It was an empty slot. I studied the directory to see if anyone else was listed for that office space. No one was. It was as if Dr. Cypher and that room and the abortion existed only in my mind.

Can you see me trying to report that to the police, even if I had wanted to, which I didn't? The police would have told me I had dreamed it all. That evening I knew it wasn't a dream, because I got severe cramps and fairly heavy bleeding. But it didn't last long, and I was fine in a couple of days. I didn't even miss any work.

You know, I used to think that, if you were white and middle-class, you had no trouble getting a nice safe-although-illegal abortion like mine. I guess that's not so. I was very lucky.

ESTELLE

I HAVE HAD LOTS OF BABIES and abortions because I could never get birth control. I had my first attempted abortion in 1948 when I was twelve. I say "attempted" because I wasn't pregnant and had never even had sex. I had just started getting my periods, and they weren't very regular. I'd miss a month, or even two or three months, and then I'd have a period. My stomach was big, but I've always had a big belly. Anyway, my mother took me to this doctor in the Hill District of Pittsburgh, where I was born and raised.

I'll never forget that doctor. He didn't even examine me. He just felt my belly and told my mother I was pregnant. My mother dragged me home and asked me if any kid had ever touched me. Well, I said yes because I didn't know what she meant. I thought she meant "touch," but she was meaning having sex. If she'd said what she meant, I'd have said no.

This doctor told my mother I was four months pregnant. I don't know why, but it might have been four months since I'd had a period. The doctor told my mother to give me some Humphreys' Eleven [a homeopathic patent medicine still sold today]. They were just pills you could buy at the drugstore, little white pills that were supposed to bring on your period. She gave me the pills, but they didn't do anything, because I didn't get my period.

My mother knew about slippery elm [see Appendix B], so we tried that. She just bought it at the drugstore. It was a piece of some kind of special bark or something. You soak it in water and then insert it. The one my mother bought was about three inches long and shaped sort of like a tampon. My mother soaked it in water, but I inserted it myself. It didn't work either, because I didn't get a period. Then one day, about two weeks later, my period just happened again.

After it was all over and I got my period, my mother and I talked. I told her I had never had sex and that if she had just asked me that, none of this would have been necessary. I think she was too mad or too upset to listen when it was happening. If that doctor had even taken the trouble to examine me, he could have told my mother I wasn't pregnant.

I had my first baby in 1957. I was twenty-one. Then I had a second baby in 1958 and a third baby in 1959. I wasn't married. My third baby died just fifteen days after her birth. They called it "crib death," but I never knew anything more than that. In 1961 I had my first real attempted abortion.

When I got pregnant for the fourth time in five years, I knew I didn't want any more children. I had just lost a child, and I had two little babies. I just couldn't handle any more children. Because I wasn't married, I couldn't get birth control. I had tried to get birth control after my first baby, but they wouldn't let me have it, so I just kept having babies. Black women living in the Hill at that time couldn't get birth control from the clinic unless they had the consent of their husbands, and there was no place on the forms for women who didn't have husbands.

I called my sister and told her I was pregnant and wanted an abortion. I knew I wasn't going to try Humphreys' Eleven or slippery elm, and I sure wasn't going back to the stupid doctor who had told my mother that her twelve-year-old virgin daughter was pregnant, but I didn't really know what to do. I didn't even bother with a real doctor to diagnose my pregnancy, because I *knew* I was pregnant. Besides, I was afraid that a real doctor might be able to do something to prevent me from getting an abortion.

My sister asked around and found out that there were lots of women in the Hill who did abortions. The black community I grew up in was like that. It was a close community, and someone always knew someone, so it was pretty easy to get names. My sister gave me two options. There was a woman in the Hill that I could go to, or there was another woman who would come to my house. I picked the option of the woman coming to me. The way it worked was that my sister gave the woman my telephone number, and then she called me. She asked me my name and what I wanted. I told her I was pregnant and wanted an abortion. She asked how far along I was, and I told her I thought it was two or three months.

I never really knew the woman's full name. When I asked, she told me to call her Mary, and that's all she would say. She worked at the Veterans Hospital, but she wasn't a nurse. I know that. She said she was a nurse's aide. She came to my house and brought all kinds of instruments and things with her. Then she examined me and told me exactly how many months pregnant I was. Imagine that! I was impressed. She really seemed to know her business. Unfortunately, she wouldn't do the abortion. She told me I was too far along. She could do it up to so many weeks, but I was beyond that. Because she really seemed to know what she was talking about, I figured she was right and that no one else was going to do it either, so I gave up and had the baby.

My next experience was just a year later. I had gotten married a few months after the baby was born, and my husband refused to sign for the birth control pills. This was like a bad dream. First I couldn't get birth control because I wasn't married, and then, the way things turned out, I couldn't get birth control because I was! I got pregnant just a few months after I got married. I had had my fourth baby in May of 1961. I got married in August, and by November I was pregnant again.

This time I contacted Mary right away. I couldn't contact her directly. I had to call someone else who would take my name and number and have her call me—just like the year before. Well, Mary called back and asked me how far along I was. I told her it couldn't even be as much as a month. Again she came to the house and examined me. Since I was very early, she could do the abortion. She told me to buy a catheter and penicillin pills. She told me what drugstore to go to and who to ask for. It was the same drugstore in the Hill where we had gotten the Humphreys' Eleven and the slippery elm when I was twelve, but they had both been right out on the shelf and you didn't have to ask anyone. This was a little bit more complicated.

Mary told me to ask for a certain man at the drugstore. I don't remember his name. He wasn't the pharmacist. She said he was the pharmacist's helper, but I think he might have been the cleaning man. I called and told him what I wanted. He told me to bring twenty-five dollars in cash and to ask for him. I did. He took my money and handed me a brown paper bag. I never saw the pharmacist, and I don't know if he knew what was going on or not. When I got home I looked in the bag, and there were twelve penicillin tablets and a catheter. The catheter was about twelve inches long. It was red and looked like it had a wire or something inside of it.

Mary came to my house the next day. I paid her fifty dollars. She spread newspaper on my bed and put those pads they put under you in hospitals on top of the newspaper. Then she had me lie down on the pads. She told me I would just feel a little pinch, and that was exactly what it felt like. She inserted the catheter in me and pulled out the wire. The whole thing didn't take more than fifteen minutes. When she was finished, she told me to start taking the penicillin pills right away, even though it would be several hours before anything happened.

She told me exactly what to expect and when to expect it— like in a certain number of hours I would start having pain, and the next day I would expel the catheter and everything. She told me how long I would bleed after the abortion and when I would have my next normal period. She told me what was normal and what to worry about. I remember that big clots or a temperature were things I should worry about, and if something like that happened, I should go to the doctor but not tell him anything about her. She was very good—just like a real doctor—and everything happened just like she said it would.

The next day I had bad cramps and heavy bleeding, and I did pass everything like she said. I just kept taking the penicillin, and in a few days I was all right.

The next year, 1962, I was pregnant all over again. Again I tried to get an abortion. I didn't go back to Mary because I didn't have seventy-five dollars. I wasn't going to spend a lot of time trying home remedies, but this time I did try Humphreys' Eleven again, and again it didn't work. Then I took quinine because someone had told me that would work. I bought the quinine at the same drugstore where I had bought the Humphreys' Eleven and the catheter and penicillin. No brown paper bags for the quinine. It was all open and aboveboard. I had to ask the pharmacist for the quinine, but he didn't ask me why I wanted it. He sold me a whole bottle of quinine pills. They made my ears ring but didn't do anything else, and I decided I better not waste any more time.

I got the name of a different, cheaper abortionist. This time I went to a doctor's office on Centre Avenue in the Hill district. I was told I had to call the doctor's office on a Thursday. The doctor wasn't in on Thursday, but his nurse was, and she was the one who did the abortions. She only charged fifteen dollars. I was told that she would give you a shot and some pills [probably Ergotrate] and you would miscarry. For each set of shot and pills you had to pay fifteen dollars, and if you were very lucky, it would work the first time. You know, I have no idea whether the nurse—she could have been just the office receptionist, for all I know—and the doctor were partners somehow or whether the doctor didn't know anything about what went on there on Thursdays.

I called and went over that Thursday for my shot and pills. Well, nothing happened. I had to wait a week and go back for a second dose. By that next Thursday she told me I was too far along, and she refused to give me any more shots and pills.

Then someone told me about an oblong purple pill [probably potassium permanganate]. I can't remember now what it was called, but I knew then because I had to ask for it at the drugstore. I remember that two or three pills cost five dollars.

Again the pharmacist didn't ask me any questions. He just sold me the pills. You didn't swallow these pills, you inserted them, and they were supposed to cause an abortion. I inserted the pills, and they did make me bleed. The flow was so heavy that blood ran down my legs, but it was kind of thick and funny-looking. It was almost rubbery, and I felt that I could have rolled it into a ball. Anyway, in spite of all the bleeding, the pills didn't cause an abortion. I was weak and nauseated and bled for about two days, but nothing else happened. I was still pregnant. By this time I was too scared to go to a doctor to see if I was all right, and there really didn't seem to be anything else to try, so I just gave up and had another baby. She was born in 1962.

After that I tried to get a hysterectomy or get my tubes tied so I wouldn't be at risk every time my husband came after me, but they wouldn't do it. They asked me why I wanted one. Why? Why couldn't they understand? I was tired. My body was tired. It is hard on your body, being pregnant every year. My marriage was going bad. My husband wasn't working. He had been laid off from the steel mill. We were on welfare. I was depressed, desperate, and frantic. I felt that I really couldn't survive another pregnancy. How many reasons did I need? Well, they didn't think my reasons were good enough, and they refused to sterilize me, so I was stuck again.

I had to do something, so I forged my husband's signature on a consent form and did get a diaphragm. If he found it, he would tear it or throw it away, and sometimes he would hit me.

In 1963 I got pregnant again, but it was a tubal pregnancy and they had to operate. They removed one tube and one ovary, but they still wouldn't sterilize me. I begged them to just take out both tubes while they were there, but they wouldn't do it. They kept saying things like, "What if all your babies burned up in a fire?" Isn't that crazy? I wouldn't have been willing to get pregnant if the whole country burned up in a fire! But I just couldn't make them understand that. If God put me on earth to have babies, I had done that. I had done more than my share!

I get so mad when I hear anyone say that women on welfare have more babies so they can get more money. Anyone who believes that doesn't know much about welfare! My husband wasn't working, we had four children, and we got a hundred and ninety-eight dollars every two weeks. Tell me six people can live on that! With every new baby we got poorer. I couldn't imagine that life would get any better or that I would ever get out of the welfare trap. With all the rules about birth control and sterilization, I felt like the welfare department or the system or something wanted me to have more babies.

I talked to my mother once about birth control, after I had children and couldn't get it "officially." I figured she would know some kind of home remedy. Well, she didn't. She had only been pregnant two times in her life—me and my sister. She had never used or needed birth control, so she had a hard time understanding why I was having so much trouble. Isn't it funny how different people can be?

In 1964 I got pregnant again, even though I had only one ovary. My husband was an ass and the marriage wasn't good, but he was working in the mill again. We were off welfare. We had money. I could feed my kids. I could afford to have a private doctor and eat the right kinds of food while I was pregnant. Things seemed better, so I had that baby.

After that my marriage just fell apart. My husband was physically abusive, and he would throw away my birth control if he ever found it. He refused to leave, and there was no place for me to go with all those kids. I had five by that time. Naturally, I got pregnant again. I still had a private doctor, but I wasn't doing as well as I had the year before. My body was all "babied out," I guess. There had just been too many pregnancies too close together.

One hot day in August of 1965, when I was seven months pregnant, my husband came home after being out all night drinking. He got mean when he drank. Me and my kids had gone to a neighborhood picnic that day. Well, he asked my older son—my two older kids weren't his—if I had talked to any men at the picnic. Of course I had. They were all my neighbors. Why wouldn't I speak to them? I'm a friendly person by nature, and I talked to anyone who would talk to me. Remember, I'm seven months pregnant with five kids in tow—not exactly the kind of woman a man is looking to pick up, or at least no sensible person would think so.

Well, my husband wasn't sensible, and he sure wasn't sensible when he'd been out all night drinking! He came into the living room and said, "Is that baby mine?" I laughed. I figured it had to be a joke. Well, he grabbed me and threw me down on the floor. Then he sat on my chest, holding my arms down with his knees, and he beat me. It was bad. He had a big ring on his finger, and it cut my face and his hand when he hit me. My youngest boy, who couldn't have been more than five years old—I had three girls, not counting the crib-death baby, and two boys—hit him with a chair. That stopped him, and he left the house.

That day I drifted in and out of consciousness at home. One of my children called my sister, who came and got me and took me to the hospital. I had a concussion, and my face was all swollen and cut. My doctor, who had delivered my last baby, came to see me, and he was really upset. He said, "Don't you tell me you fell downstairs or walked into a door, because I know what happened to you, and if you lose this baby, I'm going to press charges against him if you don't!" Imagine that. I really felt that no one cared and nobody would help me, and here was this doctor saying he was upset about what my husband had done to me. He was really a very nice person.

My daughter was born two months prematurely three days after the beating. She only weighed one and a quarter pounds. My husband came to see me in the hospital and begged me not to press charges against him. My doctor told me that I really shouldn't have any more babies and that I ought to get away from my husband. After about eight days they discharged me from the hospital. The baby had to stay until she was bigger and stronger, but she did survive.

In spite of what my doctor had told me, the hospital sent me home with no birth control, and my husband was still in the house. Well, I knew I could not survive another pregnancy, so I forged my husband's consent again, went to the clinic in the

Hill, and told them I had to have birth control pills. They wanted to give me a diaphragm, but I had had enough of that. I said, "I don't want no diaphragm. I want the pill!" Maybe the desperation I felt got conveyed to them, because somehow, for the first time in my life, I got the pill. It was wonderful. I went home and told my husband, "If you touch me or my pills, I'll kill you!"

I started taking birth control pills. I took them for the next five years and I never got pregnant. Since I grew up I had had a pregnancy almost every year, so this was a real miracle. My husband was still around and the marriage was still bad, but he wasn't hitting me and I wasn't pregnant. I wonder why I stayed in that bad marriage as long as I did, but I think I know the answer. My daddy left my mother when I was only two, and I always felt like I got cheated out of a father. But I tell you, I never had to run out of the house because my daddy was beating up on my mama. When I looked back on it, I realized that my childhood was better than my children's childhood. As long as he was around, my children weren't going to have a good childhood.

My husband kept living there. He wouldn't move, and the kids and I couldn't. My mother had moved into the projects, so she just had three rooms. She couldn't take us in. No one really wants a woman and six children, let me tell you! I called the Salvation Army. They could take me and my girls, but they couldn't take my boys. I wasn't about to leave my boys behind, so I just stayed.

I bought a gun and practiced in my basement until I learned how to use it. I wasn't going to have any more beatings or any more babies, and I figured having a gun gave me a better chance of making sure that those things didn't happen to me anymore.

In 1965, when my last baby was six months old, I got a job. It was the first real job I'd ever had. I worked for the city. It was part-time and minimum wage—no health insurance or anything like that—but it was wonderful. I felt like I had a little bit more control over my life and that I could do for my children.

Then I got a second job working nights at the museum, and a third job doing cleaning three mornings a week. I worked three jobs for eight years until I finally got a real full-time job, with health insurance and everything, at the museum. I still work there.

I ruled my kids with an iron hand, and they did what they were supposed to do. They came right home from school. They did their homework. The bigger ones watched out for the littler ones. I'd make dinner in the morning, before I left for the cleaning job, and the kids would heat it up when they got home from school. I'd eat dinner with them before I went to my night job. I ignored my husband and tried to save some of my money. I never let him have any of it because he would just spend it on booze. At that point he wasn't working at all. He was really crazy jealous after I got the jobs. He accused me of having sex with the milkman and even with an old white farmer who lived down the street from us. He and his wife felt sorry for us, and they would give us things like a bushel of beans or whatever that was still good but was wilted and couldn't be taken to the market.

Anyway, one day my husband was upstairs yelling at the kids—he never hit them, just me—and he yelled down, saying he was going to kill me. I grabbed my purse and ran out the door. He came running after me. He was mad and looked like he meant business. I decided I couldn't keep running, so I turned around and told him that if he took another step I'd shoot him. The gun was in my purse. Well, he laughed and kept coming. I took aim and shot him. I hit his arm. He looked amazed. I was amazed too. I was really kind of surprised that I had hit him, but I acted a lot braver than I felt and told him that next time it would be his head and not his arm. Big talk, but it worked. That man never hit me again—never!

By 1970 I had become a diabetic. I had been taking the pill for five years, and they told me I had to quit, so they gave me an IUD. I had it for less than a year when I got a severe infection from it. I was in the hospital, and they took the IUD out and told me I couldn't use it anymore, so I was back to nothing, this time for medical reasons. I got pregnant, but by then it was 1971, and I got a legal abortion through the clinic. A year later I had a second legal abortion through the clinic. When I came back that second time, they asked me if I thought abortion was a form of birth control. I told them I didn't but that if they wouldn't do the abortion because I was a "repeater," I would find someone who would. They did the abortion.

Now that I had jobs and a gun, I decided to divorce my husband. Well, he told me that if I divorced him I'd have to support him, because I was working and he wasn't. There was no way I was going to give that man any money to spend on booze, so I figured I'd just stay married, because no one was making me give him any money now.

After that second legal abortion, I never got pregnant anymore. I kept working and saving money. Working those three jobs was not because it took three jobs for us to live. I was secretly saving all of the money from one of the jobs. That third job was my ticket out of this lousy marriage. I figured that if I never talked to him and never gave him any money, he might get tired of me and take up with another woman, maybe even leave.

Well, it happened. One day I came home from work and he was gone, along with almost everything in the house. He left six towels and washcloths—one for each kid, but none for me. He took all the sheets and all three of our TV sets. He even took the crock pot I had bought to make it easier to cook dinner when I was at work all day. He took almost everything. But you know what? I didn't even care. I lay on my bare mattress in my empty bedroom and just grinned. Now I could really do something for my kids and for me. The next day I bought a TV set for the kids and a new mattress for me. The old one smelled like him, and I didn't want any reminders! He divorced me on December 31, 1973. In February of 1974, I took all the money I had been secretly saving and I made a down payment on this house. This is mine. I pay my bills. My kids are all grown, and they all turned out fine.

Mary, who did my illegal abortion, is still around, I think.

Do you know she guaranteed her work? If it didn't work the first time, she did it again at no charge to you. Everyone in the Hill went to her. She bought a house with the money she made doing abortions. One of my friends had an abortion done with a catheter by a woman like Mary. My friend saved the catheter and used it again *on herself* to do an abortion. I can't imagine that. It worked, too. She got so good that she could do an abortion with a well-sharpened pencil. Her mother-in-law used to do abortions too.

Abortion was very open in the black community. My sister had an abortion. It was a bad experience, and she ended up in the hospital. She also got one for her daughter, years later, when the girl was only fourteen.

In 1958 my best girlfriend, Millie, called and told me she was going to have an abortion. She had a year-old child and an infant. Her husband had started fighting with her, and he had other women. I tried to talk her out of it, but she was determined. Well, her mother called me a week later. Millie was dead. She had died from the abortion. She died from gangrene. She was only twenty-three. I was devastated. About six years ago I met her son, who had been a year old when his mother died. His aunt introduced us and said, "This was your mother's best friend." Well, do you know, he sat and talked to me for the longest time. He wanted to know everything I could tell him about his mother. He didn't have any memory of her at all. It was sad and made me cry for him and for Millie— again, after all these years.

Those years were awful, and I never want my daughters to go through what I went through. You know, I never really knew until today that the stuff that happened to me happened to white women too. I thought it just happened to me and Millie and other women in the Hill because we were poor and black and dumb. But that's not it. This isn't a black thing, this is a woman thing. Why was it that way? Why did it have to happen? Why did we let it happen?

CLIFFORD

I'M AN OLD MAN NOW—ninety-three, to be exact—but I remember how abortion used to be in the black community. I'm from Virginia, but I came to Pittsburgh in 1912.

Now, if you go way back, it was herbs and roots and special things that the people passed on, one to another. When someone found that one of their daughters was pregnant, there were certain people—men sometimes, but most often women—who knew roots and herbs, I know this. In Virginia there was Aunt Mary, and it was recognized that she had more remedies—roots and herbs for different ailments. And of course, with that, if someone came along pregnant, Aunt Mary knew what root to give, and therefore the woman aborted.

In about 1929 or so, there was a man who used to come through Pittsburgh. He had a cart and he sold roots and herbs. He came from Louisiana. We all called him "Doc Lane from New Orleans." Young men would go to him and say, "I've gotten a girl in trouble." Well, he would know what to do. If a girl missed her period, he would give her something with bluing in it. Hardly anyone even uses bluing today, but in those days the women used it to get the wash white. He'd tell the girl to take this bluing and she'd "come around," and I guess she did. I'd even heard that from girls in the South when I was growing up. A girl would say, "If I don't show up, I'm going to take me some bluing."

Now, Doc didn't just have roots and herbs for abortions. He had them for all kinds of things. People believed in him, yes they did. One night I happened to be standing in Big Track, a place where they gambled. He came in there with a basket of roots and herbs. A fellow named Jim Stone asked Doc if he had anything that could help an old man have sex. Doc said, "Yeah, I'll get you something." In about three or four days, he came and gave Jim a root and told him to make a tea out of it. Well, Jim did, and it began to give him an erection—at least Jim said it did. Jim died a week or so later, and they said he died with an erection on him. Now, people said the erection was from the root. I guess they didn't think he died from the root, because after that, Doc was famous and everybody wanted his roots for whatever it was that ailed them.

Then I remember the Italian woman in Pittsburgh's first ward—Mom, they called her. She lived down on the eleven-hundred block of Pig Alley, as we called it. That was an all-right part of town in those days. Now it's not so nice. Mom was a white woman. I don't know whether she did roots or what she did, but it was said she could help a girl who got into trouble. People went to her and thought she was good.

In those days, the best way to hear about people who could help with an abortion was to hang around the pool halls or other places where young men congregated. Then you would hear about who was around at any given time. These people changed from time to time, because they went to jail or retired or left town and then new ones came along. The pool hall was the best way to find out who was around and who was good.

In Pittsburgh one of the abortionists I remember was the Reverend Kane. He was around later than Doc and Mom. I would say he was around in the late thirties. Now, he was different, because he had originally started to medical school. In his second year of medical school he did an abortion on a girl at the college. They found out and kicked him out of school. Since he couldn't become a doctor, he became a minister. He was from somewhere in the South. He came to Pittsburgh after the war in Europe, maybe around 1920. I don't know how he

did abortions, but I know he did them, because it was common knowledge. He was arrested several times and convicted at least once. That's how come everyone knew about him.

As I say, I don't know how Reverend Kane did abortions, but I know it wasn't just giving them herbs to take. He had the custom of having the women meet him at a drugstore on Centre Avenue across from the old Wilson Theater. His fee was thirty-five dollars. Then he took them to his home or somewhere, where he did the abortion. He did something there and sent them home, and then they would abort at home.

I remember one girl who had an abortion from Reverend Kane. She came from a prominent family here. Afterward, she started bleeding badly. They took her to the hospital, and she had to have blood transfusions. She almost died. Dr. Ames was her family physician, and he put her in the hospital. He was very upset after he got her in the hospital and discovered she had had an abortion, because he was afraid that people would think he had done it.

And I'll tell you about someone else who was somewhat upset. The Reverend Kane lived in the Hill District. When he died, he had an awful lot of money and left a great deal of it to a local Catholic church. The church was a little bit concerned about what Reverend Kane was doing and where the money came from. But the church needed the money, so they took it and were glad to have it.

In the early forties there was Dr. Parker, also in the Hill District. She had been a chiropractor or something like that, and she used to do abortions. She was arrested a couple of times.

Now, remember that even when the Reverend Kane and Dr. Parker were in business, up through about 1950 anyway, an awful lot of women in the black community just did the things that their mothers and grandmothers before them had done. They did their abortions in their own homes without involving anyone. They just did it. I think the women just told other women and us men never knew about that. What I knew about was just what young black men knew about. I'm old now, and maybe things are different today. I don't know.

FAY

*She was a light-skinned black woman, wearing no makeup,
with short, white, unstyled hair, dressed in a simple pink
sweatsuit and white tennis shoes. Short and slightly over-
weight, she was one of the most strikingly beautiful sixty-
four-year-old women I had ever seen. It was easy to envision
the lovely young dancer she had been forty years earlier. I
had first heard about Fay eight months earlier, from Dr.
Clay (see pp. 109–16). He was not willing to put me in touch
with her, since I was a stranger and Fay had a new life he
was hesitant to disturb. Several months later, I tracked
down Detective Stan (see pp. 105–8) from old newspaper
clippings about Fay's arrest. He remembered her but had no
idea where she might be now. Finding Fay and persuading
her to talk to me proved a very difficult task. When an
underground abortionist from a black community gives it
up and goes even further underground in an effort to conceal
her past, she can be extremely difficult to trace—especially
for a white woman searching twenty-five years later.*

I HAVE CHILDREN AND GRANDCHILDREN. My grandchildren are in
college. They don't know anything at all about my past, and
I don't want them to ever find out! Just like you had a hard
time finding me, I don't ever want anyone to find out who I
was. I have two kids. They are in their forties now. They knew, I
think, although we never talked about it. My daughter knew
because she would answer the telephone. The caller, hearing a

female and thinking it might be me, would ask her questions that led her to guess what I was doing. My son knew too, but I don't know how he found out. Maybe my daughter told him.

When I first got out of high school, during World War II, I went into the army. I was in the army for three and a half years. I was a drill sergeant, a cadence caller—you know, "Hup, two, three, four." I was probably the smallest drill sergeant in the army, since I only weighed ninety-eight pounds.

When I was a young woman, I loved to dance, and I was pretty good too. I did dance professionally a little bit at clubs in the area. The owners liked to have good dancers around because it was good for business. People would come to watch the dancers. It didn't pay much, but I would have done it for nothing because I loved to dance. I could really jitterbug! Of course, I had a nineteen-inch waistline in those days, and that helps. I couldn't do it today.

I'm a nurse. I first learned nursing in the army, and then I learned a lot more when I worked in a big hospital in Pittsburgh after I got out of the army. I stayed at the hospital for three years, until my husband died. That was in 1952. After he died, I took my baby daughter and moved to a different part of town. I got a job as a nurse in a Catholic hospital.

I hadn't learned a lot about obstetrics or gynecology in either the army or the big hospital. I had spent most of my time on the medical and surgical floor, so by the time I left to go to the Catholic hospital, I was a pretty good nurse with not much obstetrical or gynecological experience. Everything I learned on those two topics, including how to do abortions, was taught to me by two white doctors at the Catholic hospital. Isn't that ironic? Learning how to do abortions at a Catholic hospital!

I'm not sure that either of the doctors knew that the other one was teaching me how to do abortions and other things. Each may have thought he was the only one. However, between the two of them, I sure got good training, because they were both very good doctors. They taught me lots of things besides how to do abortions. I assisted them and watched what they were doing. That's how I learned to do it myself. I learned to find the cervix—that's the opening of the uterus—and I learned how to insert a catheter into the uterus. They did some abortions themselves for their special patients, and they did them right there at the hospital, but they called it something else. Like maybe one would do a D and C and even call it a D and C but change the reasons. Maybe he would write in her chart that she had been having cramping and heavy bleeding for ten days when really she hadn't had any bleeding. In fact, that's what the problem was—no bleeding.

I can't remember when I did my first abortion, because it was such a long time ago. I would guess it was in the early to mid fifties. Most of my referrals came from doctors or nurses who knew me. At first I was always reluctant. I'd say, "Can't you get someone else to do it?" Now, that wasn't because I thought it was morally wrong. When you work in a hospital, you see lots of human suffering, and you want to help prevent it if you can. I always believed that women should be able to have as few or as many children as they wanted. I guess you could say that I believe in choice in things like that. Well, anyway, they would say that they couldn't get anyone else or they wanted me because they knew me and trusted me or because I was a good nurse or something like that. I always ended up helping them out.

I always did the abortions at my home. I really didn't have anyplace else to do them. Yet I never worried much about having someone turn me in, because in the beginning I only took cases who were people I knew or the daughters or close friends of people I knew. Usually the person I knew was the one who actually brought the woman to my house.

Abortions are easy to do, and it doesn't take long to do a good one. I could do one in less than five minutes: completely done, clean and out. Usually the woman wouldn't be at my house for longer than fifteen minutes—total.

I always used a catheter, but sometimes I took it out and other times I left it in. Mostly I left it in because you get better results that way. Catheters were easy to get. Different doctors would sometimes give them to me. I would also go to the drugstore and buy them. The pharmacist would sort of jokingly bawl me out for buying so many, but he always sold them to me. Sometimes he would even offer to order them special for me. I'd buy them in batches of a dozen or so. It was about a size fourteen regular irrigating catheter that I used. It looked sort of like what you would use for an enema, except that those were bigger—eighteens and twenties. The catheter I used was thicker than a broom straw and not as thick as a drinking straw. They were made of red rubber and were about twelve inches long. Sometimes they were just plain, but sometimes they came in little sterile individual packets. That was nice. I liked it when I could get them like that. When they didn't come in the sterile packets, I sterilized them myself by boiling them in water with Clorox.

In addition to the catheters, I had to have a speculum and a light so I could look in and see what was going on. Like, I never wanted to do an abortion on a woman who was a diabetic, and I could pretty much tell if she was a diabetic just by looking at her vagina and cervix. That was because I had spent so much time on the medical service before I ever started doing abortions. You can also tell a lot about a woman's health by looking at her eyes, lips, and fingernails, so I routinely did that as well. Also, I could usually tell how pregnant the woman was by feeling her uterus, and so I always checked that out first.

I've heard of people who did abortions in the back seats of cars. I can't imagine that. You wouldn't be able to see, and it sure wouldn't be very clean. With all the abortions I did, I had the woman lying on the bed. I had good light and good conditions. You have to be able to see what you're doing. Like, sometimes you look up there and you can't see the opening because the uterus is tipped forward. Then you have to kind of move things around and tip the uterus back so that the cervix comes into view, because that is where you are going to insert the catheter. You simply have to be able to see what you are doing.

I never was willing to do an abortion beyond the first two months or so. It could be done later, but it was more complicated and more dangerous for the patient, and I just never wanted to get involved with that. The woman never actually aborted at my house. It always happened a day or so later when she was at home, and I didn't think it was a good idea for a woman to be at home, unattended, having a late abortion.

I didn't give the women antibiotics because I couldn't get those without a prescription, so I would tell each woman to get them from the doctor who sent her to me. Sometimes I never knew who the referring doctor was because the doctor didn't want me to know he was sending people to me. Maybe he was thinking that he didn't want anything coming back on him if something went wrong. It's like they all wanted me to be out there doing good abortions so they could send their patients to me, while at the same time they didn't want to be "involved." Although I guess I understand that, in some ways it doesn't seem very fair.

As I said, often I never knew who the woman's doctor was. I knew he referred her, though, because the woman would say something like, "My doctor says that if you do this, he will take care of me, but he said that I had to come and see you first." If the woman didn't have any doctor of her own, I would call one of the doctors I knew and he would write a prescription for her.

I never had a medical problem that occurred right there, like a perforation or something, and only one woman ever got an infection afterward. Although I didn't know it at the time, she had a toothache. If I'd known, I would have made her go to the dentist first. As it turned out, when I did the abortion she already had an infected tooth, and she ended up getting an infected abortion too. When you already have an infection, that is a real bad time to decide to have minor surgery.

There were lots of other abortionists around when I was doing abortions, but they weren't doctors, and most of them weren't even nurses like I was. They were just hit-or-miss types who didn't know what they were doing. Sometimes they would call and ask me different questions. It was scary how little they knew. One woman who did abortions was a beautician. She quit when one of the women she did ended up in the hospital. That scared her into quitting.

The first abortion I ever did was for Marie, a nurse I worked with. One day she stopped me in the hall. I was surprised, because she always acted like she didn't like me. She seldom even spoke to me. I don't know if it was because she was white and I was black or what, but there it was, for whatever the reason. Well, she told me that her thirteen-year-old daughter was pregnant, and she asked me to do an abortion. She knew that I had been working a lot with the two doctors who trained me. Maybe she figured that since she couldn't get one of them to help her, I might be the next-best thing. She never really said.

When Marie asked me, it was also a shock because she was always a very religious person—a holier-than-thou type—and she seemed to disapprove of everything. Like, at work she was always talking that this was "wrong" and that was "wrong." I don't remember her ever talking about abortion, but I'm sure that if you had asked her, she would have told you it was wrong.

When I met the girl, I could see why Marie was worried about her daughter. She was a very sullen, rebellious teenager who seemed to me to be angry with her mother and intent on punishing her. This pregnancy was sure a good way to do that, because Marie was really distraught.

I did the abortion, like Marie asked me to. When it was over, I told her to be sure to have the girl checked by her doctor in a week or two. Wouldn't you know, her mother brought her to the ob-gyn out-patient clinic where I worked at the hospital. When the girl came in, I was the nurse on duty. In my presence, the doctor examined her and pronounced her to be "fine." Her mother was so relieved and so grateful. I felt good about that—about knowing that I had helped someone and that I had done a good job.

You know what that girl is doing today? She's a doctor. I think having that abortion may have turned that kid around. She quit punishing her mother—and surely herself in the process—and she quit cutting school and getting into trouble. She just seemed to get her life on track after that.

Most of the women I did were white. However, I had black women too. They tended to be more desperate, with fewer options than the white women, or maybe it was just that their economic desperation was so much greater. You have no idea how a lost soul looks until you look into the eyes of some of the poorer black women who came to me for help. I just could not look into those eyes and bring myself to say, "No. Sorry, I won't help you." Some of them had six or seven children and no place to go and no one to turn to. I certainly had some white women like that too. I just couldn't live with myself if I refused to help people like that.

When a desperate woman came to me and said, "Please help me," I usually called a doctor before I agreed to do anything—at least I did that when I first started out and was more unsure of myself. I would call either the doctor who sent her to me or one of the doctors—and there were a lot!—who regularly referred women to me. I would tell the doctor the facts as the woman had given them to me and ask what I should do. The doctor would always urge me to help the woman, sometimes saying, "I would if I could, but I can't." Well, I guess that because I felt I could, I always felt I should. Probably the main reason I quit running it by doctors first, about whether or not I ought to do it, was because I never got a "no" answer.

I probably did one or two abortions a week for ten or twelve years altogether. I certainly did hundreds, but probably not more than a thousand, if that many. I always did the abortions in my bedroom, and contrary to what the police said, my bedroom was neat and clean. So was the rest of my house.

My fees varied depending on the person. My regular charge was a hundred and fifty dollars, but I did lots for twenty-five or thirty dollars, and I did plenty for nothing. When you live in a community like mine, you see a lot of poor people who really need help. There was one white doctor I knew who was just wonderful. I once sent a real poor woman to him. She didn't have any doctor or any money, but she did have some serious health problems. He stopped me in the hall later. I was kind of nervous because I thought he might be mad at me for sending someone I knew couldn't pay. He was just wonderful! You know what he said? He said, "Anytime you have someone like that who needs help, just send them to me. I'll take care of them."

Don't misunderstand. We weren't talking about abortions here. These were just poor folk who needed other kinds of medical care. I never made a lot of money doing abortions because I kept doing them for free for poor women.

In addition to urging women to see their doctors for a follow-up, I always encouraged them to call me if they had any problems. They all had my telephone number. Maybe I should have, but I never worried about people betraying me to the police. Desperate people—especially black people—don't betray the person who helps them. The two police who set me up were white. I don't think black people would have done that. I've never gotten over it, and to this day I have a deep distrust of white people, which is kind of surprising since I've spent my whole life around them. But I just never got over what was done to me that day by two white people.

I would trust a black person not to betray me where a white one might because of the way blacks and whites feel about what I will call "the system." Whites basically expect the system to believe them and to treat them right. Blacks, on the other hand, expect not to be believed by white folks. They don't think they will do well in the system no matter what their role is. As a result, a black patient of mine was less likely to report me to the system because the system would probably somehow punish her as well as me. For those reasons, I didn't usually just take white folks on faith, although I now know that even so, I was probably much too trusting. Usually when I did a white woman, she was brought to me by a black person I had some reason to trust. I either knew the black person personally or the person was a friend of someone I did know and trust.

During all of the ten or twelve years I was doing abortions, I worked in the Catholic hospital, and I think at least some of the nuns knew what I was doing on the side. Once I had to go into that hospital myself because I was having heavy vaginal bleeding. They did a D and C on me, and I can remember the nun saying, "Now, you have to be quiet about this." She thought I had had an abortion and that the hospital was treating me for the consequences, but I hadn't. As it turned out, I had fibroid tumors, and they were what was giving me all the trouble.

That thing with the undercover cops in 1966 was the *only* time in my whole life that I got arrested for anything. I was just too trusting. When they called, they used the name of a man I did know and trust. I never knew if he set me up or whether someone else told the cops to mention his name when they called me. I sure hope it wasn't that man, because I had never done anything to hurt him. Maybe it was nothing personal. Maybe the man had troubles of his own with the cops and just needed something to throw at them to take their interest away from him. The reasons of whoever did it to me don't much matter. The harm that was done to me as a result was real bad.

You know, the judge threw it out. He called it "entrapment," what the police did to me. It was good that I didn't go to jail, but my life was ruined all the same. I got fired by the Catholic hospital. It is one thing to quietly do an abortion for a nurse at the hospital or for their doctors to refer patients to me, but it is quite another thing to get arrested for abortion and have your name printed in the papers. It didn't matter how good a nurse I was. I couldn't be a nurse there or anywhere when it hit the papers.

In 1970 a woman in the next block was doing abortions, and wouldn't you know, Detective Stan tried to arrest me. You know why? I think it was because she and I lived in the same neighborhood and we were both black women. To him, we just all looked alike. This time, though, he quickly figured out his mistake and left me alone. The woman left town right after that, and so I didn't have any more problems with the police.

I felt so horrible when I was arrested and my name was in the paper. It was years before I was willing to leave the house. I felt so ashamed. It wasn't doing abortions that I was ashamed of, it was being arrested. In my mind, the only people who are arrested are criminals, and suddenly, overnight, instead of being a nurse, mother, and productive member of society, I had become a criminal. It was awful. I did not feel good about myself, and I just withdrew from the world.

Some people were nice to me, though. Doctors told me that

the best thing for depression was to go back to work. The director of nursing at another hospital called me at home and offered me a job. I knew they were right, but I just couldn't bring myself to do it. I wish I had listened to them, because I would be in better shape today.

I never worked as a nurse again, and I never did another abortion either. I went into a deep depression and refused to leave my house. The longer I stayed home, the worse it got and the more depressed I got. I just kept retreating inward. I'm still depressed. I don't understand why one person can be so inhumane to another. I never did anything to those two people. Why did they do that to me?

DETECTIVE STAN

I'M A RETIRED CITY DETECTIVE. In 1966 I was one of two under-cover city detectives who arrested Fay.

From 1965 on, I was a supervisor in the detective bureau. We would get information about people doing abortions. Whenever we obtained that kind of information, the team, which consisted of a young female police officer pretending to be the girl in trouble, and a male police officer posing as the boyfriend, took steps to try to infiltrate and get to the abortionist. One of us would set up an appointment. Then we would let the abortionist go just so far, making the arrest before anything was actually done to the policewoman.

Someone gave us the tip that Fay was doing abortions, and they were able to give us enough information, like her address and such, that we could make an appointment. I made the tele-phone call. I don't know who I talked to on the phone, but it was a woman. I think it was Fay, but I'm not sure. She asked me what I wanted. I told her I had a girl in trouble and I needed an abortion. She was very up-front about everything, and it was a very candid discussion. She told me what it would cost. As I remember, it was a hundred and fifty dollars, but that might not be right. She gave us a specific time to come to her house and asked if I needed directions. I didn't.

The female police officer was new on the job, but I had

known her for years because she lived in my neighborhood. Before we went in I said, "Now, Mary, whatever you do, don't let her put anything in you." Well, Mary laughed and told me she sure wouldn't. It seems that Mary had had a hysterectomy, and so she didn't have a uterus anymore, which meant that as soon as Fay examined her, she would realize that Mary knew she wasn't pregnant. Then Fay would figure out that we were undercover cops, and it would all be over. I guess maybe the department should have made sure that any female police officer who did that kind of undercover work had a uterus!

We did so many of these that I really can't remember what Fay looked like. She was a black woman, and she was in her mid-thirties, I remember that. But there was nothing unusual about her looks. I do remember the house. We entered into a living room, where I was told to sit and wait. Mary was ushered into the next room, which turned out to be a bedroom. There wasn't a door between the rooms. Just a kind of drape hanging over the doorway.

The plan was that as soon as Mary handed Fay the money, she was to yell and I was to come in and make the arrest. That would have been before anything actually started to happen. I don't know how long I sat, except that it was too long. It should have just been a few seconds, but the minutes dragged by. I sat there getting more and more nervous and wondering what had gone wrong. It's true that it was Mary's first job, but she was just on the other side of the curtain, and I didn't think anything could go wrong with our plan. Finally Mary yelled and I went flying in. Mary was partially undressed, lying on her back on the bed. Fay had already inserted an instrument that I later learned was called a speculum. That was the first step before she actually did the abortion. In one more instant, Fay would have looked into Mary's vagina and seen that she had no uterus at all.

I arrested Fay while Mary put her clothes back on. I looked around the room. Fay had a piece of coat hanger she was planning to use on Mary. The only "equipment" I remember seeing was the coat hanger and the speculum—you know, a kind of thing real doctors use. She had probably stolen it from some hospital. The instruments were wrapped in an old newspaper. The room was an ordinary bedroom. It wasn't particularly clean. There were clothes and stuff like that laying around.

It turned out that there were other people in the house who we hadn't known about. One of them was Fay's daughter, who appeared to be in her early twenties. Fay was real upset. She was screaming at us. She didn't deny it, naturally. How could she? I remember that later Fay accused us of stealing money from her. When we searched her house looking for abortion para- phernalia, we did find several thousand dollars in cash in a drawer in the kitchen. I called her daughter in and counted out the cash, in her presence. Then I gave it to the daughter and told her to put it someplace safe because her mother was going down to the jail for a while. Well, if anyone stole that money, it had to be Fay's own daughter! Nice, huh?

Usually we went after someone like Fay not because a woman had been injured or had died but because an infor- mant had given us the information. I had known nothing about Fay before the day we arrested her. All we knew was what the informant told us—that she did abortions. There were so many informants over the years that I have no memory of who that person might have been.

The way the informant system worked was like this. Say you picked up someone on something minor, like a shoplifting charge. Maybe this time the person has a chance of going to jail because they've been arrested lots of times on this charge. Then the person will say to the police, "Can we horse-trade? Can't you do something for me?" And then we would say, "Well, what can you do for us?" Now, we weren't looking for just another shoplifter. That didn't get us anything. We wanted something bigger. So the shoplifter would usually try a couple of things, like, "Look, I know who is robbing this or that." In this case, the informant said, "Look, I know about this abor- tionist." We had heard there was one, but we didn't know who it was, so this was useful information—worth a horse trade. In exchange for not being arrested for shoplifting, the informant told us everything we needed to know to get an appointment with Fay.

All of these abortionists fit the same mold. It didn't matter whether they worked out of houses or the back seats of cars. It was the same dirty routine. The house was usually run-down. The room was dirty. The abortion was usually done on a bed or a kitchen table, sometimes on the floor. The instruments were wrapped in newspaper. They weren't sterilized. They weren't even washed from one client to another. It was just filth. The abortionists were black and white, men and women. Color or sex didn't matter. What drew them to it was the money. It was terrible.

DR. CLAY

ANY DOCTOR PRACTICING in the forties or fifties or sixties was surrounded by patients he knew real well, and they often had great social or economic needs that were not always medical needs. It would put him under severe pressure to help certain families either directly or indirectly. In some ways the family doctor is one of the most instinctively sympathetic people you could come to with a problem pregnancy. But the risks to the doctor—loss of license, going to jail, the disgrace—are so great that the doctor either needs to be extremely cautious or not do it at all. You would be well advised to say no to anyone you didn't know, and even if you knew them, no was a safer, smarter answer.

I graduated from medical school in the forties. In the era when I came along, doctors had big hearts. We were very compassionate, but not necessarily good businessmen. It would be much easier to be a doctor today, I think. In those days your patients expected you to solve all their problems, and you sort of expected it too. Why, in those days I did marriage counseling and everything! I had an enormous practice. I sure didn't *need* to do any abortions. Abortions are part of a problem in the community. It's the same with drugs. Compassionate doctors treat drug addicts because they are people in the community who need help.

Sometimes you could help a patient indirectly, and that was a more common and a much smarter way of handling the abortion problem. Because you were a part of the community, you knew what was going on and who was doing abortions and who was pretty good at it and who was not so good. Now, none of these people were doctors. They were just people doing abortions. Most doctors who did abortions tried to keep it as quiet as possible and hope the patient didn't end up in the hospital, because if she did, you could count on the fact that she would be intimidated—mostly by the hospital, but sometimes by police—to tell the authorities who did the abortion or even who helped her find someone to do it.

One way hospital doctors intimidated the patient was to tell her she was going to die—even when she wasn't—and that she should tell all before she did so. A woman who is bleeding and has a temperature of a hundred and four and knows she has done something illegal, if not immoral, is not in the best shape to withstand that kind of pressure. I guess the theory was that if you could scare her badly enough, she would surrender. That often worked, so if you were going to help a woman, directly or indirectly, you really had to impress on her that she mustn't tell, no matter what, because then you wouldn't be able to help anyone else. If you were a doctor, you could get into big trouble for doing an abortion, or even for helping her find someone who would.

Usually, in the black community, there were midwives who did abortions. A lot of them were nurses or at least had some nurses' training. Many of them knew anatomy and physiology. They had developed an abortion practice. People knew them and liked them. The doctors knew them and liked them. Many times these midwives would call us before they did an abortion. Then we could follow up on the patient afterward. This practice was universal in the black community, but I don't know what it was like in the white community.

The doctor certainly came to rely on these competent midwife-abortionists and to refer patients to them. They charged reasonable prices. They had set up their own facilities where they did the abortions. These places were clean and reasonably well equipped, although there were some major limitations. It wasn't anything like what it would have been if it were legal and aboveboard. When you have to hide and sneak around, then naturally there's a lot of stuff you can't do that you would otherwise do.

If the patient came to the doctor first, instead of to the midwife, you would listen to her reasons. Whether you asked or not, she would pour out her reasons. They were *always* socioeconomic. Their minds were absolutely made up, and they were *determined* not to have a baby! The doctor would examine her and find out her general condition of health, and most important, how far along she was. If the patient is only five or six weeks pregnant, the danger is much less than if she's in the second trimester. Then, if she wasn't too late in the pregnancy, you would send her to a good midwife. The doctors knew the midwives, and the midwives knew the doctors, and the referrals worked both ways. "Referral" is too open and up-front a word. It was really a little more indirect than that.

In my experience, it's exaggerated about how bad some midwives were. The ones I knew were good. I suppose in other communities—maybe white communities—you got dishwashers and mechanics, but in the black community, mine and others, you got midwives who were by and large very good. But there is a natural morbidity, and even mortality, in this procedure, which means that no matter how good you are, sooner or later you're going to get into trouble. The percentages are just going to catch up with you. You will get some patients with sepsis and pelvic infections.

Now, these patients usually had to go to the hospital. It's one thing to see a patient in your office after an abortion by a midwife, but you sure didn't want anyone using your name if she were going to a hospital. For that reason, most of these women just went directly to the emergency room, and no outside doctor referred her or admitted her or even admitted knowing anything about it. Don't misunderstand me. We would take care of the midwife's patient if the complications were fairly minor. If all the woman needed was antibiotics, something for pain, and bed rest, that was no problem, and of course you would treat her, but if she was seriously ill, you just couldn't afford to be involved.

The doctors in my community who did abortions would tell the patient, "At the first sign of hemorrhage or infection, you go straight to the emergency room. Don't call me and don't mention my name!" If you're a good doctor, you *must* tell the patient what to do at the first sign of trouble, even if it poses a risk to you.

A lot of the doctors in the hospital were very hostile to abortion. It apparently was more a function of the individual doctor in the emergency room that day than the philosophy of the hospital itself. For example, you could get kinder, better abortion care in a Catholic hospital if the right doctor was on duty in the emergency room.

Some midwives did get into trouble with the police. They had to go to court, but I don't remember any of them going to jail. The police didn't care unless someone died or someone who was hostile to abortion wanted to pursue the case. Then they would turn the heat on and get the patient to say, "Yes, Fay did it. She did my abortion."

What I am trying to convey is that the climate was so hostile to abortion and so dangerous but the need for the service was so great that we just continued on in spite of the dangers. Individual doctors did a few abortions—not many. This was true in the white community and the black community. Black doctors had to be very careful because they were watched much more closely, whether writing a prescription or doing an abortion. When a white doctor wrote the same prescription, no one was likely to be looking over his shoulder.

The black community as a whole—not the doctors—was just more open about abortion than they were in the white community. White women tended to get referred to someone in the black community, midwife or doctor, and a lot of them came, often referred by their own white doctors. Black doctors are going to be real careful about referring a strange white woman to a good midwife unless the white doctor who referred her is someone you know and trust. If the black doctor was going to do the abortion himself, he had to feel *really* safe—a close friend or relative or a highly reliable referral source. You had to protect yourself from the setup and from the patient who would crumble under pressure.

It's easy to say abortion is wrong if you've never been face to face with a desperate woman threatening to commit suicide and you have the ability to help her. But even so, you would be a fool to do an abortion on a stranger, no matter how desperate she was. She had to have some connections you could trust.

I do remember some deaths from abortions done by midwives. Sometimes there was publicity about the death, and sometimes not. The deaths I remember were in the late fifties and early sixties, maybe two in four or five years. For the most part they happened because the woman went home after the abortion and didn't get *early* post-abortion care—early antibiotics, for example. She would stay home getting sicker and sicker, and by the time she got to the hospital she was beyond help. These deaths were by and large unnecessary. They wouldn't happen with proper medical attention.

It is very important to get all of the material out of the uterus. Retained placenta must come out. If she goes to the hospital, a D and C will remove any remaining tissue. Left alone, the remaining tissue can take weeks to be expelled, and she isn't getting any better during that long wait. If it's infected, she's getting sicker. Perforation can be a much more acute medical complication than infection, but a midwife who has done five hundred to six hundred abortions isn't going to perforate the uterus. Infection is the far more likely complication. As to early abortions in our community, we did thousands with no complications at all.

Sometimes midwives would actually dilate the cervix with an instrument and scrape part of the surface of the uterus, but the most common abortion method was a catheter because it was fairly easy to do. With the catheter technique, some had the woman leave with the catheter still in place, others didn't.

Either way, the abortion happened because of the introduction of a foreign object into the uterus. If the catheter was put in and taken out immediately, there was a much higher failure rate. It was much better to leave the catheter in for at least twenty-four hours or until it came out on its own in two or three days, because you knew that when the body expelled the catheter, it would most likely expel everything else in the uterus, although on rare occasions that didn't happen.

One of the best midwife-abortionists I knew was a woman named Fay, who did the most abortions in our community. She would often send the woman directly to me or another doctor after her abortion so that we could give the woman antibiotics. Fay was good, but she couldn't write prescriptions. She was very well trained. She was a nurse, and a good one. Of course, she was never trained during her formal nursing career in how to do an abortion, but she knew anatomy, and sometimes your best training is experience. After you do two hundred to three hundred abortions, you get pretty good. In the late fifties and sixties Fay was in her thirties, I would guess. Today I'm sure she's retired. She would be close to seventy now, I guess.

Fay had a very lucrative practice. She didn't select her clientele just on the basis of money like some did. A lot of the women who came to Fay had three or four children, all by different men. Some were on welfare or didn't have much money. For them, Fay cut her prices, maybe charging no more than thirty dollars. With a good Fay out there, there was almost no reason for a doctor to take a chance and do an abortion himself—I'd say probably only for a close friend or relative, someone really special.

Fay functioned in our community for about twenty years, and there were a lot of Fays in other communities all over Pittsburgh. There were several very good midwives in the Hill District during this time. I have no doubt that there were back-alley abortionists—people with little training and little experience—but the Fays I knew weren't like that at all.

A lot of very poor women couldn't even afford a Fay. They had abortions done by friends and relatives. Often mothers did abortions on their daughters. Naturally, they didn't have the knowledge or the technique to do a safe abortion, so there were more failures and more complications in those situations. Typically, because of their poverty, these same women couldn't get birth control either, so they ended up getting pregnant every year. Those are high-risk women. Their general health is poor, and the constant pregnancies make it worse.

If abortion were to become illegal again, I'm not sure what it would be like. I guess I'm of two minds. It could be better for the woman and worse for the provider. I knew Dr. Benjamin King, who had several arrests for doing abortions and finally had a bad one. It has to happen to you if you do this long enough. With all the abortions he did, finally a woman died. He perforated her uterus, and she died. Now, this can happen in the best of circumstances, but they sure went after him. They got him, too. He went to jail and lost his license. He was in prison for maybe two or three years, but it was long enough. When he got out, he was broke and broken. He died not long afterward.

For abortion to be dangerous to the provider, even when it's medically safer, all you need are some really vicious enemies— and the enemies are a lot more vicious than they were in my day. Any doctor doing an illegal abortion in the future would have to be wary of the anti-abortion lobby, who will really be out on a search-and-destroy mission. No doctor wants to be the target of something that well organized and that vicious.

One thing that could be better than it is, even if abortion is illegal, and something that could very much lessen the need for abortion, is better birth control. As a nation, we treat birth control as a very low research priority. The diaphragm came out in the late thirties and the pill in the early sixties, but there hasn't been much research since the pill. There's a lot of work that could be done in that area. Ask any woman who's had an abortion—legal or illegal—and I'll bet she'll tell you abortion is a lousy form of birth control. It is just a necessary backup when everything else fails.

I guess I think that even if abortion became illegal again, it would be safer for women than it was in my day. I think the Fays of the world, and the doctors who were willing to do abortions, would do a better job because the technology is so much better and doctors have gotten good abortion training themselves in the last twenty years. That wasn't the case before. But they would do them like we did—very discreetly! A doctor could probably still buy a suction machine for something that was legal, like a D and C. If necessary, you could buy them illegally, just like you can buy a gun illegally, but they would certainly be available. I mean, they would still be manufacturing them somewhere—in Canada or wherever—since abortion is legal in most of the world. You just can't turn back the technological hands of time, even if you turn the legal-illegal clock backward.

DR. REBA

I GRADUATED FROM MEDICAL SCHOOL in 1934. I was twenty-three. The medical school was in a large northeastern city. Afterward I did my internship at a small community hospital. Then I tried to get into one of the few residency programs that were available to women at the time. There weren't many—pediatrics, anesthesiology, maybe one or two others. It was the height of the Depression, and times were very hard, so young doctors just stayed in their residencies since there weren't any other jobs to be had. I couldn't get a residency, but I did get a fellowship to take some graduate courses in gynecology at Columbia University in New York City.

As I was growing up, I knew abortion was against the law. Being illegal, it was a bad thing—sort of dark and dirty. It was not something that nice people got involved with. However, I was aware even as a girl that desperate women—usually the desperation was based on their social or economic circumstances—occasionally went to shady, unethical doctors, or maybe not even doctors, and got abortions. I thought it was a pretty risky undertaking for the woman. I didn't think about any risk to the doctor, because I had been taught to have a very low opinion of any doctor who would do an abortion. I think I got that attitude from my parents.

Medical school certainly reinforced my anti-abortion attitude. There I was taught that abortion was not only illegal but immoral, and that no self-respecting doctor who considered herself to be an ethical member of the medical community would perform an abortion, even if it was profitable. Abortionists were "bums," "murderers," real "lowlifes," and very inept physicians who could not make a living any other way. They were objects of scorn and contempt.

I don't recall thinking about or being taught about the non-doctor abortionist. I suppose that the medical school was only concerned with teaching us things that doctors shouldn't do. What barbers or hairdressers did was of no concern. This strong anti-abortion attitude was not limited to one or two professors or classes. It was absolutely universal in medical school.

In medical school I got no training in how to do a D and C, which was what an abortion was. That was something that no one would learn until postgraduate training. Not being trained in abortion techniques was not unusual, since we weren't trained in any other surgical technique either. That suggests that an abortion done by a medical student probably wouldn't be much safer than one done by a hairdresser. I didn't learn even as simple a surgical procedure as a D and C during either my internship or my fellowship. Interns didn't do surgery. We would hold a retractor and watch the surgeon, but there was no actual hands-on experience.

In medical school I rotated through the obstetrics and gynecology service and an ob-gyn out-patient clinic where we actually went into the home. Under the supervision of hospital residents, we did home deliveries on our own.

When I first became a doctor, antibiotics didn't exist. It's hard for people today to even imagine what it was like in those days. Infections were more common, with often fatal consequences. Antibiotics were nothing short of miraculous. I still remember vividly the first patient I treated with antibiotics. It was probably 1940 or 1941. I know it was before the war, because, after the war started, antibiotics were hard to get. The patient was a woman with a very painful pelvic inflammatory disease. I gave her a sulfa drug, and it worked like magic. I remember I came into the office waiting room a few minutes before her follow-up appointment. She and her husband were already waiting for me, and I could tell by the looks on their faces that something amazing had happened. They were smiling, and her husband leapt up and grabbed my hand. He acted like I was God or like I had performed a miracle. The miracle wasn't me, it was the sulfa. Really, I was as amazed as they were, although I didn't let on. I had never seen anyone with an infection like hers recover so fast.

Before antibiotics, there really wasn't any treatment for infection. You just told the person to stay in bed and get lots of rest, made reassuring noises, and hoped for the best. The bed rest was so their body would have a better chance of fighting back. There was nothing else to do. You usually had to hospitalize anyone with an infection because the person was pretty sick. Even then, you just treated the symptoms—aspirin or cool sponge baths for the fever, things like that. They either got better or they died. But if they got better, it was probably nothing more than luck and their own body defenses.

In my medical school days the wards always had women with post-abortion complications. There were always women being brought in who were acutely ill following criminal abortions. Sometimes the patient would admit to having the abortion; more often, she would not. But it wasn't difficult to figure out. Their symptoms were usually a heavy discharge, severe pain, and a high fever. They were very sick. A disproportionate number of these women were poor. More affluent women had family physicians who, while they wouldn't do the abortion, would have the woman with complications admitted as a private patient, so she never ended up on the ward and her real diagnosis was probably never revealed.

The hospital didn't really pursue bringing police attention to abortion cases, because the hospital's main interest was in treating these usually critically ill patients. The attending physician would generally try to get the true story, but if he couldn't, he didn't worry about it. He just worried about the patient. I don't know what obligation, if any, the doctor would have had to report the event to the police on those occasions when he did get the straight story. I can't remember ever being taught that doctors had that obligation. I was never involved in that situation, so I really don't know what other doctors did.

When I completed my internship, I went into private practice. My practice was intended to be general, but it very quickly became almost exclusively gynecology. I suppose that's because women preferred a woman doctor and there weren't very many women doctors around in those days.

Although I had great contempt for abortionists and would never have done an abortion, I had no ethical aversion to treating women who were suffering from the consequences of septic abortions. I remember in 1941 or 1942 being called to a house in the eastern part of the city. I had never met the people before. A young woman was in bed. She was obviously in pain and was running a fever. I was told by the young man who was there—I assumed he was her husband—that she had had a "miscarriage." I suspected that she had had an abortion. I asked a few questions, but their guarded answers made it very clear that I was not going to get the truth, so I just took care of her. I remember that I treated her with sulfa. She made a good recovery.

I remember another woman who came to me for some minor pelvic symptoms. There was nothing about her story that made me think of abortion. However, when I examined her, I discovered that she had very recently—probably within the last day or two—had her pubic hair shaved. She could give me absolutely no explanation for that. She professed to have no idea when, why, or how her pubic hair had been shaved! When I examined her internally, it was obvious that she had just had an abortion, but she continued to insist that she had no idea what I was talking about and could shed no light on this seeming mystery. The lie was as bald as her pubic area. I gave her antibiotics and sent her home.

I remember another woman, actually an acquaintance of mine. She lived in central New York, and I then lived in Philadelphia. I had not seen her in several years. She called and told me that she was coming to Philadelphia to visit a well-known gynecologist about some sort of problem. She asked if she could stop and visit me. When she arrived, she told me some long and involved story, but I finally figured out she was here for an abortion. Well, the well-known doctor told her that he couldn't help her. The next thing I knew, she was in the hospital with a severe hemorrhage. I don't know where she ended up going. I never asked her what happened, and she never volunteered the information.

I was in private practice, on a full-time basis, from 1936 to 1942 and from 1944 to 1947, when my second child was born. I certainly had patients ask me to do an abortion. It probably happened to many doctors during that time. I always answered by saying that I couldn't because it was unethical. There wasn't the slightest bit of hesitation on my part. I wouldn't dream of doing that. I wouldn't do what a friend of mine used to do either. After you said no, the woman would always say, "Who can I go to?" My friend would give them a hint about a certain doctor in a certain building. He never mentioned the doctor's name, but he gave them enough information so they could usually figure it out. I never even did that. I just said, "I can't help you."

I was aware of one highly respected physician who was rumored to do abortions. He was nothing like my stereotype of the incompetent marginal physician. He was well respected, and he certainly didn't need the money. I have no idea what motivated him. I really don't even know if the rumors were true.

I did sympathize with the women. They were in such impossible situations that they had to find a solution, even one that involved considerable risk. If I had been in their situation, I'd have done the same. But I couldn't and wouldn't sympathize to the point of helping. Maybe I wasn't strong enough or committed enough to put my own reputation and self-respect at issue. I certainly saw the social need to legalize abortion, but working within the system to change the law is quite different from risking your license and your livelihood! I imagine most doctors feel the same way. When abortion is illegal, that is just too big a price to pay.

DR. SPENCER

D R. ROBERT DOUGLAS SPENCER was born in Kansas City, Missouri, on March 16, 1889. When he was a child, his family moved to Williamsport, Pennsylvania, where his father was for a time the district attorney of Lycoming County. His mother was a schoolteacher. He graduated from Penn State University in 1911, briefly taught biology there, and then entered medical school at the University of Pennsylvania. After his graduation in 1916, he was on the staff of Philadelphia General Hospital. In 1920 he moved to Ashland, Pennsylvania, where he served for nine years as chief pathologist at Ashland State Hospital, a facility specializing in miners' diseases. In 1925 he entered private practice in Ashland.

Dr. Spencer was married twice, first to Julie Butler, and then, in September 1945, to Eleanor Becker, a schoolteacher from nearby Mount Carmel. A born scientist, he loved botany and zoology as well as medicine. Although raised a Methodist, in adulthood he became an outspoken atheist. A lifelong Republican, he was also a member of the Rotary Club and always sported his Rotary pin on his lapel. He liked to read philosophy and proudly considered himself a free-thinker and a nonconformist. Among his heroes were Thomas Paine and Clarence Darrow.

But there was more to Dr. Spencer, another side that earned

this diminutive man from a little anthracite mining town in northeastern Pennsylvania an obituary in the *New York Times*. Dr. Spencer died on January 21, 1969—four years, almost to the day, before the United States Supreme Court legalized abortion in America. By his own description, he was an abortionist who did over one hundred thousand illegal abortions between 1923 and his retirement at age seventy-seven in 1967. He was as open about his abortion activities as about his atheism and his enthusiasm for the Rotary. The town knew, and for the most part tacitly approved by looking the other way.

He did his first abortion in 1923, on a coal miner's wife. As he recalled, he charged her five dollars. According to Michael T. Kaufman ("Abortion Doctor," *Lear's*, July–August 1989), the woman said that she had "missed her mark," and that she and her husband could not feed and clothe the four children they already had. "Once I realized that a woman should be the dictator of what went on in her own body, I just set out to help, and I never gave it another thought," Dr. Spencer told Kaufman.

Dr. Spencer first became aware of abortion as a social problem just after World War I. His district-attorney father had a case in which the daughter of a prominent minister in Williamsport had been receiving threatening letters. As the case unfolded, it was discovered that the girl was pregnant and had been writing the letters to herself. A few months later the minister committed suicide. Dr. Spencer said that the case made an enormous impression on him, leading to his realization that a small error could have a devastating impact.

Learning how to do a safe abortion was not easy in Dr. Spencer's day. By the time he came to Ashland in 1920, he had been asked many times to terminate a pregnancy, but he had no idea how to do it. It was not taught in medical school. After the miner's wife sought his help, he discovered a German concoction he called "Lubeck's Paste," which was probably Leunbach's Paste, one of several abortifacient salves popular in Germany at the time, and widely available in the United States until 1931, when reports of several deaths from air and fat embolisms persuaded the government to ban them.

There were no doctors in Ashland or nearby areas who knew how to do an abortion. Finally Dr. Spencer obtained permission to observe an extremely rare court-ordered abortion in New York in the 1920s. He even went to Moscow in 1934, since abortions were legal and were being performed in large numbers in the Soviet Union. As an abortion education, the trip turned out to be a waste, because by the time he arrived Stalin had banned abortion and there was no longer anything for him to observe. Having no other way to learn, he essentially taught himself how to do a D and C abortion.

After that first abortion in 1923, his reputation spread and he got more requests "because I never tried to hide what I was doing," as he modestly put it. His patients would attest that it was "because he was good."

No back alleys for Dr. Spencer. He ran his abortion practice openly from an eleven-room clinic at 531 Centre Street in the middle of downtown Ashland. His chief associate was Stephen Sekunda, his lab assistant and longtime friend. Although he had receptionists and office nurses from time to time—Mildred Zettlemoyer being one of the most faithful—Steve was a constant presence, doing whatever needed to be done. After Dr. Spencer's death Steve recalled, "Oh, how we worked—seven days a week, twelve to fourteen hours a day. We did everything here, just like a hospital."

Dr. Spencer's custom was to examine the women in the evening, interview them, and record their medical histories. Then they could stay overnight at the clinic if there was room, or at the Marko Towne House just up the street, or at the Boulevard Motel. Ashland is not now and wasn't then a place that supports a brisk tourist trade, and the obvious out-of-towners—all young women—who strolled aimlessly down Centre Street looking into store windows in the evening were readily identifiable as "Dr. Spencer's girls."

The abortions were performed in the early morning, starting at 7:00 a.m., and were usually completed by 9:00 a.m., at which time regular office hours and the regular day's work began. After their D and C abortions, Dr. Spencer's patients were given a large dose of penicillin and put to bed at the clinic or motel for the rest of the day. When they were discharged at 4:00 or 5:00 p.m., they received a second large dose of penicillin, instructions for post-abortion care, and if they wanted it, a prescription for birth control.

Dr. Spencer usually did about ten abortions a day, although as he got older, he cut back to three or four a day. In the early years he charged five to twenty-five dollars, and in later years, a hundred to two hundred dollars. But abortion was not the main part of his medical practice. Starting at 9:00, and often for the next twelve hours, he conducted the general practice typical of a small-town doctor: giving eye exams and X-rays, lancing boils, setting broken bones, delivering babies, doing tonsillectomies, and treating everything from head colds to infected toes. He was one of the few doctors in the area willing to go down into the mines to treat an injured miner when there was an accident.

Dr. Spencer didn't believe in Medicaid or Medicare and refused to participate, but he never turned people away for lack of funds. He gave all his patients printed slips advising them that he wouldn't accept Medicaid or Medicare and stating, "I will expect you to pay for my medical services as you have always done. If you are unable to pay, please confide in me and I will treat you without charge, as is my custom." But his philanthropy went beyond the provision of free medical care. It was not uncommon for a poor patient who had been treated at the clinic to go home and soon thereafter receive a bag of groceries sent by Dr. Spencer. He sometimes gave his abortion patients travel money to get back home. Indeed, his first and only partner, Dr. W. A. Jacques, dissolved their joint practice in the 1920s because "the damn fool gives everything away!"

There was something special about Dr. Spencer, but there was something special about Ashland as well—a town that permitted an abortionist to function openly for over forty years when abortion was illegal. A more unlikely town is hard to imagine. In the late sixties Ashland boasted five thousand residents. There were no blacks and only ten Jews. There were eight Protestant and two Catholic churches, although fifty percent of the townspeople were Catholic. The town was overwhelmingly conservative. The Rotary met every Wednesday and the Kiwanis every Thursday at the Marko Towne House. Hardly a hospitable place for an openly atheistic abortionist.

A survivor of the long-dead anthracite coal industry, the little town perched on the side of Mahanoy Mountain now has no visible means of support or reason for existence. There do not appear to be new homes or stores. The Frackville Mall, five miles away in a neighboring town, is the new shopping area if Ashland residents need anything special. Ashland's neighbor, Centralia, now mostly a ghost town, is famous for its smoldering underground fire, almost thirty years old.

The Marko Towne House is no longer a hotel, there being almost no need for one now that Dr. Spencer is gone. One of Ashland's most striking features, and one that the natives urge you to visit, is the Mother's Memorial, a more than life-size bronze statue of Whistler's Mother. The plaque at the memorial dedicates it to mothers everywhere. No one in town seems to find anything inconsistent or even ironic about having a Mother's Memorial in what may well have been the abortion capital of the United States. Perhaps it really is a town of freethinkers.

As Dr. Spencer's reputation spread, women came to Ashland from all over the United States. They were preceded by letters addressed simply to "The Doctor of Ashland" or "Spencer" or even "Doctor." The letters themselves, often cryptically worded, testified again and again to the desperation of being faced with an unwanted pregnancy.

I am in trouble. I was married at 17, I had a daughter at 18, and my husband and I separated when I was 19. I am the sole support of my daughter, and so I consequently have little money to spare each month and none in savings. Both my parents and my in-laws live in this town, so my fear of being exposed is tremendous. I have been

almost out of my mind for several weeks because I have had
nowhere to turn and no one to turn to.

Dr. Spencer, I'm at the end of my rope. I have $123 and I am run-
ning out of time. I am eight weeks pregnant. I have nowhere to go. I
have to do something. You are my last hope of qualified help.

Dr. Spencer was arrested three times and brought to trial at
least once. In addition, there were minor bouts of harassment.
At one point the Knights of Columbus put the clinic under
surveillance, taking notes on the out-of-state cars parked at the
clinic and the strangers who checked into the Marko Towne
House in the evening and out again the following afternoon.
This information was then submitted to the county district
attorney, with a demand that some action be taken. The district
attorney would order the state police to put a watch on the
clinic. The state police would tell the local police of their plans,
and somehow or other, Dr. Spencer was always warned in
advance. He would just shut down until the troopers left, and
nothing ever happened as a result of these surveillance efforts.

Dr. Spencer's first arrest was in December 1953. He was
charged with performing an abortion on Lillian Frie of
Pottsville, Pennsylvania. There was no evidence of injury to
Mrs. Frie, she apparently suffered no complications, and the
reason for the arrest is unclear. Dr. Spencer was acquitted. His
most serious encounter with the law was in 1956, when one of
his patients died on the table during the abortion (as
recounted on pp. 129–33).

In 1964 Dr. Spencer became a political issue. The Demo-
crats campaigned against the Republican incumbent district
attorney, charging that he had failed to close Dr. Spencer
down. The electorate spoke: the incumbent won big! Dr.
Spencer was not a political liability, it seemed.

His last brush with the law was in 1967, when he, Steve
Sekunda, and one Harry Mace were arrested by state troopers
and indicted on an abortion charge. It was understood that the

real target of the arrest was not Spencer or Sekunda but Mace, a former car salesman who had managed to work his way into Dr. Spencer's confidence when the doctor was older, frailer, and less astute than he had been in his prime. Mace set himself up as an intermediary between the abortion patient and the clinic, adding as much as four or five hundred dollars to the fee and pocketing the difference himself. In failing health, Dr. Spencer died before the case could be brought to trial. Since Mr. Mace was out of business without the doctor and the problem had solved itself, the case was not pursued.

There would be no more open abortions in Ashland, Pennsylvania. Women all over the United States would have to find another way to get abortion care. It would be another four years before the Ashland experience—without the Harry Maces, public surveillance, blackmail, and other concomitants of illegality—would be available to American women. But Dr. Spencer, the freethinking Rotarian in the little anthracite mining town, had provided a model.

COMMONWEALTH V. SPENCER

O N DECEMBER 9, 1956, Dr. Spencer's luck finally ran out. So did the luck of Mary Davies, a twenty-six-year-old New York City woman who died in his Ashland office that Sunday morning.

Ms. Davies, a part-time student at Columbia University, worked at Irvington House, a research and treatment center for children with rheumatic fever. She had come to Ashland with $66 in her checking account, $153 in cash, an unwanted pregnancy, and a bus ticket back to New York.

Dr. Spencer was arrested and charged with involuntary manslaughter, abortion, and abortion resulting in death. His jury consisted of seven men and five women. In his written statement, submitted at trial, Dr. Spencer described what happened.

At approximately 10 a.m. on December 9, 1956, Miss Mary Davies, 110 W. 96th St., New York City, came to my office alone. She was also at my office December 8, 1956, about 3 p.m. On her December 8 visit she was alone and told me that she had been bleeding for the past two weeks. I did not examine her, I told her to come back to see me Sunday—I gave her pills for pain and ergotrate tablets to stop bleeding. She left and returned this date, for the purpose to do a D and C. I put her to sleep with 13 cc's of Evipal made into a solution to make it a 10% solution. I injected that solution into the vein of the left arm and in ten seconds she was asleep.

The next I noticed, she was not breathing very well and her face appeared blue. I gave her five cc's Metrozol into the muscle of her left leg. When I saw that she did not respond, I gave her an injection of five cc's in the vein. When this did not work, I started artificial respiration and used my oxygen tank, placing a tube into her throat. When that failed, I gave her an injection of adrenalin. One injection into the vein and two injections under the left breast. I tried more artificial respiration and pulled on her tongue, but got no response. I worked on her a full hour and did all I could think of, but she expired about 11:30 a.m.

The assistant, Mildred Zettlemoyer, was called in to help me and give artificial respiration. Then I went for adrenalin in my laboratory in another office on the first floor. I had my assistant, Mrs. Zettlemoyer, call Steve Sekunda, Walnut St., Ashland, who is employed by me as laboratory technician and works every day but Sunday. I was going to go into air passages in the trachea. This would give light to see into the trachea. However, the battery was dead. I could not use this. When Steve arrived I told him it was too late, that the patient had expired. . . . When the patient expired, I placed the body in another room and took care of my other patients. . . . I believe that this patient died in my office from some heart disease.

Several medical witnesses, among them Dr. Milton Halpern, chief medical examiner for New York City, testified at the trial. Their testimony established that Ms. Davies had been pregnant and that the pregnancy had been terminated right before her death, that she had been in good general health prior to her death, and that she had died from the administration of a drug used for anesthesia during the performance of a D and C. The jury deliberated for only four hours, including time out for dinner, and found Dr. Spencer not guilty on all counts.

I asked Dr. Bert, a retired surgeon (see pp. 192–95), to review the news reports of the death of Mary Davies and the trial of Dr. Spencer, and to comment on whether Ms. Davies received proper medical care and might have survived if abortion had then been legal.

Of course, anything I say is highly speculative because I am doing this only from newspaper reports. I never saw the patient, and I never saw the medical records.

It is certainly true that anesthesia deaths are a continuing problem, even today, and what we appear to have here is an anesthesia death. This occurred in 1956, and certainly toxic reactions to anesthesia or airway problems developing during anesthesia or sudden cardiac arrest during anesthesia are things that happen in a certain percentage of surgery cases. Sooner or later, anyone who does enough surgery will have someone develop cardiac arrest. This is one of the reasons patients are monitored all the time. If cardiac arrest occurs, resuscitation can be done immediately.

The resuscitation attempts that Dr. Spencer made were the ones in use at the time. We have better ones now. However, if this patient had been under the management of an anesthesiologist, or even a nurse-anesthetist, she might have survived. There is a certain deterioration in the quality of any medical procedure when it is being done surreptitiously. Today a doctor could do an abortion in an office like Dr. Spencer did. That is certainly legal. But what we have here is general anesthesia, and that changes things. It increases the risks, no matter what medical procedure is being done.

Dentists have been doing something similar for years—nitrous oxide in the office for a tooth extraction. But nitrous oxide is a lighter level of anesthesia, sort of in and out. Evipal is intravenous, more like sodium pentothal. Today it would not be good medical practice to give a patient a drug like that without a competent anesthesiologist or nurse-anesthetist.

The problem here—and it may have been a result of the clandestine nature of an illegal medical procedure—is that the doctor was alone. In my view, to give a general anesthetic alone is below good medical care, even in those days. The patient may have swallowed her tongue, or her head could have dropped forward, obstructing her airway, and if he was alone, the doctor probably didn't notice because he was intent on the procedure he was doing. Another person monitoring her vital signs would have noticed it immediately. By the time he looked up and realized what was happening, it was too late.

Of course, we will never know whether Mary Davies would be alive today if abortion had been legal in 1956. But Dr. Spencer, who certainly appears competent if he did a hundred thousand abortions and had only one death, would have been able to provide a higher standard of care. Legality might well have made the difference for Mary Davies.

Apart from the medical aspect, as a legal and political matter the jury's verdict is nothing short of astonishing. The grand jury indicted Dr. Spencer for involuntary manslaughter, abortion, and abortion resulting in death. However, the district attorney sought conviction only on the two counts of abortion. The trial took place in 1959. All the Commonwealth had to prove was that he did an abortion. It didn't matter at all whether Mary Davies' reasons, or Dr. Spencer's, were good or justifiable. It didn't matter whether she died or lived, or whether she suffered any ill effects. The law didn't even require that she be pregnant. It only required that Dr. Spencer had acted with intent to perform an abortion.

Dr. Spencer did not admit in so many words to having performed an abortion on Mary Davies, characterizing her death as a heart attack or anesthesia death. Nevertheless, his own testimony, coupled with the testimony of other witnesses and the common sense jurors are presumed to bring to the courtroom, made the case virtually airtight. Mary Davies was pregnant, and she had an abortion very close to the time she died. A D and C would have resulted in an abortion. Mary Davies died during a medical procedure done by Dr. Spencer, in Dr. Spencer's office. But the jurors found him not guilty. What's more amazing, they did it in only four hours, counting time for dinner.

Not one juror was from Ashland. When the press asked why they had failed to convict Dr. Spencer, an unidentified juror said, "There is nobody in Schuylkill County that the doctor hasn't helped. He's a good doctor and a good person." While that may be true, as a legal matter it is no defense. As a political matter, it tells the whole story.

Here are a few typical comments on Dr. Spencer, from people inside and outside the community.

Dr. Spencer was our family doctor for years. My wife went to him, and he took care of our children. My wife and other women in town used to worry about what people would think. My wife would say,

"How will they know I went for a sore throat and not for an abortion?" I told her it was no one's business and not to worry about it, but you know how small towns are. Everyone knows everyone else, and people do talk. She fussed, but we all loved him, and so we just kept going to him.

I'm not going to say whether I believed in abortion, but I would never have lifted a finger to harm the doctor, because he did so many wonderful things for our community. He was a definite plus for the whole area, and I'm just one father, but I'd say I represent the mainstream. When my sons were in high school, they got interested in fossils. When they went to the library, they couldn't find any scientific treatises on fossils, and I certainly didn't know anything about it. The librarian told my boys that Dr. Spencer knew more about fossils than anyone in town, so they called him and asked a question or two. That night Dr. Spencer knocked on our door and handed my boys a wonderful book on fossils. That's just our family. He did things like that for everyone. Do you see why no one in town wanted to crucify him?

I grew up in Frackville. As a girl I never met Dr. Spencer, but my parents knew him. It's funny, my parents are opposed to abortion, but they thought Dr. Spencer was a wonderful doctor. I guess if you're good enough people just overlook things they don't approve of.

And this from Dr. Clay (see pp. 109-16).

Dr. Spencer was in an almost rural environment, a small-town setting. In the urban setting a doctor had to be more or less "permitted" to do illegal abortions. There is no way you could do three or four abortions, or ten or twenty, without the word being passed around, and eventually someone who had a problem with that took it to the law. It's not amazing that Dr. Spencer did them. What's amazing is that people permitted him to do them. And they really did, you know. That doesn't happen by accident.

I think that the urban versus small-town environment made a difference. But if you look at Dr. Spencer and Dr. Benjamin King, race makes a difference! A black doctor like Dr. King is just not given the benefit of the doubt in the same way that a white doctor is. If Dr. Spencer had been a black doctor in Pittsburgh, he simply would not have been treated as he was—either in his practice or in his trial.

MRS. SPENCER

Twenty-two years after Dr. Spencer's death, his widow, Eleanor Becker Spencer, is a white-haired matronly woman with sparkling dark eyes and a warm smile. Marrying "Doctor," as she frequently calls him, and being part of his life for twenty-five years, was the most exciting and wonderful thing that ever happened to her, she makes very clear. His books and his hobbies still remain very much in evidence in her home. She speaks of him so vividly and with such animation that the listener half expects him to come bounding through the door calling, "Ellie, I'm home!"

MY HUSBAND WANTED TO BE A DOCTOR from the time he was a little boy. That's all he ever wanted to do. He was always interested in living things and what made them work. His mother used to tell me how he was always studying flies and bugs, trying to understand why they were the way they were. He had a religious upbringing as a Methodist, and he used to pass out hymnals on Sunday mornings. Then something happened to change his thinking, and he became an agnostic. He believed there was a supreme being and that we couldn't live without the sun, which made everything go. Maybe science *was* religion to him, I don't know. I'm a traditional Lutheran, but he didn't hold with that at all!

In those early days I was young and really didn't know anything about abortion, but I had been raised to believe that it was a terrible thing. Then, when I got to know Douglas and to know *why* he did abortions, my attitude began to change.

The Catholic church is very active in Ashland, and his reputation was very controversial. The Catholic church was very much against him, but the criticism was muted. There weren't pickets or letters to the editor or anything like that. No one was out to get him because he was such a good doctor. Besides, he was benefiting the local economy. People were coming here from all over the United States. They spent money in the hotels and restaurants. The local merchants, no matter what their attitudes about abortion, knew a good thing when they saw it, and they weren't about to kill the goose that laid the golden egg.

There weren't more than four or five doctors in Ashland. My husband was the only one who did abortions. I don't know what they thought of him, but there wasn't a lot of camaraderie. I recall that from time to time there would be discussion in the county medical society about the need to "discipline Dr. Spencer," but no one ever did anything more than talk about it—at least we assumed they never did anything, because nothing ever happened.

The politicians never bothered him either. Once, when he'd been arrested, the county detective who picked him up was almost apologetic because he had to take my husband to jail. The detective kept saying things like, "Gee, I'm sorry, Doctor. I hate to do this, Doctor." In one of those tough times, when an arrest was pending, Douglas said to me, "Ellie, if I open up and tell what I know, there will be a lot of red faces among the politicians in this town! And a cabinet member from Canada will also be embarrassed." He never told, though.

Most of the women who came to Ashland to see my husband traveled by bus, but we had a lot of out-of-state cars, and many came by train. We didn't have any real cab service, so they just walked from the hotel to the clinic. Not too many women called for appointments. Most of them wrote letters. Then Doctor would write back and set up an appointment. Sometimes when he examined the woman she was too far along and he couldn't do the abortion, but if he could, he always put her to sleep first, with a general anesthetic, and he always gave her antibiotics afterward. Sometimes women had complications and had to stay two days at the clinic. Sometimes they went home and got an infection and had to come back. When they stayed overnight at the clinic, they would call up Wayman's Restaurant and place a dinner order. Steve would pick it up and bring it to them.

There was a woman from Hazelton, Douglas told me, who he did an abortion for against his better judgment. She had a number of children and a husband with a relatively low earning ability, and she just didn't want another child. She didn't die, and she didn't even have any medical problems, as I recall, but after the abortion someone persuaded her to go to the authorities. My husband was arrested for doing an abortion, which was, of course, an illegal act. He actually had to stay in jail until our lawyer could arrange bail. It was only for a few hours, but it was a very scary time for us.

I can't remember if my husband was acquitted or whether the case was dismissed. I remember that the woman's husband tried to shake Doctor down for a money settlement, but Douglas wouldn't have any part of that! I don't think it was a set up as much as it was just a shake down. Her husband thought he saw a way to make a little extra money, I guess. Anyway, that attempted shake down came out in the middle of the trial, and that was the end of the trial. Everything just ended.

My husband trusted everybody—too much, I thought. We used to have whole stacks of checks that were uncollectible for one reason or another. When the women wrote them, I guess they didn't have any intention of paying.

The death of the New York woman was by far the worst thing that ever happened. That's the only abortion death he ever had in forty-four years! It was a Sunday evening, and I can remember it so clearly. He came home and he was all quiet—not his normal self. I said, "Something happened today, didn't it?" He looked at me and said, "Yes. A patient died, and I don't understand why. I don't understand what happened to her. " He was shocked and shaken. He had given her an injection of Evipal. He used that on most of the abortion patients, and nothing about it had ever been a problem. He wasn't frightened for himself as much as he was terribly sad that the woman had died.

She died in December of 1956, and the trial didn't happen until January of 1959, but during all that long wait, nothing really changed in the way people treated my husband. He was still the family doctor, and he had just as many regular patients and just as many abortion patients as he had ever had. The other doctors in town didn't act any different than they ever had, and neither did the politicians. Maybe it was because Doctor knew too much about too many people. I don't know. I just know that nothing much changed.

He had three defense attorneys—Mr. Stutzman, Mr. Sidoriak, and Mr. Kilker—and two of them, Mr. Sidoriak and Mr. Kilker, were among the most important, influential Catholics in town. They were both very good lawyers, but I wondered if they were chosen in part because of their religion. Here were two prominent Catholics defending an abortionist.

Douglas dreaded the trial, not so much because he thought he would lose his license and go to jail, but because he dreaded having to deal with and talk about the actual fact that he lost a patient—for reasons he didn't understand. But I was terribly worried, much more than he. I didn't go to the trial because he didn't want me to. I just sat home and worried. I'll tell you, I didn't think about anything else. We didn't talk about it at night either, because he didn't want to talk about it. He just wanted to get away from it for a few hours.

After this big one—this trial and all—I thought, "Well, now he will quit. He just won't do them anymore. " I asked him if this would end the abortions, and he said, "Yes, Ellie, I think I am through." He did stop for a month or so, and it was heaven! But then, first thing you know, a woman would bring her thirteen-year-old daughter in, and he couldn't refuse her. Before you knew it, we were right back to where it had been. He just couldn't turn anyone away!

The business with Harry Mace, in 1967, should never have happened. Harry would bring an awful lot of women and girls here for abortions. It just got to be awful. Harry lived in Williamstown. He sold cars. He had a friend, Willie, a nice young man in his twenties. Somehow or another, my husband was so busy and jammed up with all these abortions, and Willie offered to help. He wasn't a medical person. He did other kinds of helping, like lifting the women off the table and things like that. He was sort of a gofer—"Go get me this, go get me that." Douglas was in his seventies then and not as energetic as he had been.

Well, it got too busy and too open. It got sloppy in ways that would never have happened earlier. Harry was driving women to the doctor. We found out later that he was charging them money for that, and the more women he brought in, the more money he made. Harry was so busy that he was bringing in more women than my husband could handle. Well, Harry also hustled the women out sooner than they should have been, because he wanted to make room for more. These women had had a general anesthetic, and they were leaving sooner than they should have. They would go out on the street and fall down. It was bad, and people got upset. I worried.

There was a bad case where a woman was there an unusually long time. That took all of my husband's attention. He was not able to do more abortions, and logically patients began to back up. Well, Harry just kept bringing more women, and pretty soon it was a real mess. Cars were parked all over, and people were spilling out into the street. It got to be a nuisance, and the townsfolk didn't like it.

During the "Mace period," where things got so bad, my husband's health really began to fail. He had angina. He'd come home and say, "Ellie, I thought I was going to die today. I had to take thirty nitroglycerins." Well, I said, "You *know* what you should do!" So he would stop for a while and then start again. But he was really failing rather badly. When letters came in, I answered them and said that the doctor was sick and wasn't doing abortions. I had to do something.

Doctor wasn't arrested, but he was indicted in connection with the Mace problem, even though it had quieted down because of Doctor's health. The feeling in the community was that had my husband gone to trial with Mace, he would have been convicted. Things weren't like they had been in 1959. Instead of this beloved family doctor doing abortions at a low fee because he wanted to help people, you had this unsavory Mace gouging women and making money hand over fist. It just all seemed so sordid.

My husband was so wonderful—interested in everything and everybody. Did you ever spend an hour or two watching a trap-door spider? Well, he did, and he would call me to watch with him. He would grind and polish rocks, climb mountains—there was nothing he didn't do—and he would take me with him. I'd be sitting in the living room, reading the paper, and he would be in the back of the house, studying things with his microscope. He'd call, "Come out here, Ellie, and look at something. I want you to tell me what it is. " Well, I didn't have any idea, I can tell you. He'd say triumphantly, "That's the brain of a flea!" He thought I would be as fascinated as he was. I wasn't, quite, but I never told him that.

Once we got robbed by four armed men who broke into our house and tied us to chairs. Oh, it was terrifying, but he was never afraid. He identified all the men and they went to jail. Whether it was robberies, mountain climbing, abortions, or whatever, it was a fabulous life I lived with him! I miss him still.

DETECTIVE JACK

I WAS AN ALLEGHENY COUNTY DETECTIVE for almost thirty years and I have been retired for sixteen years. In that almost thirty-year period, there were a lot of people we suspected of doing abortions. But suspicion is one thing, and catching them is something else. Most of my memories come from the fifties and sixties, because it quit happening after about 1970 or so. There were a lot of abortionists out there. Some were doctors, but most of them weren't. Keep in mind that the only ones we knew about were the ones we were getting complaints on. We didn't even know about most of them.

Sometimes, even if the woman complained, she couldn't lead us to the abortionist because she had been blindfolded to get there, and sometimes blindfolded during the procedure itself, so she could never say who did it. Facts like that can make it real tough to arrest or convict someone.

I remember these two girls from New Castle in Lawrence County. They were admitted to the hospital there in New Castle, both suffering from septic abortions. Because they said their abortions had been done in Allegheny County, the hospital called us. One of the girls told us what had happened. They were friends, they were both pregnant, and they made appointments to go to the same abortionist on the same day—appointments back to back, so to speak. The charge was five hundred dollars apiece. Afterward they both got sick, and one damn near died.

Well, on the basis of their statements we went out and arrested this guy. He was a real doctor out in South Park, and he had a fine reputation and an impeccable medical background. He had never been arrested and never been in any kind of trouble. He was convicted, but as I recall, he was placed on probation since it was his first offense, or at least the first one we knew about. That was the one and only dealing I ever had with him. I don't know if he left town or just quit doing abortions.

Once, in the early sixties, a young man—nice-looking, wholesome kid—walked into the office on a day when I was on duty and said, "I want to turn myself in." I was sort of surprised and said, "Why? What happened?" He explained that he and his girlfriend were from Mercer County. She was pregnant. They had tried certain things or certain people in Mercer County in an effort to end the pregnancy, but they were all unsuccessful, so they had come to see this doctor in Pittsburgh. The doctor had his office on Fifth Avenue right across the street from a hospital. The boyfriend had made the appointment and driven her there. She had died right there in the doctor's office, and the doctor just called the coroner and had her body taken away.

This young man just kept crying and rocking back and forth and saying, "I love my girlfriend. I just killed her, and I have to pay for what I have done." As it turned out, we weren't able to charge the doctor because the evidence wasn't clear enough as to whether he had done the abortion or whether someone in Mercer County had done it and the Pittsburgh doctor was just treating her afterward. Although we were never able to know exactly who caused her death, her boyfriend was absolutely convinced that he had—convinced and inconsolable.

Another one was Dr. Ludlam. He was one of the most distinguished and most interesting doctor-abortionists. This man was a very respected and influential member of the medical community, but for years we had heard rumors that he did abortions. He had never been arrested. He was a wealthy man and certainly didn't need the money. Apparently he did abortions out of principle. He believed the law was wrong, so he broke the law. Simple as that. There was nothing sleazy about him. No way! If anything, he was a pillar of the medical community, a big man.

Once we actually got some complaints about him, and it was my job to go and arrest the doctor. I won't forget that in a hurry! Dr. Ludlam seemed to have a busy and reputable practice. I went to his office, and the waiting room was just filled with these very pregnant ladies, all there for their monthly checkups. This fellow was their obstetrician, and from the looks of things, he was soon going to be delivering a lot of babies. I felt pretty conspicuous and out of place in that waiting room, even though I wasn't wearing a uniform.

When I told him why I was there and that I had a warrant for his arrest for doing abortions, I will never forget what he did. He opened the desk drawer and showed me a gun he kept in there. He said, "I might just as well take this gun and blow my brains out if you go ahead with this." I had a horrible mental picture of this respected doctor blowing his head off in a waiting room full of women who looked like they were going to deliver at any moment. I tried to be very calm and soothing, but I did tell him that there was nothing I could do about it. We had gotten these complaints. None of the complaints involved a woman dying or anything, but still, they couldn't be ignored. We had to follow up on them.

Here was this man, at the height of his career, and it was like he just crumbled before my eyes. He began to cry and shake. It was awful. I had a hell of a time with him. He said, "If I'm taken out of here now and all my patients see it, I am destroyed!" So I said, "Listen, Doctor, here's what I'll do." I was a captain then and had enough discretion to use my own judgment about a thing like this. "Call your lawyer right now," I told him, "and as soon as you finish with your last patient, you and your lawyer can come down to the police station. You don't have to walk through the waiting room with me now." I did that partly as a courtesy to him, but mostly as a courtesy to all those pregnant ladies, because it seemed like the right thing to do.

However, before I left, I tried to make sure that he wasn't going to kill himself. I waited while he called his lawyer, and then I talked to the lawyer. I explained about the gun and asked him to talk to his client. He did and then reassured me that Dr. Ludlam was not going to do anything with the gun. Last, he guaranteed that he would have the doctor at the police station as soon as the last patient was finished. That all seemed like a reasonable compromise to me, so I left and went back to the station without him. Unfortunately, I got chastised for not bringing him back with me immediately. They wanted him right then and not four hours later, but they hadn't seen that waiting room.

Well, he and the lawyer appeared as promised. We arraigned him and he was indicted. I know he wasn't convicted, and maybe he didn't go to trial. I don't remember what happened. But I sure remember him and his tears and the gun— and all those very respectable, very pregnant women who obviously had a lot of faith in this guy.

There was a doctor on Mount Washington, one in Duquesne, and one on the Northside. These guys were kind of "regulars," and they each seemed to have their own neighborhoods. Dr. King, the one in Duquesne, was real bad news [see Dr. Clay's remarks on this same Dr. King, pp. 115, 133], and we wanted to get him before he killed someone. Unfortunately, we failed. He used to spread the word to college campuses in Ohio and Pennsylvania that if you had a certain kind of a problem, he could solve it for you for a certain price. The sad part about it was that he had a legitimate medical practice in the community, and it's too bad that he resorted to this kind of stuff. He was a very intelligent man, interesting to talk to. His medical training was good. He was a competent doctor—at least at one time—but he sure took a wrong turn somewhere.

I first arrested him in the early sixties. He had done an abortion on a young woman from another county. She got a bad infection and had to be hospitalized. She sure was sick, but she didn't die. She told the people at the hospital that Dr. King had done the abortion in his office. Because the crime had occurred in Allegheny County, the hospital called us, and I went to the doctor's office and arrested him.

He had a lot of friends in high places, and he was able to do lots of things to prevent his cases from coming to trial for years. I don't know who he knew or how he did it, but he sure could do it. Like in this case, he was indicted, but when it came time for trial, this young woman disappeared, and without the key witness there simply was no case. He walked.

His next arrest for abortion, or at least the next one I knew about, was two or three years later. He did an abortion on a twenty-six-year-old Pittsburgh woman. On the scheduled day, the woman and her boyfriend paid two hundred and fifty dollars to the doctor's wife, who functioned as his nurse-receptionist. Then, following instructions, the boyfriend left and waited down the street while the woman had her abortion. Afterward she had to be hospitalized because she got a bad infection. The hospital notified us when they found out what was wrong and who had done it, and we went out and arrested the doctor.

There was no real way to put Dr. King under surveillance and catch him in the act, because there were so many legitimate patients coming and going—men, old people, children. There were women too, and we could hardly stop each woman and ask why she was there. It's true that most if not all of the legitimate patients were black and in the three abortion arrests that I made the women were white. But I'm sure that the abortion practice was both black and white, so you couldn't tell the legitimate patients from the abortion patients—at least not just by looking. We had to sort of wait, and if we were lucky and someone got sick and didn't die, we might be able to arrest him. It was very much a hit-or-miss sort of thing.

Unfortunately, with the next case involving Dr. King the woman did die. That was in December of 1967. She was a nineteen-year-old girl from Youngstown, a freshman at Ohio University—a nice girl from a nice family. It was tragic what happened to her. Her nineteen-year-old boyfriend got the doctor's name from somewhere—maybe this was one of the college campuses he targeted. The appointment was made for December 27th, and a price of three hundred dollars was agreed upon. The abortion was done in Dr. King's office, after which the young couple returned to Ohio. She died the next day at a Youngstown hospital.

Once again we went out to arrest Dr. King. Now, he and his wife knew that this one was more serious than anything that had happened before, and when we got there, the community was ready for us. This time we nearly had a riot on our hands. There were all kinds of people waiting for us. The wife wasn't going to let us take her husband, and she had assembled a good-sized crowd to meet us and prevent that from happening. These were not ordinary neighbors, mind you. These were some real tough types! I don't know where they came from, but there were thirty or forty of them and they were mean! We had to call in reinforcements to help us make the arrest. They had to form a cordon so we could get him to the police car without the crowd getting to us. It was wild.

Abortion was not his only problem with the law, though. In 1968 he was arrested and charged with failure to report a gunshot wound and with being an accessory after the fact in connection with his treatment of a wounded robbery suspect. In 1970 he got fined and sentenced to ninety days in jail for illegally selling narcotics. He was a real bad actor, and I'm just sorry we couldn't put him away before that girl died.

Some of the smarter doctors covered their trails and didn't do abortions right there in their own offices. Most of the doctors had some sort of middleman who made the appointment and things like that. If the middleman was a real stand-up kind of guy, the police never got to the doctor. For a lot of reasons it was real hard to get to these people, and the ones we did arrest had to be just a small part of all the people doing it.

It seemed to me that there was a pattern with some of the doctor-abortionists. Once they did one illegal medical activity, they just seemed to drift into others. The "big three" for the doctors seemed to be abortion, illegal drug sales, and treating bullet wounds without reporting them. That's probably because they were all basically easy money. But this pattern of other illegal activity wasn't true for all doctor-abortionists. Like, the doctor with the New Castle girls didn't do other illegal things so far as I knew. And I bet that Dr. Ludlam never even got a parking ticket!

The abortionists who weren't doctors didn't do any other illegal medical things. They usually just did abortions. But sometimes they would be involved in some other kind of illegal activity, like gambling. Sometimes, even if they didn't do anything illegal except abortions, they would be married to someone involved in criminal activities, but I never thought organized crime was involved in this. The criminal stuff was pretty small-time.

As I say, there were lots of abortionists who weren't doctors. I remember—and this was way back in the fifties—that the biggest one up the valley east of Pittsburgh was a doctor's widow. She wasn't a doctor, and I'm pretty sure she wasn't a nurse. She just inherited all of his instruments and books, and she figured that was all she needed to set up shop, so she did! She used to put on a surgical gown and even a mask. She really dressed the part. She also didn't see too well and wore these real thick glasses.

We got a policewoman to make an appointment with her for an abortion, and to set it up so that it was right after a real pregnant woman who actually wanted an abortion. Like, the policewoman's appointment was at nine p.m. and the real patient's was at eight-thirty or something like that. We got there at quarter of nine with a police photographer. Since this woman didn't see too well, it was harder for her to figure out what was going on when something unexpected happened. We kicked in the window of her "operating room," and there she was—all gussied up in this mask and gown. The real patient was on the table with her legs up in stirrups and the abortionist had this catheter in her hand. When the window smashed in, the abortionist whirled around so she was facing the camera. She actually had the catheter still in her hand. Now, that was a great picture, and there was no way she could talk her way out of it! The picture and the look on her face just told the whole story.

Then there was a white woman in Braddock and two black women in the Hill. None of them were doctors, and they did abortions in alleys and places like that. They would get arrested periodically, but that didn't seem to bother them. They would pay the fine or serve the time and just keep doing abortions, sort of like you see sometimes with arrests for prostitution.

When a woman from an affluent family had an abortion and was admitted to the hospital, do you think the family would call us? Hell, no! Those were covered up. Even if the woman died, a rich family, or even a middle-class family with the right connections, could arrange to have the family doctor list something else as the cause of death.

There was one thing I never understood. These women were having abortions done with coat hangers, under horrible conditions, and the women I would see in hospitals were in terrible shape. Hell, a lot of them were sick enough to die! But they wouldn't talk. They simply wouldn't tell who did it or where it was done. I'd plead with a woman to tell me, and she would just look away or turn her head to the wall. Even when they thought they might die, they wouldn't tell. That just made no sense to me. If one of these people who did the abortion had robbed her on the street or done any other criminal act, she would have told, real quick. But there sure was something different about this. No one talked about it, especially the women. In those days, a lot of women were losing their lives or their health as a result of abortions, but still they wouldn't talk. Why?

MARIE

I N 1957 I WAS LIVING IN PITTSBURGH. I had graduated from high school a little more than a year earlier—the first person in my family ever to do so—and was working as a secretary. We were West Virginians. I was one of thirteen children, and we were what are known as "country people."

Having all those babies wasn't a religious thing, and I don't know how much it was related to a lack of birth control, although they certainly didn't have any. It was more than that. They were country people who had very little education, money, or material possessions. Having babies was just a natural thing to do. It was sort of like planting a crop. A family needed babies because they needed people to help work the farm. It was good to have a lot of babies because some always died in infancy. My mother lost three children, all of whom died before their first birthdays. My mother and father liked having babies, and they had pretty babies. As soon as one got old enough to walk, it seemed to my father that it was time to have another one.

My childhood experiences had a lot to do with the decisions of my adult life. I suppose that is true for everyone, but it is particularly so for me and is very vivid in my mind. When I first set foot in the door of my high school, I vowed that I would graduate, even though no one in my family had ever done that. I was not going to get pregnant before I got an education, and I was absolutely not going to live the kind of poverty-stricken life I watched my mother and older sisters live. My oldest sister had six children, no money, and no education. There seemed no way for her to ever climb out of the trap she was in. I promised myself that would never happen to me. My idea of how to prevent that life of poverty was to get an education and avoid sex, or failing that, avoid pregnancy.

I graduated from high school still a virgin, so I felt I had a good chance of surviving the trap all the women in my family had fallen into. My mother and sisters all were married with several children before they reached eighteen.

When I was nineteen or twenty, I met a sophisticated older man. Ray was twenty-five years older than I was. He had been married and had children older than I was. In addition to his maturity and sophistication, he had, by my standards, a great deal of money. He owned a nightclub and drove a big fancy car. I had never even been in a nightclub until I met him. He showed me a lifestyle I hadn't even known existed.

With him, I embarked on my first sexual experience. His sophistication and affluence overwhelmed me. I suspect that my naiveté and docility enchanted him. I was pretty and pliant. He was the strong male figure I had never had.

In those days there was really no birth control—at least so far as I knew. Ray told me that if you douched every time after you had sex, you wouldn't get pregnant. What did I know? I did what he told me. Now we know that douching is one of the most dangerous things in the world to do after having sex. It doesn't get rid of the sperm, it just washes it into places where it's more likely to meet the egg.

At the time, I had no attitudes, religious or otherwise, about abortion. In fact, I don't know that I had ever even heard the word when I was growing up. I never was aware that this was an option people had. When I was in high school, I was aware of pregnancies before marriage, but the couple always just got married. It never occurred to me that people could do anything else. Joyce, one of my classmates in high school, had a baby out of wedlock and kept it. That was a very daring thing to do in my community in the fifties. My high school sweetheart was the one who got Joyce pregnant. She would and I wouldn't, so his choice was fairly easy.

Then I had that morning so many women face—when you look in the mirror and say, "Oh, my God!" You spend your time running back and forth to the bathroom, hoping against hope to see that magic spot of blood, but it doesn't happen. Finally, you reluctantly admit that it just isn't going to.

When I finally admitted to myself that it wasn't going to happen, I told Ray I had missed my period and thought I might be pregnant. I didn't have a pregnancy test or anything, because in those days they weren't easily available, but I didn't need a pregnancy test. I was nauseated and my breasts were sore, so I was pretty sure I was pregnant. I wasn't living with my mother and all of the babies when this happened. I was living in an apartment with a roommate. Maybe that made everything easier. I don't know.

Ray said, "Of course you have to have an abortion." The only thing I'd ever heard about abortion was listening to my mother talk about jumping off kitchen tables, falling down flights of stairs, and taking hot baths—or maybe cold baths. I never really knew that there was any other way to have an abortion. Ray said, "Oh no, it's not like that. There are other ways." Ray was very—what shall I say?—well connected. He had many connections with organized crime in western Pennsylvania. Many of his close friends were gangsters and people who lived outside the law. Ray said he knew of a good person to go to, and the reason he was good was because that's where all the gangsters took their girlfriends and their wives. Anyone involved in organized crime seemed to do nothing but the best, so this abortionist was sure to be "the best money can buy." It certainly made sense to me. Think about it. Abortion was illegal, so why wouldn't gangsters, whose business was illegal activity, know the best place to get an abortion? So, like everything else he told me, I believed this as well.

Ray made all the arrangements and told me that he and

another man would pick me up and we would drive to Youngstown, Ohio. For some reason—and this doesn't make any sense—Ray told me I would be up all night and that I should take a Benzedrine to stay awake. I never took drugs, so I had no idea how to get medicine like that without going to a doctor, but Ray had no trouble getting prescription drugs. I don't know how he did that either, but it was probably even easier than the abortion for him to arrange.

At the appointed time, at night, Ray and his friend Lloyd picked me up. We started to Youngstown, but first I took the pill Ray handed me. Maybe it wasn't really intended to keep me awake but instead had something to do with the abortion. A pill to keep me awake was unnecessary, even if it had made any sense, because there was no way I would have been relaxed enough to fall asleep. I bet even a sleeping pill would not have put me to sleep.

I had met Lloyd before. He was a convicted murderer. I don't know who he had killed, but he had served his time. He was out of jail, working as a bookie.

That late-night car trip to Ohio happened many years ago, but I can see it as vividly as if it was yesterday. I sat in the front seat of this shiny new big black Chrysler Imperial with Ray in a black cashmere coat on one side of me and Lloyd, the murderer-turned-bookie, sporting an elegant camel's-hair coat on the other. Lloyd drove. All the way to Ohio, the two men talked exclusively to each other, mostly about sports or gambling. I sat silent between them, feeling like I was no bigger than a candle flame in the dark. I felt almost nonexistent, like I was in some other world. The trip had a strange quality of unreality about it.

I was beyond fear—truly beyond it. I was so terrified I couldn't move or speak or even think. I just huddled there in the front seat. I didn't know where I was going or what was going to be done to me. I had no idea. Was someone going to cut my head off or cut my belly open? Either was equally possible in my mind.

Once I began to tell a few people what I was doing, I began to hear horror stories. I heard about kitchen tables and knitting needles and coat hangers. It was horrible. It couldn't be true, and it couldn't be happening to me. One of the worst things about it was that I had no control over my life. I had taken such pride in never being as stupid as my mother or my sisters, who had quite literally given control of their lives over to men, and now I was speeding west with two men, both of whom thought boxing and gambling were so important that by comparison I wasn't worth talking to. No wonder I felt like a flickering candle flame about to go out. To them, that's all I was.

Both of these men were old enough to be my father. Maybe that had some sort of psychological significance, I don't know. My own father had just died, and I hadn't really lived with him or spent much time with him since my mother had taken "her babies" and left him. Ray was an authority figure, and like any good girl of that era, I didn't question him or what he said.

When we got to Youngstown, Lloyd drove to a very run-down part of town. The houses all had a ramshackle look about them. We pulled up behind a run-down old house. It was frame and looked like it hadn't been painted in at least twenty-five years. The two men sat in the car, and I went up to the door by myself. I supposed I was expected, so no introduction was necessary.

An old black man with springy white hair opened the door and let me in. I found myself standing in a very small room with a wooden kitchen table in the middle. Although the table needed a new paint job too, it had seen a paint brush much more recently than the exterior of the house. There was a twenty-year-old calendar hanging on the wall. I thought that was odd, but no more odd than the entire surreal trip. I could hear men's voices in what sounded like the next room, but I never saw anyone else. I think it was a bookie operation, judging from the bits and pieces of conversation I could overhear.

The 1937 calendar has special significance for me. I was born in 1937, so I was convinced that its appearance on the wall could only mean that I was going to die. It had to be a sign, since why else would it be there? The only things in that little room were the table and the twenty-year-old calendar.

My fear drove me into what must have been an altered state of consciousness. I didn't ever lose consciousness, but I have very little memory of what happened next. To this day, I cannot recall what that old man did to me. He was the abortionist. No one else came into the room. The last thing I remember was climbing up onto the kitchen table. I don't remember anything else until it was over. The next thing I remembered was the old man looking at me and saying, "Now, you are going to have a lot of pain, but you are going to be all right. Just take some aspirin. Don't worry about it, and don't go to a doctor." When I came out of the house, Ray and Lloyd were waiting in the car. I got in and we drove back to Pittsburgh. At that point I felt fine—no pain or bleeding or anything.

I lived in a small apartment with a roommate, a young woman about my age. The men dropped me off at my apartment. They didn't come in or anything. Ray just said, "I hope you're all right," and they drove off. I went to bed and waited for something to happen.

The next day the pain started. The cramps were terrible— unlike anything I had ever experienced. Aspirin did nothing for the pain, but I didn't call a doctor. After about two days of severe cramping, I began to hemorrhage and did miscarry. I remember going into the bathroom and having blood and clots just pour out of me. The blood was very dark, almost black. There was blood all over the bathroom floor. It was frightening.

When I began hemorrhaging, my roommate, who knew about the abortion, said, "We've got to tell your mother. We've got to call a doctor." I refused. She was scared, and frankly, so was I, but I had been told not to call a doctor. I was afraid that a doctor would call the police and I would go to jail. My roommate kept arguing that they wouldn't put me in jail, but I was sure they would. Not only had I done something illegal, but I had been driven there by a gangster. How much more illegal could it get? Besides, I figured that even if the police didn't put me in jail, gangsters might do something even worse to me if I told. It was much better—and safer—to just keep my mouth shut.

Ray came to see me once or twice. I can remember him bending over the bed looking at me. I kept hoping he would just pick me up and take me to an emergency room. He didn't, though.

My roommate and I just toughed it out without involving anyone. The pain and the bleeding gradually subsided, and after about ten days I was able to drag myself back to work. Everyone had been told I had the flu, and I looked the part. I had lost weight to the point where I was sallow and scrawny-looking. I was weak, and it was an effort to drag myself through the day.

About three weeks after I had gone back to work, and more than a month after the abortion, I began to have a new and ominous symptom—a discharge. It was very different from the hemorrhaging, although it was almost as heavy. Instead of dark red blood, it was a pale pink fluid with a putrid odor. The smell, which seemed to pervade my whole body and not just the discharge itself, was so bad it made me gag.

My roommate again begged me to go to the doctor, and this time I was willing because it seemed to be a different medical problem, one for which I might not get arrested. However, it took me another two weeks to get up enough nerve to call a doctor, so by the time I actually got medical attention, it was five or six weeks after the abortion.

I found the doctor in the Yellow Pages. I didn't know him or anything. I just picked him at random. His last name did start with an A, so I might well have just picked the first gynecologist I came to. He was very nice to me and very kind. Of course, I didn't tell him about the abortion. All he knew was that I seemed to have a severe infection. He told me he was going to test me for venereal disease. I felt ashamed that he thought I might have a venereal disease—that was something else that didn't happen to nice girls—but it was infinitely worse to admit to the abortion, so I said nothing and let him do the test. Then he did some other tests and announced that I was extremely anemic. Again I told him nothing about the weeks of heavy bleeding, so there was no readily apparent explanation for the anemia or any of my other symptoms.

Because I had, to him at least, a bafflingly innocuous medical history that did not match the severity of my symptoms, he decided to hospitalize me. Although that made me somewhat fearful, I was really too sick to offer much resistance. After lab tests ruled out a venereal disease as the cause of my symptoms, he informed me that he was going to do a D and C because I had a severe infection of unknown cause. Before I could have the D and C, however, I had to have a blood transfusion, because I was too anemic to have even a minor surgical procedure.

My mother and brother came to visit me in the hospital. They seemed frightened. Partly it was just having someone in the hospital—country people didn't have much experience with that—and partly, I am sure, it was the way I looked: thin and pale, with IVs in my arms. Of course, they didn't know what was wrong with me. I told them I had an infection, and that seemed to satisfy them. They didn't ask any questions.

After the D and C, the doctor came in, and I'll never forget this. He leaned over my bed, looked into my eyes, and said, "Young lady, why didn't you tell me you had had an abortion?" I looked back at him and said, "Because I thought you would put me in jail!" He patted my hand—he was very kind—and said, "No, no. We'll take care of you. It's all right. No one will hurt you. It's over now, and everything will be all right." Well, I started to cry, and I just lay there crying, and he stood there patting my hand, telling me not to worry. He was really a wonderful human being, and for the first time I felt that things really might be all right after all.

I didn't see Ray at all during this period of my life. I just didn't want to be around him. He was an unpleasant reminder. He did pay my hospital bills and doctor's bills, but I think he was secretly relieved that I was handling this on my own, without any emotional help from him.

I finally did recover from the abortion and the infection,

but it was a very slow process. It took several months before I got over the anemia, but finally I did, and ultimately I got back to where I had been before the Youngstown trip. Actually, I never got back to where I had been, because the infection left such severe scarring that I was never able to get pregnant after that. I ultimately got married and adopted two children. I adore my children. They are both wonderful people and are the high point of my life, but I was always disappointed that I could not become pregnant.

I had no doubt and no mixed feelings about having an abortion. I desperately wanted that abortion. I could always have gone home to my mother. She would have welcomed me with open arms and would have loved the idea of another baby. But I didn't want to grow old before my time like my mother and my sisters had. I didn't want to lose my teeth before I was thirty like my sisters did. I didn't want to spend the rest of my life like I saw my sisters living theirs: with lots of children in dire poverty. I saw what early pregnancy did to women.

I was not taught, and I did not believe, that abortion was morally wrong, but I did feel that I was a bad person because I had committed a criminal act. Abortion was against the law, and I had broken the law. That made me a bad person, because in my mind there was no such thing as "good criminals" and "bad criminals."

It took me years to get over that feeling. A big step toward getting over my guilt and shame occurred in the seventies quite by accident, when I was reading an article about well-known women who had had illegal abortions. I had always felt so alone—like I was the only woman who had this dark and dirty secret. Finding out that there were so many of us made me feel less like a criminal, because I knew those well-known women weren't bad people. My guilt went away completely, I think, when abortion became legal. I felt that although what I had done was illegal then, it shouldn't have been. It wasn't that I did something "wrong," it's that I did what I did at the "wrong" point in the history of this country.

DR. JAMES

I GRADUATED FROM MEDICAL SCHOOL IN 1954. We didn't receive any training about how to do a D and C, and the subject of abortion wasn't even discussed. We did receive training in how to treat the consequences of induced abortion, but there was absolutely no training in how to do an abortion. Later, as a resident in ob-gyn, I learned how to do a D and C, but again we never learned how to do an abortion.

During my medical training, I saw women being treated for septic abortion, and as a resident I took care of lots of them. There was a special ward in the hospital. It had four to eight beds filled with women who had either pelvic inflammatory disease, usually from gonorrhea, or septic abortion complications. The septic abortion patients were usually looked down upon as having done something illegal, probably because just about everyone grows up with the idea that bad people do illegal things and good people don't.

There were ways around being identified as an "illegal abortion patient" if you had the right kind of connections. When I was an intern, the daughter of one of the head nurses came in, supposedly with appendicitis. I was called to examine her, and I discovered that she had a catheter still in her cervix. That was kept very quiet, and she was treated as having a "bladder infection." To my knowledge, only a handful of people knew, and the hospital records didn't show that she had had an illegal abortion. Her records said she had a "pelvic infection," but they sure didn't say that it came from a dirty catheter! She was not on the ward with the other septic abortion patients or even the pelvic inflamatory disease patients. She was in a private room, which made the whole thing a whole lot easier to cover up!

But it was more than just the head nurse's daughter. If a private doctor's private patient got into trouble after a back-alley abortion—the doctor certainly hadn't done the abortion, he was just treating her later—that patient could get follow-up hospital care in a private room. Her diagnosis would be "pelvic infection—cause unknown." Think about what all the mislabeled "bladder infections," "appendicitis," or even "pelvic infection—cause unknown" did to abortion statistics in those days.

These women we're talking about—the head nurse's daughter and the doctor's private patient—weren't getting safe abortions. Their abortions were just as bad as the women's on the ward. They were just getting anonymous postabortion care. Having an illegal abortion or an illegitimate child was something to be ashamed of in those days, because they pointed to illicit, if not illegal, sex. Women went to great lengths to conceal the fact that they had had an abortion. They never went near a hospital unless they really had no choice because they badly needed medical attention.

That always full ward was by no means an accurate measure of the incidence of abortion or even the incidence of complications of abortion. The ward was a small part. By the mid-fifties antibiotics were in use, so not only did we have all those private hospital patients, but a lot of doctors could now treat their patients with out-patient antibiotic therapy, so these people also missed the statistics.

Even with the patients on the ward, we didn't put into the chart everything we knew, because if we did, the hospital would probably have to call the police. It sure wasn't going to help her get better, and it wasn't going to solve the abortion problem either, since other abortionists, no more skilled, would simply take their places. Of course, it was different if the woman died. Then the coroner got involved and there were lots of police.

I have no idea what the real abortion numbers were in those days, but I'm pretty sure we just saw and identified as "abortion patients" the tip of the iceberg—women where something went wrong *and* they had no private doctor. I suspect that no more than one in five abortions was actually listed as an abortion, maybe even less.

The women on the wards were generally more seriously ill than the private patients. Now, that may be due to their generally inferior health status. They didn't have the advantages of good nutrition, good hygiene, and so forth. They didn't get regular health care or any kind of maintenance health care. They also tended to be black, and the private patients tended to be white, but this was probably typical of the times. However, it didn't mean that white women got better abortions. They *all* got lousy abortions.

The technique of the criminal abortionist wasn't limited to a catheter or coat hanger. Many of them injected some kind of caustic substance—bleach or something like that—into the uterus. The uterus would contract to get rid of the irritant, but there was a high risk of complications.

Potassium permanganate was another common choice. The abortionist dissolved some of the crystals in water and inserted the solution into the uterus through a syringe or catheter. On the street, women heard that potassium permanganate would work, but they didn't get all the details of how to use it, and we would see women who would just insert the crystals into the vagina. By the time these women got to the hospital, they would have terrible burns or even actual holes in the vaginal lining, because the crystals had simply eaten away the tissue. The irony is that placed in the vagina, potassium permanganate didn't abort the pregnancy, but it sure did a lot of damage to the vagina! Women who describe the abortionist as inserting a catheter but not leaving it in place were probably having some solution inserted into the uterus through the catheter.

The complications we typically saw on the ward were severe pelvic inflammation and infection, with pelvic abscesses which had to be drained. Many women got an ileus, or shutdown of their intestines. They had to have a nasal-gastric tube so we could just keep their intestines quiet until they started to function again. They would also get a generalized peritonitis. Some patients died of "uremia"—at least that's what would be written on the death certificate, again leading statisticians to miss the abortion connection. Uremia is an extremely severe infection with septic shock and kidney shutdown.

The lay public, reading an abortion death certificate—does the lay public ever read things like this? Maybe their next of kin do. Anyway, the lay public is always surprised to see death due to gas gangrene or tetanus. The public associates gas gangrene with battlefield wounds and tetanus with stepping on a rusty nail. Bacteria in the vagina and cervix, however—even in fairly healthy women—are a relatively virulent type of bacteria. *Clostridium,* which causes gas gangrene, is an occasional cause of a severe non-abortion vaginal infection. In an illegal abortion, where nothing is sterile, you would just be introducing into the uterus all those virulent organisms living in the vagina. In the vagina, they don't do any harm. In the uterus, they create death certificates.

Hemorrhage was sometimes a complication, although often these women died at the time of the abortion, before they ever got to a hospital. With a perforation in certain parts of the uterus, where the blood supply is concentrated, it would take only a few hours—a day at most—for the woman to bleed to death. If it isn't that part of the uterus, perforation could take several days to cause death.

With a bad infection, the time of death is going to depend on the type of infection. With *Clostridium*—gas gangrene—death probably comes in twenty-four to forty-eight hours. With *E. Coli,* the normal organism in the bowel and a common contaminant in an abortion, it takes longer to die—probably days or even weeks.

With illegal abortion, there were lots of ways to die. The lucky ones made it through. The not-so-lucky ones died fairly horrible deaths.

As a child growing up, I did learn attitudes about abortion. My father was a doctor. He was a general surgeon, and before World War II he had a general family practice. After the war he did general surgery. I was probably in my teens then. I graduated from high school in 1947. He talked about it, usually at the dining room table—all doctors talk about medicine at the dining room table. Maybe it's because that is the only time the family sees each other. Anyway, I can remember him saying that this certain doctor was doing office abortions. This was probably in the late forties. His feeling was that these doctors were "fringe people." Certainly what I learned is that this is not the kind of doctor I wanted to be associated with.

What I got from my doctor-father was not that it was "immoral"—I really don't recall a moral judgment—but rather, that it was illegal. When I started to be involved in what I guess we could call "the movement"—the efforts to legalize abortion—my father was still alive, and he was what I would call passively accepting of my decision and my involvement. We would often discuss it, and he had come to the view that it was something that ought to be legally available. His attitude had changed over time, and much of what had caused the change may have been that abortion techniques had greatly improved.

I recall doing an extremely rare hospital-approved abortion in the early sixties, before we had suction abortions. The woman's pregnancy had to be terminated for medical reasons. Even though she was only eight weeks pregnant, it was extremely difficult to do a D and C on a pregnant uterus. In terms of technique, it was very hard to do. Because the pregnant uterus was soft and not as firm, there was a much greater chance of perforating the uterus than there would have been with a nonpregnant uterus. I'm sure that's why my father and other physicians felt it wasn't a good procedure.

I do recall two women who died from the complications of illegal abortions. One happened in 1955. A young woman—she was only seventeen or eighteen—died of a ruptured uterus and an absolutely overwhelming infection. She had originally been admitted to a smaller hospital, but then, because she was so critically ill, she was transferred to the university hospital where I was doing my residency. Even with antibiotics, the infection simply overwhelmed her body. She died of septic shock. Afterward there were spirited discussions among the doctors about whether we might have been able to save her if we had done something differently—maybe different antibiotics, things like that. But no one talked about or even seemed to notice the really obvious solution: making legal abortion available.

The second woman I remember probably died in 1957 or 1958. She was a young woman too, but not a teenager. She had had an abortion, and when she was brought to the hospital, she had gas gangrene. She was in shock by the time she arrived, and nothing we did made any difference. She died quickly—in less than twenty-four hours.

After I finished my residency, I spent three years in the service. There I never saw a woman with an abortion complication—not dependents and not female military personnel. I suppose it happened, but they just didn't go to the military hospital for treatment, because in those days, if female personnel got pregnant, they were bounced out of the service, even if the abortion had been successful so that they were no longer pregnant. I'm sure they went to the local hospital if they got into any post-abortion medical problems.

I started private practice in ob-gyn in 1961. I took care of a few women who had complications from illegal abortions, but there weren't many, not like what I had seen during my residency.

I remember a patient I saw in 1961 or 1962. She had been exposed to rubella early in her pregnancy. She had a well-documented case, and the risks of fetal abnormalities as a result were very well known. She and her husband wanted an abortion, but no hospital would permit it. They asked me what to do, but I had no real help to offer them. I didn't know any reputable abortionists to refer her to. They eventually went to Mexico and she had an abortion there. When she came back, she was fine. She was my patient for many years after that, and I delivered several children for her. But I always felt bad because I couldn't help her at one pretty critical time in her life when she very much needed help.

By the mid-sixties, the suction abortion had been developed, which made abortion much easier and safer for women. I did my first suction abortion at the hospital in 1968 or 1969. By that time New York had changed its laws, and so had several other states, so things had loosened up a lot. At that point the hospital would most certainly have permitted an abortion on a rubella patient.

There is a big battle going on right now to keep RU486 out of this country. That is really unfortunate, because it has medical uses which go beyond abortion. We can certainly bring it into this country whether it is legal or not. Anyone who doubts that just has to look at all the illegal drugs we already have. If RU486 is illegal, it will just be more expensive and perhaps dangerous due to contamination.

If abortion were illegal, RU486 would not save us from the return of the coat-hanger abortionist, because there is such a relatively brief period in pregnancy when RU486 is effective. Besides, it would probably take a prohibitive amount of money and some unusual "connections" to get it as a black market drug. A lot of women just don't have that kind of money and connections or couldn't get it in the short time period when RU486 could help. Of course, we could send women to Canada for RU486. We used to do that when Flagyl was not approved or available in this country. I suspect that as people continue to do research on RU486 and related compounds, they will doubtless improve on it and find a drug that is effective for a longer portion of the pregnancy.

Maybe a revisiting of the bad old days wouldn't be as bad as what I remember, because the technology is so much better. If nurses, or even nonmedical people, could get access to suction machines, they would be less likely to have as many complications as they had in the forties, fifties, and sixties. It isn't a hard technique to learn. However, the first time I did a suction abortion, I did perforate the woman's uterus, so it's not foolproof under the best of conditions.

In the fifties and early sixties, in spite of that always full hospital ward, no one talked about abortion as a public health problem. It was just a fact of life, and you dealt with it the best way you could—taking care of the complications. It was the women's rights movement and not public health concerns that made abortion legal. I remember that when I first went into private practice in 1961, if a woman wanted her tubes tied, she had to get her husband's written permission. I thought that was way out of line. Her body didn't belong to her husband! Besides, she didn't have to sign for his vasectomy. But that's how it was in those days.

For as long as I can remember, I have been in favor of making abortion legal, because I always thought that a woman ought to have the right to control her body. Pregnancy is a real parasite that invades all of a woman's body systems, and that ought not to happen unless she is willing. I'm not sure where I got that idea. My mother didn't have it, and my wife actively disagrees with my views on abortion. I have two daughters. One very strongly shares my views on this topic and the other one just as strongly shares her mother's views. We talk about being a pluralistic society, especially where abortion is concerned. Well, I'm living in a microcosm of that pluralistic society.

JULIA

I HAD AN ILLEGAL ABORTION IN 1958. I was living in White Plains, New York, working at Saks Fifth Avenue as a salesclerk. I had graduated from high school in 1957. Even though I was only nineteen, I was living alone, rather than at home, which was the normal pattern in those days. My mother had remarried, and my stepfather—well, I don't know if it's fair to say he disliked me. Let's just say I was "in the way." I knew it and went out on my own.

I was dating the same boy I had gone with all the way through high school. He was in the navy. We were very much in love, and he was my first sexual experience. He taught me about my body, about the rhythm method and things like that. My mother never told me anything when I was growing up. She just said, "Here's a Kotex and a belt. Someday you'll need it. I'll tell you the rest later." Well, she never did, and I just got bits and pieces from friends and what I heard at school.

I knew absolutely nothing about birth control; any access to it was out of the question. I was raised Catholic, and I had heard of the rhythm method. The only other thing I'd heard of was condoms, and I knew my church didn't approve of those. I was taught that abortion was a sin. I went to a Catholic girls' school, a convent school. I didn't want to be there, and I was very rebellious. I wanted to go to the public school where my friends all went. I was smart, a straight-A student. I wore the medal and said the prayers, but I misbehaved just enough so that I finally got my wish: I got expelled.

Now, I had no real knowledge of how the rhythm method worked. I had just heard the word. My boyfriend, Bill, told me that from the fourteenth to the seventeenth day after the first day of my period, it wasn't safe to have sex because I might get pregnant. Any other time was safe, he said, and I didn't know any different.

When Bill, with whom I was so madly in love, came home from boot camp, he was only going to be home for a few days, and I hadn't seem him in a long time. We were going to a Valentine's Day party. Remembering what he had told me, I warned him that it was my fourteenth day. "No problem," was his response. I guess he felt more confident than I did that our emotions would not cloud our judgment. Well, it didn't work that way, and of course we had sex. Since it was unplanned, we had no alternate means of protection, and I got pregnant.

It took me a while to realize that I was pregnant. I never had a very regular cycle, which made our fourteen-day rule particularly dangerous and ineffective, I now realize. I missed a period and noticed that my breasts were sore. At first I thought they were sore because my period was about to start, but that didn't happen.

Two or three weeks after the missed period, I borrowed a car from a friend of mine, and my girlfriend and I drove to New London, Connecticut, where Bill was stationed. I told him I had missed a period and thought I might be pregnant. He swung me in his arms, grinned, and said, "That's great! We'll get married." That was what was expected in the fifties, and it sounded fine to me. I was nineteen and he was eighteen; everything seemed easy to us then.

We bought rings and set out for a place in Maryland because he had been told that we could get married there at eighteen. Well, his mother found out somehow and called the police. We never got to Maryland. The police picked us up in New Jersey and brought us home. Bill's older brother had run off with a girl, and Bill's mother wasn't about to let that happen again. Besides, they were Swedish and I was Italian, and I don't think they wanted me to be part of the family.

I really dreaded telling my mother, because it would just prove to her all the bad things my stepfather always said about me. I had lived with my aunt Helen during my senior year in high school. She was my father's sister. My father had died several years earlier. My mother had asked me to leave home after my junior year because of the conflict between me and my stepfather. My aunt was very good to me and let me stay with her. She loved me, and I adored her.

Reluctantly, I told my mother I was pregnant. Her response was to call Bill's mother. Then they got together and essentially planned my abortion. Isn't that something? My Catholic mother planned my abortion. I didn't want an abortion, but I seemed to have no say in the decision. Once Bill got the message from his family that marriage was out of the question, he never mentioned it again. My only other option seemed to be unwed motherhood, and in 1958 that was not easy to do. Abortion was the group decision made by Bill's parents and my mother, but I really didn't resist too much. My mother told me that if I had a baby, she would be "humiliated" and would do nothing to help me. I knew Bill wouldn't do anything because his parents wouldn't let him.

My mother found the abortionist, I don't know quite how. She was Catholic and her doctor was Catholic, so I don't think her doctor made the referral. My mother had been an unwed mother in 1936. I didn't discover until I was a grown-up that the woman I thought was my sister was really only my half-sister. The fact that my mother was herself an unwed mother probably explains why she was so strongly opposed to my making that choice and why she felt so strongly that I should have an abortion. She had also had at least one abortion, and having done both, she knew far better than I what was really involved with each choice.

As I said, my mother couldn't call her doctor because he was Catholic, so she called another doctor she knew. She always called him "the Jewish doctor," which in her manner of speaking meant that he was more sympathetic than her own doctor. The sympathetic doctor said that he couldn't do it himself but he could arrange for us to go to a hospital in Havana, Cuba.

Now, at nineteen I paid little attention to news. I was dimly aware of people fighting somewhere in some country to the south of us. I had heard people talk about a man named Castro who was engaged in some sort of guerrilla warfare in an attempt to topple the existing government, but I knew nothing more than those bare facts. It certainly had nothing to do with my life in New York.

I don't know whether my mother knew any more about international events than I did, but she made the arrangements for me to go to Cuba to have an abortion. She didn't go with me. My aunt Helen went with me, the same aunt who let me live with her when I was in high school and my mother wanted me out of the house. The fact that my mother was so insistent that I get the abortion but wouldn't even go with me made me feel really unworthy. It wasn't that she was ill or had a demanding job she couldn't leave or anything like that. She just didn't want anything to do with me.

The abortion itself cost about six hundred dollars. There was also the expense of plane fare for two people and hotel accommodations. That was a great deal of money, especially in 1958. Bill's parents and my mother got together and figured it all out. I don't know who paid for what, but my aunt was given our tickets, the hotel reservation, and the money for the Cuban doctor. We also had to have passports, and that was the most time-consuming task facing what I thought of as the "abortion committee." I had gotten pregnant at the Valentine's Day party, but it was May by the time my aunt and I were able to go to Cuba.

When we got to the airport in New York, they said to my aunt, "Do you know there's a revolution going on?" Batista was in power, but Castro was in the mountains, and there were reports of fighting in or near Havana. The airport people told us that if we went, we went at our own risk. My aunt said, "We *must* go!" Confronted with her determination, they just said okay and let us get on the plane.

Even though my aunt was insistent that we go, once on the plane she began wringing her hands and saying, "You're going to come back in a box. I know you will! What would your father say if he knew what I was doing? He'd be rolling in his grave. He'd never forgive me!" She was my father's favorite sister, and she could never bear to displease him, even though he had been dead for several years. She didn't think abortion was wrong. Her own daughter had had an abortion. Maybe she'd had one too. She just thought that going to a Cuban doctor in the middle of a revolution was not a safe thing to do and not something my father would have approved of.

Neither of us spoke any Spanish. All we had, in addition to the money and our passports, was the name of the doctor and the name of the cab driver who was supposed to meet us at the airport. We got to Havana and found the cab driver. It wasn't that he was easy to spot, because to us, in a strange place, all the people at the airport looked pretty similar. On the other hand, we must have been fairly conspicuous. We were probably the only American women entering the country in the middle of the revolution.

The cab driver was very nice and very friendly. I don't remember his name, but he had a little old 1952 Plymouth, which he drove like a wild man. He just walked up to us in the airport and asked if we were so-and-so—whatever the code word was. We told him that we were, got in the cab, and were taken to the hotel. I remember that it was called the Hotel Presidente and was very elegant-looking.

Aunt Helen spoke Italian, which helped her understand, at least a little, the Spanish everyone kept speaking to us, but it was strange and confusing trying to register at the hotel. The cab driver helped us to get checked in and told us that the doctor would come to the hotel later that day to examine me.

To this day, my aunt likes to believe abortion was legal in Cuba in 1958, but I can't believe that it was. Cuba was a Catholic country, so it seemed highly unlikely. Besides, if it had been legal, would it have been set up as it was—with cab drivers acting as "agents" and exams being done in hotel rooms? I don't think so. (In pre-Castro Cuba, abortion was illegal but widely practiced.)

In about an hour, the doctor arrived. Heavyset and dignified, he certainly looked like a doctor. He was soft-spoken and very gentle in his manner, which both my aunt and I found reassuring. He didn't do an internal exam but just had me lie down on the bed so he could feel my belly. I suppose he wanted to confirm that I really was pregnant and get some idea of how far along I was. With a very thick accent, speaking broken English, he explained to me the medical procedure he was going to do. Although he was hard to understand, he seemed to be describing a D and C. He said that he couldn't tell, just from feeling my belly, whether I was beyond sixteen weeks— getting passports really had taken forever!—but that if I was, the abortion was going to be a lot more complicated. Then he explained what I now know is a saline abortion. He described sticking a long needle into my abdomen. I shuddered: "Then what?" "We wait," he said.

Late that night, the cab driver came back and took us to the hospital. I became even more convinced that abortion could not have been legal, since that was not the normal time to check into a hospital. We didn't go through the hospital's main door either. We went in by an obscure side door. We weren't exactly hiding or sneaking in, but it was definitely different than any hospital visit I had ever made before. There were almost no people around. I met the doctor, who had two nurses with him, but I didn't see any receptionists, patients, or any other medical personnel. The place was very quiet, and our footsteps echoed as we walked down long, dark, deserted halls.

He gave me a pelvic exam and announced, to my great relief, that he could do the first procedure he had described to us. He told me to take off my clothes and put on a gown. Then, leaving my aunt behind, he and the two nurses wheeled me into an operating room. It was very clean but very old.

They put my feet up in stirrups and tied my arm down to some kind of board. Then they told me, in broken English, that they were going to give me sodium pentothal and that it would make me sleepy but I should count backwards from one hundred in Spanish. I didn't know how to count in Spanish, and that made us all laugh. The last thing I can remember was thinking that here I was, late at night in a strange hospital, in a strange country, with a revolution going on, separated from my aunt and surrounded by strangers I couldn't understand, with my great love affair and romantic dream about to end, and all I could do was laugh. I didn't understand how it could be funny when it seemed so scary, but I laughed anyway.

When I woke up, it was all over. I was in another room, but still at the hospital. They asked me how I felt. I felt okay, but Aunt Helen didn't! In spite of my saying "*malo*" over and over, which I understood to be the word for "pain," I looked all right when she came in to see me. But she looked really odd! She'd been so nervous that she had tweezed one of her eyebrows almost completely out. She had one normal eyebrow and one that was only an inch long!

Although I was free to leave the hospital right away—I really think they wanted me out of there before the regular staff came to work in the morning—I was told to stay in bed and eat nothing for the next twenty-four hours. All I was permitted to have was fruit juice, but the fruit juice in Cuba was fantastic! I had never had any so delicious in the States.

After the first twenty-four hours, my doctor came to the hotel to examine me. He pronounced me "*bueno*" and gave me permission to eat real food, but he told me I needed to stay in Cuba for another twenty-four hours so that he could be sure I was well enough to travel back to New York.

Since I had to stay another day, our cab driver volunteered to show us the sights of Havana. He took us all over. In spite of obvious signs of fighting, Havana was a beautiful city, and my last day there more than made up for my first thirty-six hours. We went to a casino that was so opulent it made Las Vegas and Atlantic City look like nothing. Havana appeared to be a city of dramatic wealth and dramatic poverty.

At night, in the hotel, we heard gunfire, and if we went out on the balcony, which we weren't supposed to do—we were instructed to stay inside, keep the shutters closed, and stay away from the windows—we could see what looked like fireworks. It was really flares, explosions, and small fires.

We were there for a total of four days. That means that the total cost of my 1958 abortion had to be two thousand dollars. How many women could have afforded that? What would that be in today's dollars? Four thousand? Six thousand? It might be even more, because now you would have to go farther away than ninety miles off the coast of Florida. Cuba was certainly a convenient location for American women who had to leave the United States to get an abortion.

In 1936 my mother got pregnant when she wasn't married. I don't know whether she tried to get an abortion and couldn't or whether that wasn't something she even considered. She was completely ostracized for being pregnant and unmarried. It was considered shameful and sinful. I suppose it was less sinful than having an abortion, but it was more obvious, because everyone could tell by looking that the woman was a sinner. At least abortion was not so obvious to outsiders. My mother ended up going to a home for unwed mothers. It was run by stern, judgmental nuns who reminded her of the Catholic orphanage she had grown up in. Both her parents had died in the influenza epidemic. Having a baby when you weren't married was pretty shocking, especially in 1936, but then she did something even more shocking. She refused to put the baby up for adoption. She kept the baby and just let people think whatever they wanted to think. Then she married my father and had other children. My mother may sound like a strong woman who somehow rose above it and was unscarred by her experience, but I don't think so. The "shame" was still very vivid to her when I asked her about it forty years after the event.

When I accidentally discovered, in a conversation with one of my mother's sisters, that the woman I had always thought was my sister was only my half-sister, I asked my mother to tell me about it. She put her hands over her face and began to cry. "How did you find out? Who have you told?" she wanted to know. It was a major problem for her that I had discovered her long-hidden secret shame. She was fearful that I would tell the other children, particularly the out-of-wedlock child. That out-of-wedlock child is now fifty-seven years old, and to my knowledge, she still doesn't know.

My mother also had an abortion, in 1952. Her doctor said, "You know, Lucille, you're going to die if you don't stop having babies." She had six at that point. He said, "I can't do anything for you if you get pregnant again, so don't let that happen." He was Catholic, and there is no way he could or would have helped her end a pregnancy. I think she also went to Havana for an abortion. I remember that she had been frequently nauseated. She took a little trip—I never really knew where—and when she came back a few days later, she wasn't nauseated anymore. Also, when she sent me to Cuba, only six years later, she seemed to be awfully knowledgeable about how to get an abortion in a foreign country—not what one would expect of an average housewife.

My younger sister Dorcas had a baby when she was an unmarried teenager. Unlike my mother, Dorcas gave her baby up for adoption. She was only fourteen or fifteen years old at the time. My parents sent her to some sort of home in California. The place was run by a minister and his wife. She stayed there until she had the baby and then gave it up. That haunts her to this day. She never had any other children. At family gatherings, where my sisters and their children would be present, Dorcas would become quiet and withdrawn as she watched the children. I could see that it pained her to watch her sisters with their children. Mother's Day was especially hard for her. She would usually stay home alone rather than come to any family gathering.

The hardest day for her was the birthday of her lost child. She seemed to be very depressed for at least a week before the birthday and for several days after. In a shopping center or any public place, I'd catch her watching any boy-child who was the same age as her son. It was painful to see. She was looking for him, I know she was. I wonder if she will ever find him. Maybe he's looking for her. I hope so.

You know, it never seemed to get any easier for Dorcas, even thirty or forty years later. Years after the events, she and I used to talk about her adoption experience and my abortion experience. It was clear that hers was the more difficult. I never would want to go through that.

There was an interesting footnote to my story in 1961. By that time, I was married to an alcoholic who was physically abusive, and I was pregnant with my first child. And then the great love of my youth, my navy hero of the Valentine's Day party, came back briefly into my life. It was so wonderfully romantic, but so absolutely impossible. Here I was, married and pregnant, but not so pregnant that it was obvious, and here was the great love of my life telling me that now we would get married. He would make up for all the things our parents did to us when we were kids, and like any impossible fairy tale, we would live happily ever after. It seems he had never known exactly what happened in 1958 because his mother protected him from all the facts of what I got to experience in such exquisite detail. I had to tell him that I was married to another man and had just discovered I was pregnant.

I still lived in New York, and later had a second experience concerning abortion. By this time, I had two small children— still both babies, born only fifteen months apart. I had no job skills to speak of and no job. In 1965, because of the continuing abuse, I took my babies and fled to Pennsylvania, where my sister and her husband lived. Being unemployed, I had absolutely no financial resources I could count on. My sister and her husband were really wonderful to me. I arrived on their doorstep with two babies, no money and no skills. Her husband said he could help me get a job at the university and we could all stay there until I saved some money and got on my feet. Unbeknownst to any of us, I was also pregnant.

I kept saying to my sister, "I'm sick. I always feel like I have to throw up." I had had three menstrual periods during this long interval of chronic nausea, and I'm sure that's why I didn't realize what was wrong with me. My sister was by now a very strong feminist, but she was also a good Catholic, with six children. When we realized I was pregnant, she said, "What do you want to do?" I said, "My God! How can you even ask? I want an abortion. I can't feed the two children I have." Of course, my abusive husband didn't send us any support. He hadn't spent money on us when we lived together. Why should he do it now? Well, my sister was good. Whatever personal feelings she might have had about abortion she put aside, and her husband and I went on a search for an abortion.

Abortion was still illegal in the United States in 1965, but things were changing, and it was somewhat easier to find a sympathetic doctor who was willing to help. We found a wonderful doctor. He examined me and said, "I can't help you, because it's too late. I can't do it in my office, and there's nowhere else you can go in Pittsburgh or anywhere in the United States." Of course, by that time, Cuba was no longer an option for American women.

He was very kind and I was very hysterical. He said, "We're trying to change the law so we can help women like you, but aren't there yet." I barely heard him. I cared nothing about that. What did I care about the women of the world? I only cared about me and the children I couldn't take care of already. I cried. I screamed. I was distraught. I remember grabbing his lapels and screaming, "What will I do? How will I survive?" He gently disengaged my hands and said, "You will put another potato in the stew." I screamed, "Is that all you have for me? An extra potato?" He didn't answer.

I got through it and had the baby, and of course we all loved him, but it was terribly hard. There were many times I thought I wouldn't make it and my kids wouldn't make it.

I'm a grandmother now, and I work as a counselor in an abortion clinic. Every morning, when I see that waiting room full of women, I remember the time when all we could have given them was an extra potato, and I'm glad to be at work.

BRUCE

I'VE DONE THREE ILLEGAL ABORTIONS IN MY LIFE. I'm not a doctor, but as an Army corpsman I worked in a hospital in the orthopedics department. I worked in the casting room, putting casts on people and cutting casts off. I knew absolutely nothing practical about gynecology, but at the hospital library I had access to books about anatomy and gynecology. Also, working in a hospital, I had access to some kinds of medical equipment, if I could figure out what equipment I would need to do an abortion.

My first real awareness of abortion was in 1948. I was eighteen at the time and was in the army. I was working a night shift at the hospital, and it was real quiet. Not much was going on. In the middle of the night they admitted this woman, an army nurse I knew. Her name was Shirley. I'd been working in the same department with her just the day before, and she had been fine. I asked what was wrong with her and got a vague response about "female troubles." What they did on her in the middle of the night was an abortion—a D and C. She wasn't kept in the hospital or anything, and I think no one other than me and the people actually involved in the D and C knew she had been there. It was a big secret, and I never heard it mentioned again. Shirley was back at work two days later, acting like nothing had happened. Maybe the fact that she came back so soon helped to convince me that an abortion wasn't really too complicated and that I could do one after just reading a book. I don't know. Maybe not, because when it got right down to it thirteen years later, I was terrified.

The first abortion I did was in 1961. I really don't remember much about it because I was drunk when I did it. I got drunk because I was scared. I thought it was odd that the woman didn't seem scared. If she had known how little I knew, she would undoubtedly have been as scared as I was. I did the abortion because I had gotten the woman pregnant and I felt responsible. Besides, I was involved with another woman at the same time, and that made me feel guilty. The woman had tried to find a doctor to do an abortion, but no one would. She had gotten some ergot from a pharmacist and had taken that, but it hadn't done anything. From the books I read, I decided that ergot was the best there was of pills and things you could take. If that wasn't going to work, no pills or medicine were going to work. Finally I decided that the only way she was going to have an abortion was if I did it myself.

I was totally terrified. I was afraid that the woman would hemorrhage or get an infection or something that would mean she had to go to the hospital, and a hospital was likely to ask tough questions. I figured I could be arrested and sent to jail if anyone found out, even if the woman was okay.

I took a catheter from the hospital where I worked. I didn't take anything else that I can remember—no antibiotics or anything like that. I just stuck the catheter in my pocket. I did the abortion at her apartment. She lived by herself, so I didn't have to worry about other people being around. I didn't know any more about how to do an abortion than what I had picked up in the books I'd read. They say you can't learn to swim by reading a book, but I'm proof that you can learn to do an abortion by reading a book.

I just had her lie down. I took the catheter—it was in a little cellophane package—and inserted it in her vagina, or actually into her cervix. When I pulled it out, this little bit of mucus came out with it. I didn't know exactly what I had done, but I figured something would happen. With a lot more confidence than I felt, I told the woman she would miscarry in a few hours. Then I left and went home and got *real* drunk. The next day I was even more scared. Every time the phone rang, I jumped. I was afraid it would be her or the hospital or the police. The days went by and nothing happened. I guess she was all right. After a while I got over being so scared and I quit worrying about it.

I ultimately did two more abortions. The second one was a year later, in 1962. I didn't do abortions for money, I did them for guilt. Like the first one, the second one involved a woman I was having a relationship with. Her name was Lois. She was only seventeen and I was thirty-two, so that added another complicating and scary dimension. She wanted to get married. I didn't want to get married to anyone, and certainly not to someone whose main interest was cheerleading! When she realized that marriage wasn't a possibility, she wanted an abortion, and I certainly wanted her to have an abortion. I halfheartedly looked for someone to do it, but because the person wouldn't have been a doctor and because I felt guilty since I didn't want to get married, I figured I was more competent than some unknown and I volunteered to do it.

I was still working in the same hospital, so I got the "equipment" in the same way. The first time I had been so scared and so sure that I would never do it again that I threw the catheter away right after the abortion. Again I just stuffed a catheter in my pocket, but this time I also grabbed a bunch of antibiotics and a curette just in case. I had learned after the first abortion that just dislodging the mucus plug—I had discovered that that was what it was called—frequently wasn't enough to cause an abortion, and that I had been lucky it had been effective.

I did this abortion at my apartment. I used the same technique I had used before, but this time I did some scraping with the curette to be sure, because I didn't see any mucus plug. Have you ever cooked a spaghetti squash and then scraped the spaghetti strands out of the cooked squash? You know how the squash feels when you start scraping? You know how it feels when you've scraped it all off? You know it's all off because it just feels different—kind of a harder, less spongy surface. Well, that's sort of what doing an abortion by scraping—or a D and C—feels like. That kind of scraping abortion was easy to do, but I think it's probably also easy to perforate the uterus, and that can cause real scary complications, like hemorrhage. When I look back on it, I can't believe I did three. I'm real lucky that nothing ever happened!

With the second abortion, everything went okay while I was doing it. I took her home and told her to stay in bed and that she would abort the next day. That night she called me. She was crying and hysterical. She was having bad cramps and heavy bleeding. She also had a temperature of a hundred and four, and that did scare me. Besides being hysterical, she was a real sick little girl. All I could think was, "Okay, you tried, but you screwed up and you're going to jail!" That was my only thought. I hadn't been as scared while I was doing that second abortion, but this aftermath just overwhelmed me with fear.

I went to her apartment. She was a student and had a roommate, but luckily for me, the roommate wasn't home. Lois was crying and yelling at me. She kept saying she was going to die if I didn't do something and that it was all my fault. I figured she was right on both counts, but I didn't really know what to do. Again, acting a lot more confident than I really felt, I gave her a big dose of antibiotics and instructions about how to take them over the next few days. I told her everything would be fine. I went home, but I was much too frightened to sleep. I think my fear was more for me than for her. I figured the antibiotics would probably work and she would be fine, but if she told anyone, I'd be put away for a long time. The antibiotics did their job and she was okay. I never saw her much after the abortion. She went off and married some guy, and I guess everything was fine.

The last abortion I did was in 1964. I was living in Idaho then, and I wasn't working at a hospital. I was a teller in a bank. Again I got involved with a woman and she got pregnant. That just kept happening to me, it seems. Anyway, it wasn't a big romance or anything, and I had actually quit seeing her. One day I got this telephone call. It was her. She said she was pregnant and it was my fault and I needed to help her fix it.

After my last experience, I knew I was never going to do another abortion, so I took her to a doctor I had heard about. It was awful. My information sure was wrong, because he treated us like scum, both of us—her for being pregnant and me for asking him to help. He was angry that we had even asked. He wouldn't do it, and he wouldn't even tell us where to go, except out of his office! Well, I reacted just like I had before. If I could have gotten her to a doctor, I would have. When that choice wasn't possible, I again figured that I was better than any non-doctor abortionist, and I did it myself.

It's interesting. In spite of how scared I was after number two, I had kept the equipment—just in case I ever had a need for it. I did this abortion like I had done the second one, with some scraping. Afterward I gave her antibiotics left over from the second one. She was all right, no infection or anything. Maybe it helps to give antibiotics before the infection even starts. I hadn't done that either time before.

This woman called me a couple of months later. She said she needed money. There was something about the way she said it that made me think she might be planning to blackmail me. Maybe she wasn't, but I got that impression. I told her I had just lost my job and didn't have any money. Then I quit my job and left town. I guess she made me realize how vulnerable I was making myself. I sure wasn't about to go to jail for someone I hardly knew and had no reason to trust!

When I left town, I threw the equipment away so that I would never be tempted again. I figured that since I didn't work in a hospital anymore, I could never replace it. It seemed to work, because I never did any more abortions. And a few years later the law changed, so I never got in that situation again.

AUDREY

I NEVER ACTUALLY DID ABORTIONS MYSELF. I arranged the appointments and brought the women to the person who did the abortions.

I'm from western Pennsylvania. I was born in 1933. My mother died when I was five years old, and I was raised by my grandparents, actually my stepgrandmother. It wasn't a very happy childhood. When I was nine, I was already running away from home because of the abuse—both physical and sexual—that I got from my grandmother. I would run away and get picked up and sent to some kind of juvenile detention center. Then, after a few weeks or months, I would get sent home, and I would just run away again. From the time I was nine until I was sixteen, I was almost never home. Most of that time was spent in institutions.

I have been married twice, and then I had a relationship that lasted over twenty years. Between 1951 and 1958 I had five children. I really didn't have any good birth control. Back then, women just had the rhythm method and creams and jellies and those kinds of things, but they really didn't work very well. I used them too, and they didn't work for me either.

After I became pregnant in 1959, I felt that I couldn't handle any more babies. My oldest child, who was eight, lived with my aunt, and the four youngest lived with me. I couldn't handle but four of the five I already had, so I was real sure that I couldn't handle six. As soon as I realized I was pregnant—and after five children you get pretty good at recognizing things like that—I got myself some potassium permanganate because I had heard that worked. I inserted it like I thought I was supposed to do. Well, it burned my insides and really hurt! It even made me bleed, but it didn't cause an abortion.

When I was sure that the potassium permanganate wasn't going to work, I went to my girlfriend Val and said, "You know, I didn't get my period." She said, "Oh, I can take care of that." "How are you going to do that?" I asked, and she said, "I know someone who can get it started. That is all you need." She took me to this woman. Her name was Flo. She lived in East Liberty. I lived in McKeesport, but that wasn't too far away. She did abortions wherever, mostly in her basement, sometimes in a car. She never did one on me in the car though. It was always in her basement.

Flo was a nurse's aide. She worked full-time at a hospital and did abortions in her spare time. When I knew her, she was in her mid-fifties. She had a house out on Frankstown Road. She didn't have a husband or children that I knew of. She just lived there with her brother. She's dead now. So is he, I guess.

I paid Flo fifty dollars for that first abortion. Val set up the appointment, but later I found out how to contact Flo myself.

Val and I went to Flo's house. Flo took us down into the basement. It wasn't dirty or anything—she was very clean—but it looked like a basement, boxes all around and an ironing board and things like that. There was a couch down there, and that's what she used. She also had a table, and sometimes she used that. She would put you on that table and spread your legs apart. Then she would just take her two fingers and go up in you and find the womb. She knew exactly what to do.

After she found the womb with her fingers, she used a long, reddish-colored rubber thing to do the abortion. It looked kind of like a skinny hose. On the end of the hose it was closed, and then it had holes that air could be forced through. The tool she used with it looked like a coat hanger. The coat hanger was threaded up inside the rubber tubing to make it rigid so that it could be pushed in without bending. The tube was about eight or ten inches long, and on the other end she had about four inches of string. The little bit of string hung out of the vagina, and that's how you could tell that the thing was in the right place, that it hadn't gone anywhere it wasn't supposed to be. Well, trust me, it *never* went anywhere else. This woman was real good!

That first time I went to Flo, I was scared to death. I was about twenty-four or twenty-five, but what did I know about something like this? Nothing. I didn't know then how good Flo was. All I knew was that I was going down into this basement to have something done to me by a woman I had never seen before. How would anybody feel? That is just real scary!

But Flo was fast! The whole thing took about one minute. She took the coat-hanger part out, but the rubber thing and the string stayed in. Then she gave me a pad because she said I would start to bleed almost immediately.

She also gave me instructions. The tubing was to stay in for twenty-four hours. At the end of that twenty-four-hour period, I was to pull it out—I could reach the string—and my period would start.

Flo didn't give antibiotics. What she did was make you take penicillin for two days before you came to see her. In those days it was easy to get penicillin from the drugstore without a prescription. When you called Flo to make the appointment, she would never let you come in that same day. She told you to go to the drugstore and get two days' worth of penicillin. Then she gave you an appointment for two days later.

I got the penicillin from my neighborhood druggist. It wasn't a problem at all. I didn't do anything special, and no arrangements were made in advance. I just walked in and asked for it, and he sold it to me. Simple as that. One other time I did have trouble getting the penicillin without a prescription, but that was no real problem either. I just told my family doctor I needed it, and he wrote me a prescription. Nothing to it. I never flat out told him why I wanted the prescription, but he knew.

My doctor would always tell me, "You've got too many kids, too many kids. You have to stop having babies. It isn't good for you." But he was very clear that he wouldn't do an abortion. I never asked him directly to do one, but I'd say things like, "What am I going to do? Do you know anyone who can help me?" He always said that he didn't know what I was going to do or who could help me. Instead he'd say, "I won't do it, but whatever you do, come and see me after you do it, because I want to be sure that you're all right." He was a nice person and a good doctor. He cared about what happened to me, and he tried to take care of me as best he could under the circumstances.

After that first abortion, Val took me home and stayed with me quite a bit of the time. I was bleeding when I left Flo's. She had said it would start right away, and it did. Flo had told me that when I took the tubing out, I would get a real heavy period and start to pass clots. She told me that was real important and I should call her if I didn't pass clots, because I would need to come back. So I watched for the clots, and it happened just like Flo said it would. The clots looked like veiny small pieces of liver.

I went to see my doctor about a week later, when the bleeding had stopped. He checked me over and said, "I don't know where she learned it, but this woman is real good. You don't have a mark in your body to indicate that you ever had an abortion." I was fine, and I could tell that he was impressed by what a good job Flo had done.

Flo had a wonderful bedside manner. She was a stout light-skinned black woman. She had a nice home. She was very clean, and her home was clean. She was a warm, nice, caring person, and I could tell she felt bad for us—the women who were pregnant and didn't want to be, and came to her for help. I think that's why she went into it.

Because I still didn't have any good birth control, I kept getting pregnant when I didn't want to. The man I was dating wouldn't have anything to do with rubbers or anything like that. As a result, it seemed like every time I turned around I was pregnant. I don't remember when it happened the next time, but it was pretty soon, maybe six months later. Over the next few years I had about four more abortions—all with Flo and all with no problems, all in her basement and all for fifty dollars each.

The last abortion was probably around 1965. This sounds crazy, I suppose, but around 1966 I decided that I wanted to have another child, so I started trying to get pregnant. That was a whole lot easier for me to do than trying not to get pregnant, and my son was born in 1967.

At some point after I had the five abortions, I started working with Flo. At the time I was separated from my second husband and I was dating a young white Italian guy, and it seemed like everyone he knew was pregnant. Tony was a bartender, and people would come into the bar and ask, "Do you know where I can get an abortion?" He'd call me, and I'd call Flo and set up the appointments. For them her fee was always a hundred dollars.

I started doing it because I felt bad for other women who were pregnant when they didn't want to be—just like I felt bad when it happened to me, and I guess just like Flo felt bad for all of us. These were women with impossible problems. Some were unmarried and involved with a guy who had run out on them, or maybe he was married to someone else. Some were married to abusive husbands. Some had five children, all under the age of five, and just couldn't handle another. Whatever it was, it was a tough problem.

Most of these women never knew my name, but I knew their names because I was the contact. Every once in a while today, I pick up the newspaper and read about one of them. Some of them are doing very well. One is doing extremely well. I saw her picture in the paper just last week. As I read the article about her latest accomplishment, I found myself wondering what her life would have been like if she hadn't been able to get the abortion she wanted. Would she have achieved all the things she has? I kind of doubt it.

The referral system with Tony wasn't planned or anything. It just happened because there were so many women who were pregnant and didn't want to be. After Tony and I started dating, he knew I had had abortions, so when the guy would come into the bar and ask if he knew anyone who could help, Tony called me. It was as simple as that. Nothing fancy. I didn't really charge for what I did. I just added twenty-five dollars or thirty dollars to Flo's fee as a sort of tip for myself.

Sometimes I would actually stay with the woman at her home during the twenty-four hours before it was time to take the catheter out. I didn't do this often, and I only did it with women who were really scared and who lived alone. There were only a few women I stayed with, maybe four or five at the most. They were people who were either friends of mine or friends of Tony's. In addition to being scared and alone, they were special people I thought I could trust. They already knew my real name. Most of the women didn't know my name, because I was always real careful to keep that a secret. I always used a false name. I mean, you just had to build in some protection for yourself, because this was all illegal. Flo had been arrested any number of times, and I sure didn't want that to happen to me.

No one was ever permitted to go to Flo's house except after dark. Like, even though I worked with Flo sometimes, I never went until after dark, whether it was done in her basement or in a car. Flo trusted me, but she wasn't taking any chances. When I'd call her and ask what time I was to come, she would always say nine, ten or even eleven-thirty at night. It was never before nine.

Flo had a really big following. I mean, she did this for women all over the whole county, not just in the city. I don't know how many white clients she had, but she had a lot of black women. I wasn't her only "referral source" either—not that she needed any referral sources! She had more business than she could handle. Sometimes when I would go there to pick her up for one of the "car abortions," other people—other drivers or maybe other clients—would just be leaving. I've been there sometimes when it was actually crowded.

The women I took to Flo were all white. They were white because Tony was white, and it is white people who ask a white bartender if he knows someone who can help them. I never took black women to Flo. They didn't need help. They could find Flo, or other people who did what Flo did, by themselves. It was only white women who needed help like that. Another reason I took only white women is that they were not from my community and I was not likely to accidentally run into them ever again. Flo was leery about letting white women know where she lived, though. She would meet us on a corner somewhere, or behind her house, but never where she thought they could pick up her address.

Tony did a lot of weeding out of the requests he got. He didn't even call me unless it was a friend of his or a regular customer that he trusted. Another built-in safety factor was to only do it for someone who was running around cheating on his wife and got his girlfriend pregnant. That guy isn't going to ever tell, because he has too much to lose. If Tony called me about someone, I felt pretty safe to begin with, but still, I was always very careful.

Val brought women to Flo too. Val ran a sort of—I don't know what you would call it, but guys came to her house on weekends and played cards and drank. Val never had anything to do with the gambling. She never cut the cards or anything, but she sold them drinks. She was raided lots of times for selling drinks. Val was on welfare, but she did this on the side to make money so she could get things for her kids. All the guys would come after they got off work. If their shift at the plant ended after all the bars had closed, Val's house was a place they knew they could go and drink and gamble. They were all white guys. Val never had black guys in there. That was because it was probably true that most of the guys were cheating on their wives. If Val had had black guys in there who were cheating on their wives, she would have had trouble with the black women in the neighborhood, and she sure didn't want that. It was the white guys who would ask Val if she knew anyone who could do an abortion, and if she trusted the guy, she might help his friend get to Flo. She never did it as much as I did, though, because she didn't have someone like Tony as the contact person, so she could never be as anonymous as I could be.

I know of only one woman that Flo had any involvement with who died, and that wasn't Flo's fault. The woman had gone somewhere else before she went to Flo, but it hadn't been successful. Evidently the first one had been so badly done that gangrene had already begun to set in. The woman died, but Flo was not even arrested. I can't remember if the person who did the first abortion was arrested, and I can't remember if there even was a newspaper story or whether the family managed to hush it up. But everyone on the street knew what happened to her.

Let me tell you how the car abortions worked, because that's what I did with Flo. Everyone talks about back-alley abortions. Well, you could call these "back-seat abortions." They were always done at night so that they would be safer. I have no idea how Flo did them without any light. I guess she didn't need light. She was so good that she could do it blindfolded.

The way it worked was that the woman—let's call her Jane Doe—would call Tony. He would get basic information like the date of her last period. Then he would call me, and I would call Flo. Flo would ask me questions about how far along the woman was and if she was a "snowball." She always called them that. It was her name for white girls. She wasn't mean or anything—that was just the word she always used. Then she would give me a time, like three or four days from now, maybe at ten at night. She always reminded me to tell these women to get the penicillin. How could I possibly forget when I knew how strongly Flo felt about that?

So I called Tony and told him the appointment time, and about the penicillin and all of that. I would tell him to have the woman meet me on a certain street corner at a certain time and that he was to tell her my name was Carol. So Tony would call Jane Doe back with all those instructions. He also told her how much it would cost and that she was to have the money in cash. If the woman was too far along for Flo to be willing to do an abortion, Tony just told her that he couldn't find anyone to help her.

On the day of the woman's appointment, I'd be standing on the corner, and she would drive up in her car, roll down the window, and say, "Are you Carol?" I'd say, "Yes. Are you Jane Doe?" When she said yes, I would get into the car and direct her to the spot where Flo wanted to be picked up. It was usually a corner in the downtown area so that Flo wouldn't be identified with any particular neighborhood.

Flo would get into the back seat, and I would direct the woman to drive to wherever Flo wanted to go—where she thought it would be safe for her to do an abortion. She would usually want to go in some back alley or dark street somewhere—certainly never anywhere near her house, particularly with a snowball. I'd take the money from the woman. Then she'd get into the back seat with Flo, and while Flo did the abortion, I counted the money and took out my twenty-five dollars.

When Flo was done, the woman got back in the front seat. I passed Flo's share of the money back to her, while we drove to where she wanted to be let out. Flo got out and sort of disappeared into the night, and we drove on to where I wanted to be let out. I never had the woman let me out at my house, because I never wanted her to know where I lived. But it would be somewhere close by or where it was easy for me to get home by bus. Before I got out of the car, I gave the woman instructions— what to do if this happened and what to do if that happened. Then I got out and the woman went on her way, and that was all there was to it.

Flo got arrested several times. I don't know what happened that would lead to an arrest. Maybe a woman got sick and when she went to the hospital they got her to tell who had done it. Now, if it was one of the car abortions, the woman wouldn't have known who did it, so she couldn't have told even if she wanted to. Flo never got arrested when I had been involved. I know that the police raided her home a couple of times, but there were never any newspaper stories or anything. I'm sure she never went to trial. Either the charges were dismissed for lack of evidence or someone got paid off. I don't know.

I do know that there would be times when Flo would just lie low. Like sometimes I'd call and she'd say, "I can't do *anything* right now. I'll call you when I can." It might be several weeks, and the pregnant women would just have to wait, getting further along in their pregnancies, so that it was more dangerous to have an abortion. I'm sure that some of them did something else, because pregnant women don't like to wait. Once they know they're pregnant, they want to get that abortion as fast as they can. I know I always did.

I probably did about twenty-five of these car abortions, and I never got into any trouble. I was very careful to make sure that no one ever knew anything about me—not my name, not my address, nothing. I couldn't afford to have any trouble. I was a single parent, and my kids needed me.

I quit before legal abortions came in. I decided it was getting too dangerous. The money I was making just wasn't worth the risk. Besides, my conscience was starting to bother me. I cry about it often now and I feel guilty. I love kids, and I think, as crazy as I am about kids, how could I have done what I did? I don't feel guilty about the women I took to Flo. That's up to them and their consciences. I just feel guilty about what I did to myself. I had six children and five abortions. I guess I could have had eleven children. People do. I just love kids, and I wish I had more. There could have been five more kids of mine out there today, and that makes me feel real bad. I converted to Catholicism in 1971, and that's when I started feeling so guilty. Before, I guess I just didn't know what I was doing.

But you know, if I had it to do over, given the same circumstances, I would probably do exactly the same thing, because you do what you feel you have to do. Now I have a job and some money. Then I didn't, and that makes you feel more desperate. I did what was right for the time, but now I wish I hadn't done it—even knowing I would do it again if I had it to do over. I suppose that doesn't make any sense, but that's how I feel.

And in spite of how conflicted I feel about it now, I still do believe that Flo was so good and we were all really very lucky to have someone like that. You know, it sounds sort of horrible to say it was good, but it was good because abortions were illegal and women who didn't have someone like Flo were dying. It was good that we were lucky enough to find someone who was clean, who knew what she was doing, and who was nice to the people. Lots of women weren't that lucky, I guess.

DR. BERT

I WAS BORN IN 1924. Now I'm sixty-seven and retired. I graduated from medical school in 1948 from the University of Pennsylvania in Philadelphia. I grew up in a small town in western Pennsylvania. I was brought up in a very strict Scotch Presbyterian environment. My father was very active in the church. My mother sang in the choir. Her parents were strict Calvinist types, and in her family, abortion was one of the many things that was a sin—along with card playing and dancing and all kinds of things.

On the other hand, my father was a physician, a small-town general practitioner. He took care of a lot of people in the outlying farming communities and saw his share of botched abortions. I know he was very hostile to the abortionists, but he saw the women—his patients—only as victims. In those days, in my father's view, an abortionist had the same social status as a child molester or a rapist.

I didn't have any sisters, and when I went off to college at the University of Pennsylvania during World War II, I had never really had any contact with abortion. No people in my world had this experience. While no one in my world had had an unwanted pregnancy that I knew about, I was aware of girls in town who "got into trouble," as we called it in those days. They discreetly dropped out of school and left town for about six months or so. Then they came back, and no one said a word about where they had been and what had happened. In spite of having no real experience with abortion, I had strong opinions about the scum of the earth—abortionists.

We went through our pre-med courses in only two years in an accelerated program because the war effort needed more doctors. I had just turned twenty when I started medical school. I didn't learn how to do a D and C. We did pelvic exams, but never anything as sophisticated as a D and C. I did watch D and C procedures, both in medical school and in my father's practice. He was eager for me to become a doctor, so he kind of introduced me to the mysteries of medicine early on. He had me reading his medical books when I was in high school and college. In medical school I got a very strong message that abortion was immoral as well as illegal. Good doctors simply didn't do things like that.

In medical school we rotated through eight or ten Philadelphia hospitals, but the main one was the hospital of the University of Pennsylvania—HUP, we called it. It was in West Philadelphia, and it had a lower-middle-class and lower-class clientele. However, the hospital also had a "gold coast," and anyone who was anybody went there for surgery or whatever. The physicians were among the best in the country, and one of the men high up in FDR's administration went there by choice when he had a serious medical problem. But the plain people were just on the wards and not on the gold coast. I now realize that there were probably septic abortion patients there—probably lots of them, given the patient population and the unavailability of antibiotics. I just don't remember them. Probably it was listed as something else on their charts, or maybe it just didn't make an impression on me.

The first time I have a vivid memory of an abortion patient is during my 1948–49 internship at a Catholic hospital in Pittsburgh. The hospital functioned like any big-city municipal hospital. That was where the police brought all the stabbing, shooting, traffic accident victims and all the other medical emergencies common to a big city. I was thrown into the hospital emergency room, and I'll tell you, that was a real quick eye-opener! We had twelve-hour shifts every day for a full month. It was wild! It was the equivalent of New York City's Bellevue Hospital or something like that. The interns were thrown into this thing without any training or any supervision, and we just sort of handled it all as best we could, hoping for the best. Nothing I had ever been taught by my father or in medical school adequately prepared me for that experience, and my colleagues weren't any better prepared than I was.

We saw lots of patients with pelvic sepsis. You get pelvic sepsis from a venereal disease like gonorrhea, but you can also get it from a dirty abortion. The woman I remember most vividly was not a patient I saw in the emergency room. She was brought in when I was on the gynecology service. Now, this was a strict Catholic hospital that had very strict ideas about abortion. We weren't even permitted to do a pelvic exam unless the woman was under anesthesia—I guess on the theory that if she was unconscious, she wouldn't know what was happening to her. It wasn't so much that we were men but that female sex organs were somehow "off limits." The whole thing was bizarre, and there was a real gap in my training.

This patient was in a private room. I even remember the room number—724. That was one of the gold coast rooms. The woman, in her early or mid-thirties, was married to someone really important, with a lot of connections. She came in with severe pelvic sepsis and she died. I remember her so vividly because she was one of the most beautiful women I had ever seen. She was also one of the sickest. She was ashen. When I first saw her, she was still conscious and lucid. I think she suspected she might die. She had kidney failure. Then all her other systems failed as well. She got ecchymosis—these red blotches all over her skin. Her blood vessels were just breaking underneath her skin, sort of like what happens when you bruise yourself, but this was happening all over her body without anyone even touching her. It was due to a disturbance of her coagulating mechanism as a result of the overwhelming sepsis. She died two or three days after she was admitted.

I remember thinking, "My God! How could anyone do that to this beautiful young woman?" But I completely misunderstood what I was looking at. In those days the tendency was to treat the woman as the helpless victim of this monster called the abortionist. I completely missed the fact that she had obviously sought it out, and with her connections, it would have been one of the better ones that money could buy. I was so shocked by what happened to her and the way she died that I actually was physically ill.

My political ideas in those days were pretty primitive. Like most medical students, I was just trying to survive it all. However, primitive though I was, she did touch something at some level in me. I was angry that she had died, and I was angry at a system that let her die. As I said, in those days I thought the solution was to jail the abortionist. It took me another twenty years to fully understand that it was the system and not the abortionist who killed her. The system forced her away from the medical community and into the shadowy world of the illegal abortionist. By the time she got to a doctor, it was too late. The system, and especially the lawmakers who left her with no choice, killed her just as surely as if they had held the catheter or coat hanger or whatever. I'm still angry. It was all so unnecessary.

GLORIA

I<small>N</small> 1950 <small>MY MOTHER DIED</small> from an illegal abortion. She was twenty-seven years old. I was almost six, and my brother, Eddie, was four. Her name was Vivian, and I always thought it stood for "vivid," because that's what she seemed like to me. She was very outgoing and friendly. She could strike up a conversation with anyone, and everybody seemed to like her.

She was only eighteen when she got married. She had graduated from high school and was working for the Internal Revenue Service. I think she was just a clerk, but it was a good job for a young black woman with no particular skills. She came from a very religious family of staunch Baptists. Everyone in her family was real active in the church. My mother continued that tradition after she got married. She started two black women's groups that are still going strong more than forty years after her death: the Tina Taylor Guild, which does missionary work, and the Phillis Wheatley Society. The Society members were high-society black women who wore white gloves and had teas and raised money to send poor black kids to college.

I thought my mother was terrific—alive and active—and her friends were as vibrant as she was. Today her "girlfriends" are strong and important women in my community. They are now in their sixties or seventies, and they are still a little "in crowd." They are as full of life as old ladies as she was at twenty-seven, when she died.

We lived in Duquesne, a little mill town on the Monongahela River in western Pennsylvania. My father worked in the steel mills until he died. I guess it was a good thing that the steel mills and my father died at the same time, because he wasn't equipped to do anything else.

My father was at least twenty years older than my mother, and I think he was probably jealous of her. He was very quiet and serious. Years later, he told me that when he and my mother were going together, his friends told him she would give him "trouble" because she was much too independent. In the forties, women were expected to be passive and obedient. My mother just did what she wanted to do at a time when most married women would either ask permission, or more likely, never even consider doing something just because they wanted to. But she was pretty and "vivid" and only eighteen, and my father was in love. Maybe he thought he could change her.

My mother's family was interesting, and I guess that explains why she was so independent. She came from a family of six children. She was the oldest, and the only girl. Her mother, Rebecca, was another unusual woman, especially for her time. When I knew her, she was jolly and fat and grandmotherly, but when she was younger, she was also very gregarious and outgoing. One day she just up and left my grandfather and all those six children. My mother was about eleven then. Now, in those days women didn't just up and leave, no matter what. Well, she did. When I was grown, I asked her why she left. She said my grandfather hit her once and she was going to be sure there would never be a second time. But she knew there was no way she could support all those children, so she figured they were better off with him. He was a good father and never did anything to the kids. Even after she left, my grandmother saw her kids often and they remained very close.

My father was active in his union and in the Democratic Party, and he used to travel a lot in connection with those activities. My mother and the women in her church group started taking trips together. They weren't long trips, just a weekend here and there, but my father didn't like it. They argued about it, but she wasn't about to stop. I think her little social trips with the ladies were her way of saying, "If you can do it, so can I!"

Finally, my parents separated. My father moved out, and my mother, brother, and I stayed in the house. I think she had a hard time, working full-time and trying to raise two small children. I don't know what happened, but I think that after my father moved out, my mother had an affair. I don't know who or what or anything about it, but she must have had an affair, because she got pregnant. This was in May of 1950. I was five, but I was going to be six in June.

I don't know anything about the abortion or who did it, because her family and friends would never talk about it. Several days after the abortion, my mother got a severe infection. When she began to realize that something was wrong, she took my brother and me to my grandfather—her father—and my stepgrandmother. Then she sent a message to my father. I don't know what happened, but he didn't get the message until about twelve hours later. When he did—and I have no idea what it said—he came and got her and took her to the hospital.

We tried to see her in the hospital, but they wouldn't let us in because we were too young. Then one day, after she had been there for about a week, the hospital called and told us to come. By that time she was very sick. My grandfather and his wife took us to the hospital. This time, even though we were little, they let us in, and I remember seeing her there.

She told my brother and me that she was going to die and that we had to be good children and be strong. I didn't feel strong. I started to cry. My little brother didn't know what was happening, but when I started to cry, he cried. My mother was crying too. I remember standing there, holding my brother's hand, not really understanding what was happening, but being terribly frightened. My mother was a very religious woman, and maybe that gave her serenity in the face of this incredible thing. She didn't seem frightened. She was calm—just sad.

Then the nurse came and told us we had to leave. They let us stand out in the hall, and within an hour, she died.

I never even knew what she died of, because that was hidden from us as well. When I was eighteen, I needed her death certificate to cash in some bonds she had left me, so I could get some money to go to college. I had always been told that she died of peritonitis. I didn't exactly know what that was, but I can still remember the shock I felt reading her death certificate and seeing that she died of "spontaneous abortion." Although I wasn't sure what "spontaneous" meant, a whole lot of things I had never really understood suddenly made a lot of sense.

My mother's brothers and my father said they tried to find out who did the abortion but they never could. At one point I thought I could find out, but I could never get anyone to talk to me about it. My parents were friends with a couple, and the man was in the underworld, sort of. He was a numbers writer, which was illegal. His wife was my mother's close friend, and he was my godfather. I remember, when I was in my twenties, asking the man if he knew. He said he knew but he couldn't tell me, and he sent me to ask his mother. She was an old lady in her eighties, and she just wouldn't even talk to me about it. After his mother died, my godfather said he would tell me sometime when the time was right. I don't know what he thought was the right time, but it never happened, and he died last year without ever telling me.

To this day, my grandmother Rebecca refuses to admit what her daughter died of. She must know. She too refuses to talk to me about it, even after all these years.

I remember my mother's funeral like it was yesterday. The church was packed. My mother's aunt was the organist. In addition to the family, all the Phillis Wheatley and Tina Taylor ladies were there, as well as people from my mother's job and people from the community. There were one hundred cars in the funeral procession to the cemetery. I remember that during the service they had an open casket. My father walked up to the front of the church with my brother and me and lifted each of us up for a final look.

My father tells me that for a year afterward, I wouldn't eat or talk. He says that every time he came to visit, which was about every two weeks, I would want him to take me to the cemetery. At the funeral, and after, they kept using euphemisms like "She is just asleep," and when my father lifted me up, there at the church, she looked like she was asleep. In my young mind, I thought she really was asleep, and I was patiently waiting for her to wake up. I kept wanting to go to the cemetery to see if she was awake yet. I just sort of stopped functioning while I was waiting. When my father realized what I was thinking, he gently but firmly made me understand that she wasn't going to wake up and we couldn't just bring her home. After that I began to come out of it. I started eating and talking, and stopped being obsessed with visits to the cemetery.

My brother and I were raised by my grandfather—my mother's father—and my stepgrandmother. Our strict religious background included no discussion about abortion, so I don't remember being raised to think abortion was a sin or anything. When I was growing up, in spite of what happened in my family or maybe because of it, I don't even remember hearing the word. However, there were very strict teachings that sex was wrong if you weren't married.

Our church was sort of a country church, and I know that these church people used to send their daughters to relatives down south if they got pregnant. That's why no one actually saw unmarried pregnant women. No unmarried women ever had babies, at least not that anyone knew about. If you were a single woman and were having an affair—not pregnant or anything, just an affair—they would call you both up before the whole congregation on a Sunday morning and ask you to ask the church for forgiveness. My mother had been raised in this kind of environment and was active in the church, so I suspect that there was no way she was willing to have a baby without being married. Besides, she could barely support us.

I became very attached to my stepgrandmother. Her name was Mildred, and she really raised me. She hadn't raised my mother, since she and my grandfather didn't get married until after my mother left home. She had married late in life and never had any children of her own, so my brother and I were her first experience. Mildred was very different from my grandmother and my mother. She was not an independent woman. She was a homebody who never went anywhere except to church. She took good care of us, but I felt a sort of psychological pressure from her. When I was about eight, she said, "If you are going to stay here, I think you should call me Mommy." Well, I wouldn't do that. It had nothing to do with her. It had to do with my mother. I called her Grandma, which also seemed right to me since she was married to my grandfather.

When I was nine, my father remarried. His new wife was very young, even younger than my mother. Her name was Ethel. My father's plan was for Eddie and me to come and live with Ethel and him. He brought her to my grandmother's house to meet us. Well, right away I didn't like her, and I made it real obvious that I was not going—at least not willingly! I felt that she was an intruder in our lives, and I didn't want things to change. My brother liked her okay, but I didn't. My father filed for custody and we went to court. The judge asked me where I wanted to go, and I said, "With my grandparents." When the judge asked Eddie, he said he wanted to go wherever I went. The judge ruled that we would stay with my grandparents.

When I look back on that, it is kind of a surprise. There was certainly nothing wrong with our father. He was good to us, he kept in contact with us, and he wanted to have us with him. I'm a police officer now, and I see lots of kids the same age as my brother and me that no one wants. Eddie and I were luckier than many, I guess. I had a pretty good life. We never thought we were poor, although maybe we were. Even though we had lost our mother, we had a lot of other family members who loved us.

Ethel and I did become close years later. When I was twenty-eight, I was married and had two small children. We were living in Massachusetts. I had to have an emergency hysterectomy because of a problem with an IUD and a ruptured uterus. My husband was in the army overseas. Things were fairly desperate, and I called my family for help. In spite of the way I had treated Ethel, she came. She stayed for six months and took care of my kids and me. We are very close today.

After my brother graduated from high school, he went into the Marine Corps. He is still in the marines. We were inseparable when we were children. Now we're close when we're together, but he refuses to come back to his childhood home. He says he'll come, but he never does. I think it's too painful for him. He probably felt more lost after our mother's death than I did, because he kind of just followed me around doing whatever I did. When I try to ask him about her or how he felt about what happened to her, he changes the subject. He won't look me in the eye, and he won't talk. He just acts like he doesn't hear me. He was so little when she died, I can't believe he remembers anything about it. But something is wrong.

As a child, and even now, I would never lie on my back, because it reminds me of my mother in the casket. I so desperately wanted her to be "just asleep," but she wasn't. Maybe I'm afraid that lying like that means you aren't just asleep. Because I didn't know why she died, I grew up thinking that people just died suddenly for no reason. Once I found out what happened to her, I was terribly sad and angry, because it was such a tragic waste, but on another level I was reassured to know that healthy young people didn't just die for no reason.

Even though I was pretty young when my mother died, I have some special memories of her. I remember a birthday party. I was three. All the neighborhood children came. We had Kool-Aid and cake, which I loved. I remember going shopping with her. We would take the train into town. I thought the train ride was the best part! She had matching pink crystal lamps in her bedroom. They had teardrop prisms hanging down, and I loved the tinkling noise they made when I tapped them with my finger and set them swinging. Every time I see anything with prisms, it brings back very strong memories of her, even after all these years. In my mind, or maybe it's really in my heart, I think she never died.

JANET

T ODAY ONE OF MY SONS ASKED ME what I was doing this
afternoon. When I said I was being interviewed about
abortion, he couldn't imagine why and was stunned
when I told him that I had had an illegal abortion. Maybe
because it's difficult to contemplate a parent—especially the
grandmother of his children—ever having had a sex-related
problem. Or maybe because I carried on and covered up all my
life as I did during two nightmarish weeks in 1957.

I was twenty-eight at the time, married, and the mother of
two small children. One was five, and one was not yet two.
Although I had always worked outside the home during most
of the marriage, I was not employed at the time.

It was a very bad marriage, horrible from the beginning,
and it seemed to get even worse after my first child was born.
My husband was physically and emotionally abusive. To the
extent that he was capable of it—and he had some real limitations in this area—he was verbally abusive as well. A real brute
of a man. I don't know what made me stay in the relationship
as long as I did, since I really knew from the beginning that it
couldn't last and that it was never going to get any better.

I knew immediately when I was pregnant. I am one of these
women who immediately become nauseated. I didn't have to
miss a period to know what was happening. I knew that I was

pregnant and that I had to have an abortion. I could not possibly have continued the pregnancy. I was barely surviving with two little kids, no job, and an abusive husband. With a third child I would never have gotten away or survived.

I started asking around immediately, looking for a way to end the pregnancy. I asked doctors. I asked my women friends. I asked everyone. I don't know how much actual experience my women friends had had with abortion at that point, but no one would admit to really knowing anything about it, even though we were close friends and shared many confidences with each other. The same group of women remained friends for years, and only later, when we were all safely in our fifties, did I learn that almost all of us had actually had illegal abortions. But in those days we didn't admit to anything like that, so none of them told me anything useful. Maybe I was the first in our group to face the problem. Maybe they were being truthful when they said they didn't know. I never knew.

I didn't ask any family members for help. To my knowledge, no one in my family had ever had an abortion. In my family there were five girls—cousins and sisters—who were very close. I found out years later that the oldest one, my cousin, who has been happily married to the same man for more than fifty years, had two abortions, as a teenager and then as a young woman. It was sure a well-kept secret. I never heard a word about it when it was happening. Maybe her parents didn't know either, but I think they did know, at least about the first one. I think my mother might even have helped her parents get that abortion.

Abortion was never discussed in my family, so my parents never imparted any "abortion values," good or bad. The one value that was imparted, over and over, was the importance of being chaste. It was absolutely unthinkable for a young unmarried female to be sexually active. Abortion was never discussed and birth control was never discussed because a chaste female had absolutely no need to know anything about either of those things, right? The reason I married the abusive man was because I went to bed with him. Who else would have me? I really must have believed that. Guilt can be a very unhealthy emotion.

Although people never seemed to have any firsthand experience, they always seemed to "know someone" who knew someone or something that might help. One of my friends told me about a doctor right there in the neighborhood who might be able to help me. He had an office above a drugstore, right in the next block. He was in his mid-thirties. I am sure he was a real doctor. I think he was a general practitioner. Though I had never been to him before, I was pretty up-front about my problem. "Doctor, I'm pregnant. Can you help me?" I didn't quite dare to use the word "abortion," and I sort of whispered my request to him, in case saying the word out loud would make him more likely to call the police. Even though I didn't come right out and say I wanted an abortion, he knew exactly what I meant. The first thing he did was to give me a prescription for something called ergot. They were big, black, nasty pills. The prescription was to be filled by the drugstore right downstairs, which was a pretty handy arrangement for everyone. Maybe he and the druggist had some sort of partnership, or at least a reciprocal referral arrangement.

Then he did something that I thought was very strange and that I have always been convinced was for his benefit, not mine. He had me take off my clothes from the waist down and lie on this table in his office. There was no nurse or anyone else present. He began to do this weird "manipulation," as he called it. He put his hand in my vagina and kept touching my clitoris. Because I had absolutely no romantic interest in him and was totally absorbed with my problem, it had no effect on me. I just lay there waiting for it to be over. Does it surprise you to learn that the "manipulation" did absolutely nothing to dislodge the fetus? Well, it didn't. When it was over, he told me to get dressed and go down to the drugstore to get the prescription filled. That was it. That was all the help I got from him: a piece of paper and a "manipulation" for which I paid money.

I took the big black pills, but they didn't do anything either. The doctor, or maybe the druggist, told me that if the pills were going to work, something would happen in a few days. Well, they made me nauseated—or maybe I was nauseated from the pregnancy—but they didn't do anything else. When it became clear that the pills weren't going to work, I called the doctor back, but he really didn't want to see me or even talk to me. He made it real clear that there was nothing else he was willing to do.

I tried home remedies: jumping up and down, running up and down stairs, the hottest possible tub baths, the coldest possible showers, things that made me throw up, and things that gave me diarrhea. I continued to ask everyone I knew for ideas or help. Anything that was ever rumored to have caused an abortion I tried. Nothing worked. The days and weeks went by, and I was getting increasingly panicky as my pregnancy continued. It seemed to go on forever.

Finally someone told me about a nurse in Turtle Creek. All I knew was a phone number and a first name: Barbara. I called her and said I needed to come and see her because I had this "problem." She knew exactly what I meant and set up an appointment for me. I was to bring two hundred dollars in cash and plan to stay overnight. That was a lot of money in those days, and I can't remember how I got it. It must have been as difficult as finding an abortionist, but it must have paled in comparison to the totality of my problems. I can't remember who took me to Barbara's, but I know a friend drove me.

Barbara lived in a lower-middle-class neighborhood. It wasn't a slum or anything. It was a residential neighborhood with duplexes and little row houses close together. I was so frightened that I really didn't pay a lot of attention to my surroundings. I had absolutely no knowledge of this woman's medical competence, but I sure wasn't going to ask. I didn't care. That isn't exactly true. I cared a lot. I had two small children at home. I didn't want to die and leave them alone with a brutal father. But I didn't have a choice. Barbara was all there was. She was the first one who seemed to be both willing and able to help me. That was a winning combination, in my view.

Barbara was a woman in her mid-thirties. She seemed kind

of uncared-for. No makeup. Her hair wasn't cut or styled or anything. It was just there. The abortion was actually done in Barbara's kitchen. I don't know if it was on her kitchen table, but it was a table in her kitchen. She had me remove my underpants and lie down on the table. Then she inserted something in me. I didn't see it, but it felt like some sort of rubber tubing. In about ten or fifteen minutes I began to feel cramps, and she took the tubing, or whatever it was, out. She told me to lie there for a few minutes, and then she moved me to a little room that had a cot in it. That was where I was going to spend the night. She checked on me a few times during the night, took my temperature and asked me how I felt, but she didn't do any more talking than was necessary. No one else seemed to be in the house.

I was having intermittent cramping, but I wasn't bleeding. In fact, nothing at all seemed to be happening. Now I was really scared, because in the morning, even though I hadn't aborted, she told me to go home, saying there was nothing more she could do for me. That was just like the "manipulator" and all the other things I had been trying so unsuccessfully for the last eight or ten weeks: no good. She told me something might happen in a few days. What did that mean? That it might not? That it might never happen? Was I still pregnant? This seemed even more nightmarish than before. When I pressed her—I was probably close to hysterics, and she knew it—she told me not to worry about it. She said that sometimes it took a while but I absolutely would miscarry. She was certain of it.

With that assurance I went home, but I was a wreck. You know, I can't remember what I told my husband about where I had been all night. He had no idea I was pregnant, because if he had known, he would never have let me get an abortion. He didn't want a divorce, and this would have given him enough control to keep me where he wanted me forever. Well, he never knew. I went about my daily chores, taking care of the kids, cooking meals, and trying to act normal. But I was really frightened. I had no cramps, no bleeding, no nothing! In spite of Barbara's assurances, I kept thinking, "What if I'm still pregnant? What will I do?" I tell you, those were the longest days of my life, and it was very hard to act normal, but I did it. I don't know how, but I did. No one ever suspected.

Finally, a full two weeks after my trip to Barbara, I miscarried. I went to the bathroom one day and just passed it in the toilet. There was no bleeding or cramping. I fished it out of the toilet and looked at it. It was a glob of tissue. I felt bad. Don't misunderstand me. I don't regret it. I didn't regret it then, and I never have. I just felt bad about the circumstances.

My husband didn't know, and he doesn't know to this day. No one knew.

You know, I was never so vulnerable again. I got out of that abusive marriage. I raised my kids to be wonderful, loving husbands and fathers. I went to college. I got a degree. I went to law school. The abortion gave me a chance. I shudder to think what would have happened to me and my boys if I hadn't gotten that abortion.

I had a second abortion, in 1961. I fell in love with a married man. The best men are always married—except, I guess, the one who was married to me. Preston was a lawyer and a really terrific guy. At the time, I was divorced. I was working full-time as a secretary and was raising my boys, essentially by myself. I hadn't gone back to school, but he was encouraging me to go back and get my undergraduate degree. He was offering to loan me money or even pay for it. He kept telling me I had the ability to do it. That was incredible. I wasn't used to such support, financial or emotional. He was really great, and I was madly in love. I was thirty-two.

By now I really was used to making it on my own. The boys' father paid a hundred dollars per month until they were eleven and thirteen. Then he never paid another dime. He never bothered to send birthday cards, graduation presents, or anything. He never even bothered to see them. My family wasn't any help either. My father died young, before I was married. My mother was a widow for five years. Then she remarried and moved to Florida, so she wasn't even around. But she wasn't a supportive person anyway.

Preston had more connections than I did, certainly, and he was able to find a real doctor who would do the abortion. I know he was a real doctor. He was listed in the telephone directory under "Physicians." He had an office in a medical building. When I called the doctor for an appointment, he told me to bring five hundred dollars. This time money was really no problem. Preston was going to pay the costs. But for some crazy reason I will never understand, I thought five hundred dollars was highway robbery, and I told the doctor so. As you can imagine, we did not have a very cordial conversation from that point on. I hung up and told Preston that I would not go to such a person, that I would simply go back where I had gone before.

So I made the arrangements with "Babs the Butcher," as I came to call her. I had saved her telephone number in case I ever needed it. In fact, I had actually given her name to other women who went to see her, and it had worked out fine for them, just as it ultimately had for me. It worked out even better for them because they hadn't had two nerve-racking weeks to wait, as I had.

Anyway, I called Barbara. When I went back, she went through the same procedure. I don't remember anything being different. Same house. Same kitchen. Same Barbara. But later something was horribly different. Within hours of leaving her house—again I stayed overnight—I became really sick. I had a high fever, my belly began to distend, and I had horrible gas. There was a red line on the skin of my belly, and it seemed to lengthen as I watched it. The pain was severe.

My friends were immediately alarmed, not only because I was so sick, but also because it was getting worse so rapidly. One of them called my regular gynecologist, Dr. Hughes. He was a wonderful man. He had delivered my two children. I had asked him to help me when I first found out about this pregnancy. He was appalled by my request. He was Catholic and was horrified that I would even consider having an abortion. I should never have asked him, and I don't know why I did. I guess it was because I felt mixed signals. On the one hand, I knew he was Catholic and would probably have strong negative feelings about what I was asking. On the other hand, he was a doctor, and a good one, a compassionate one. He wanted, almost instinctively, I think, to help me.

Preston was even more frantic than my friends. He had found a real doctor whom I had turned down. He had impregnated me. He had paid for Barbara. He even drove me there. I could tell that he felt terribly guilty about what was happening to me.

When I called my gynecologist, I told him what I had done and what my symptoms were. He was obviously alarmed and told me to come *immediately* to the hospital emergency room. A friend drove me out, and Dr. Hughes was there when we arrived.

Think about my children. They were only seven and nine. Their father lived in the same city, no more than a mile from my apartment. I wasn't dumb. I had figured out that this was serious and that I might be dying. I called the boys' father and told him that I had to go into the hospital for a medical emergency. I think I told him that I had a ruptured ovarian cyst. I asked him either to come and stay in my apartment, or if he preferred, to pick up the boys and take them to his apartment. Do you know what he said? He said no. No explanation, just "no." Even though I think I'm dying, I'm not asking him to help me. All I want is for him to take care of his kids, and he can't be bothered. I said to him, "But what if I die?" His response was, "Well, we'll cross that bridge when we come to it." Unbelievable! They're his kids, but it was all just too much trouble.

I had to do something in a hurry. Because at this point in my life I was working full-time, I had a whole string of babysitters who came after school to watch the boys until I got home from work. I persuaded an intermittent, casual babysitter to actually move into my apartment and take care of the kids. She stayed the whole time I was in the hospital. I don't really know that she provided very good care, because when I got home a month later, the carpet was literally worn down between the couch and the TV, not the couch and the children's bedroom.

They treated me with Chloromycetin in the hospital. I found out later that a side effect of that drug, particularly in the high doses they were giving me, was aplastic anemia. Wow! If you don't die of the abortion, you die of the anemia.

I have no memory of much that went on in the hospital. I remember hemmorhaging. Also, I remember a nurse. Anytime she had to do anything for me, especially anytime she had to touch me, I know she must have literally dipped her hands in ice. She never made eye contact with me, and she also let me know by her body language that what I had done so offended her that she could not or would not treat me like a human being. I remember her more vividly than anything else about that month in the hospital. I'm convinced she did everything she could to make me uncomfortable. Because I was so sick, I was really at her mercy. She seemed to love that—and hate me. Finally I asked Dr. Hughes if she could be kept away from me, and he made sure that she was never assigned to me again. Even though he was Catholic and probably felt much like the nurse did about what I had done, he was so caring and so good to me. I don't know why he was so kind to me. Maybe he felt guilty. He wouldn't help me, and because he wouldn't, I had gone to Barbara. Maybe it was the Hippocratic oath. Maybe his religion taught him compassion. Whatever it was, he was the most compassionate doctor I have ever met. He kept reassuring me: "Don't worry. You'll be fine, and this will all be okay." That meant so much to me, because I was frantic with worry about my children and what would happen to them. Dr. Hughes saved my life. He showed no disapproval, just sorrow.

Preston was great too. He came daily to the hospital, which couldn't have been easy for him. After all, how did he explain that to his wife?

No one at the hospital put any pressure on me to reveal the identity of the abortionist. Maybe Dr. Hughes was responsible for that too. I don't know. Everyone seemed more interested in helping me recover than in punishing me or Barbara.

After the infection began to subside, I started to pass huge blood clots. That was frightening to me, but Dr. Hughes assured me that it was all right and meant I was getting better. Recovery was a slow process, and I was impatient because I was so worried about my kids. After a month, I signed myself out of the hospital, against the advice of my doctor. A very serious step on my part, but I just had to get home.

My boss was very good to me. He didn't know what was really wrong—he had been told the ruptured cyst story—but he knew I had two kids and really needed the job. Besides, he knew I had been a good worker before the "cyst." He actually installed an office telephone in my home so that I could work from there until I got my health back. I was home for another full month before I was able to go back to work. I was totally incapacited for two months, and though I was a young and basically healthy female, it took me another four months to get back to where I had been before.

Many years later I had to have a hysterectomy because I had fibroid tumors. The surgeon told me that my reproductive organs were in incredibly bad shape. One ovary and one tube were completely destroyed by scar tissue. It was a good thing I had my children, because I never got pregnant again, probably because of the terrible scarring and damage left by the peritonitis.

It was a terrible abortion and a terrible experience. My children spent all that time being raised by an uncaring stranger. It was a nightmare. I feel very angry, especially now that I know what a medically safe abortion can be like. I felt some considerable guilt about it all. Not guilt over having an abortion, but guilt because I was so dumb or so stubborn that I had refused to go to the doctor and went instead to Barbara. If I hadn't been so stubborn, none of this would have happened. That is really a heavy trip, and in a very real sense, if I had died, it would have been my own fault.

CAMPBELL, ENSOR,
AND LANG

YORK COUNTY, IN SOUTHEASTERN PENNSYLVANIA, rests on the
Mason-Dixon line. It has only two towns of any size—
York, with a population of 44,000, and Hanover, with a
population of only 12,000. York is the county seat. Hanover was
the scene of a brief Civil War battle two days before the battle
of Gettysburg. A century later, it was the home of one Charles
Christopher Campbell.

Mr. Campbell was arrested on November 21, 1958, as the
head of an "abortion ring" operating out of a secluded one-
story ranch house in Heidelberg Township. He and Thelma
Adele Ensor, posing as Carroll G. and Orta M. Harrison, had
rented the house several months earlier. Hanover is twelve
miles from Gettysburg and less than ten miles from the Maryland state line. Campbell's colleagues, Mrs. Ensor and Charles
William Lang, were from Boring and Manchester respectively,
small towns in northern Maryland. Campbell had previously
been convicted of performing abortions in Maryland, which
might well explain his decision to move his operation north of
the Mason-Dixon line, out of Maryland's jurisdiction.

The 1958 raid climaxed a four-year investigation and intermittent surveillance by state troopers. The police had become
suspicious because of reports that there was never anyone at
the property in the daytime. The lights burned around the

clock, even though the place appeared deserted, and the shades were drawn at all times. At night, however, the house bustled with activity, with cars coming and going at odd hours. One of those cars was a Ford of uncertain ownership. Another was a Cadillac registered to C. C. Campbell of Hanover, Pennsylvania—not a name recognized by the landlord. A neighbor who shared a party line with the mystery house reported overhearing a phone conversation in which a female stated that her daughter was pregnant. She wanted to know how soon it could be "taken care of." Things sounded suspicious.

State Trooper Smith described the raid.

There were twelve men in my detail. Some were hidden in a nearby farmhouse. Others were hidden in a field between the houses. We all had walkie-talkies and field glasses so we could stay in contact with each other. I had earlier obtained a search warrant for the house we had under surveillance. Because of the overheard telephone call, we had a pretty good idea what was going on in the house, and the warrant was for items used in the performance of abortions.

We started our stakeout on November 18th, but nothing happened until the evening of November 21st. At 6:10 that evening, a Cadillac and a Ford arrived. Then the Ford left. It returned a short time later with two women.

We entered the house using a key we had earlier gotten from the owner of the house. There was a long hallway, with bedrooms off the hallway. In the first bedroom was Nancy R. She was sitting on the bed wearing a slip, but no dress.

There was another bedroom adjacent to that, and there were two women in bed in that room. One said her name was Hazel R. and the other was Ann T.

As I continued down the hall, I came to another bedroom, and there were two more women in there. These women were not in bed. They were fully dressed, sitting on the bed. In answer to my questions, they identified themselves as Roxie W. and Barbara P.

Mrs. Ensor was in the back bedroom. I went back and asked her for the money she received in connection with the abortions. She gave me two envelopes—one with $175 and one with

$250. I also found an envelope with $200 on a counter in the kitchen.

Mr. Campbell was dressed in a set of white clothing with a white cap like a surgeon would wear. He had on a surgical mask, and on a table in front of him were various surgical instruments.

Barbara P. told about the events of November 21, 1958.

I am from York, Pennsylvania. On November 21, 1958, I was about four and one-half months pregnant. At least that is what I was told by the doctor I consulted.

The way it worked was that I was to go to Lee's Diner, park my car in their parking lot, and put a magazine on my windshield. I did that. And then the man that I later found out was Charles Lang came over and met me. There was another woman in the parking lot at Lee's Diner. She, too, had a magazine on her windshield.

Mr. Lang told the two of us to drive our cars to the Hill Cafe. He would meet us there and drive us to the place where we were to have our abortions. Our cars would just stay there at the Hill Cafe until we were finished. We did what he said. He met us at that second parking lot and drove us, in his car, to the place where the abortions were to be done.

Mrs. Ensor met us at the door. Well, really, she met us outside, because she stepped outside before she let us in and told me that I had to get rid of my cigarette before I could come into the house. She was wearing a nurse's uniform.

Then Mrs. Ensor took the two of us to a bedroom and told us to take off our skirts and underpants, which we both did. Mrs. Ensor asked me how pregnant I thought I was. I told her, and then she gave me a shot in my leg.

My purpose in going there was to have an abortion, but it didn't happen because the state police broke in before my turn came. The police took our pictures, names, and fingerprints and then loaded us into cars and took us to be examined by a doctor. It was Dr. Hart, the same one I had consulted earlier in November. There were three of us girls altogether. After the doctor examined us, they took us to the state police barracks.

Dr. Hart described his examination of three of the women.

> The police brought three of the women to me on the night of November 21st—Nancy R., Hazel R., and Ann T. I examined Nancy first. She had a moderate amount of vaginal bleeding and she had packing in her uterus. The only medical reason to do that kind of packing is after the delivery of a baby, to stop post-partum hemorrhage. This patient had not just delivered a child, which gets us to the other reason to do it. The introduction of a pack into the uterus is like the introduction of any other foreign body into the uterus. In most cases, it will produce an abortion.
>
> I examined Hazel R. at about 9:15 p.m. on the night of November 21st. This woman had no marks of any instruments and no pack was present. It is my belief that no operative procedure of any kind had been attempted on this woman.
>
> I examined Ann T. at about 10:30 that same night. She was bleeding moderately from the entrance to the uterus. The opening to her uterus appeared to have been dilated and she, too, had a pack in her uterus. Like Nancy, Ann had not just had a baby, so, in my opinion, the only reason for her uterine pack was an attempt to produce an abortion.
>
> I had been consulted earlier by Barbara P., who had come to my office on November 14th. On that visit, she identified herself as "*Mrs.* Barbara Jones." She revealed that her last menstrual period was in June of 1958. I examined her, found her to be pregnant, and advised her of that fact. Then she left.

At the trial, a chemist for the state police described his analysis of the fluids and tablets found in the house on the night of November 21. They included potassium mercuric iodide, quinine sulfate, Ergotrate maleate, diethylstilbestrol, aspirin, and penicillin. Dr. Hart then described the purpose and effect of some of the various substances. "Ergotrate maleate and quinine sulfate make the uterus contract. Diethylstilbestrol is an estrogen compound used to control uterine bleeding." Also removed from the house were a cardboard carton of rubber tubing, rubber gloves, a metal table, towels, gauze, surgical cotton, a box of tampons, surgical instruments, two kidney-shaped hospital pans, rubber sheeting, and Mr. Campbell's surgical mask.

The three defendants described their backgrounds, as well as their roles in the abortion operation. Campbell, who was married and gave his address as RD 2 in Hanover, described himself as being fifty-two years old and five feet seven inches tall, weighing one hundred fifty pounds, and having blue eyes and brown hair tinged with gray. He gave his primary occupation as farmer. Specifically, he said he owned and operated dairy farms—which did not prevent him, alone among the nonmedical abortionists I interviewed, from passing himself off as a doctor. The women who sought his services thought they were going to someone like Dr. Spencer, not to a dairy farmer.

My name is Charles Christopher Campbell. I am not a doctor and I never have been a doctor. I get patients because thousands of people know my number and they call when they need my services.

That night I made arrangements to have three people picked up in a parking lot in Hanover. They all wanted a D&C—that is to dilate the cervix and scrape the uterus. One was bleeding and the other two thought they might be pregnant. If a pregnant woman has a D&C, she isn't pregnant anymore. Five girls came to me for abortions that night. I had done D&C abortions on three of them when the police arrived.

My normal fee is $200 for an abortion. The girls pay me directly before they go home. I pay the expenses. Like, the rent for the house where we do abortions is $125 a month.

Thelma Ensor's role is to give the girls water and aspirin and to administer to any needs they may have after the abortion is performed. Mr. Lang works for me on the farm. That is his main job and he is on the payroll there. His job in the abortion business is to transport the girls from the parking lots where they leave their cars to the house where I do the abortions. Then he drives them back to their cars. He drives the Ford. I drive the Cadillac. Mrs. Ensor and Mr. Lang do just what I tell them to do.

Thelma came over with me from Hanover on November 21st.

> Lang drove his own car and brought the first three girls. Then he went back for the other two. Those last two didn't get done, because the police came before I could get to them.

Mrs. Ensor stated that she had worked for Mr. Campbell for approximately fifteen years as his secretary, but that in the abortion business she functioned as his nurse. She was not a registered nurse, but she had once worked for eighteen months as a practical nurse, she said, which gave her the experience necessary to do this job. She said that all she'd done on November 21 was to administer to the wants of the girls, but that she hadn't given anyone any shots and she never gave shots.

Mr. Lang gave his primary occupation as carpenter and said that he had worked for Mr. Campbell for approximately three and a half years as a carpenter on one of his dairy farms. He was also Mrs. Ensor's son-in-law. His job on November 21 was to pick women up at various locations and times and to drive them to the house using back roads, as Mr. Campbell had instructed him to do. He picked up three women in Hanover and took them to the house. He then went to York, again using back roads, and picked up two more women in the vicinity of Lee's Diner. When the police arrived, he was sitting in the living room, waiting to drive the first group of three women back to Hanover.

Campbell, Ensor, and Lang were arrested, and each was charged with three counts that involved performing abortions. The first count alleged administering drugs and other substances to cause an abortion, the second alleged administering certain poisons, and the third alleged using certain instruments to cause an abortion. All three defendants were acquitted of the first two counts and convicted of the third.

On May 15, 1961, Campbell was sentenced to not less than one and a half and not more than five years in solitary confinement in the State Correctional Institute of Philadelphia. Ensor and Lang were each sentenced to eight months in prison.

Either the abortion business or the dairy farm had been

profitable enough to give Campbell the financial resources to fight on. Taking his case first to Pennsylvania's state appellate courts and then to the federal courts, he argued that he was unfairly convicted for an assortment of reasons based on certain evidence submitted at his trial. No one was persuaded, and his conviction stood.

It is not known whether Campbell later moved on to a new state and again set up shop as an abortionist, or whether he decided to stick to dairy farming or take up some other occupation. While dairy farming may not generate such immediate profits as performing abortions, it does entail considerably less risk. So too with carpentry and secretarial work.

DR. DON

IGRADUATED FROM MEDICAL SCHOOL IN 1961. Then I did an internship at a Catholic hospital. After that I did a two-year residency in anesthesiology at a large teaching hospital in Denver. I don't remember abortion being discussed in my home when I was growing up, and I don't recall being taught any values or attitudes about it. I really don't remember much about attitudes or moral judgments in medical school either.

In medical school we did a three-month rotation through ob-gyn, and I remember receiving training in how to take care of someone who had had a septic abortion. That was mostly antibiotic therapy, as I recall. I don't have any particular strong memories of the patients. I just know there were some.

During my internship at the Catholic hospital, I received a very strong message that abortion was evil, and I am quite sure there were no septic abortion patients there. At the Catholic hospital I did learn how to do a D and C, though, since it would be appropriate treatment for things other than abortion. It wasn't until I did my residency in anesthesiology that I became more aware of illegal abortion. Even then I was not as aware as I would have been if I had been in an ob-gyn program, since I only saw surgery patients.

During my residency, I remember one young girl. She was probably no more than nineteen. When she was admitted to the hospital, she had peritonitis and septicemia. Now, either of those things can kill you. She was in bad shape when she was brought in. Her body was covered all over with horrible boils, and she had gangrene. She was one very sick kid! It took weeks, but she finally did recover. She was really very lucky to have survived. She was one of the sickest people I have ever seen. She would never tell us what happened to her—who did it or how it was done—but there was talk around the hospital of a coat hanger or slippery elm or something like that. Whatever was used on her sure wasn't sterilized first for her to get an infection like that.

The hospital where I did my residency was a large municipal teaching hospital. A substantial portion of the patient population was indigent. The hospital always had so many septic abortion patients that I don't think they could have bothered trying to find out the identity of the abortionists. The young girl with the boils created more of a stir because her condition was so horrible. As an anesthesiology resident whose job was anesthetizing people for surgery, I didn't have direct contact with nonsurgical patients, and most abortion patients didn't require surgery. The girl with the boils did. I don't remember why. Maybe they were repairing a perforation.

In Denver, at the time, the significant minority groups were Negroes and Hispanics. The septic abortion patients in that public hospital were disproportionately black or Hispanic and disproportionately poor. I don't remember that they were disproportionately young, but they might have been.

As for the attitudes of the medical community toward these women who got coat-hanger abortions, it's not that the doctors were judgmental or hostile as much as they were kind of contemptuous. The attitude was "How could these women do anything so stupid as to get such a dangerous abortion?" or "Why would any smart person take such a stupid chance?" I don't recall any discussion about the need to provide women with safer options.

I have no idea how many years it covered, but the pathology department at that municipal hospital had a rather large collection of jars of preserved organs that had been removed for one reason or another. Many of the organs were uteruses with the abortion instrument still in place. Some of the instruments were knitting needles, and some were coat hangers, and there they were, neatly labeled and lined up, each floating in its jar of formaldehyde.

Colorado legalized abortion in 1967, so they probably haven't added much to that part of the collection in the last twenty years. I wonder if those bottles are still there. If they are, I wonder if today's medical students understand just what they mean. Coat hangers and knitting needles probably seem very strange to them. They must wonder, even more than we did twenty-five years ago, "Why would any woman take such a chance?" I don't know why, but I know a lot of them did.

PAULA

T HE SOON-TO-BE EX-WIFE of a brand-new doctor, I had an
illegal abortion in 1963. I had just finished putting my
husband through medical school, and we were trying to
have another child. Our son Jeff was not quite two years old. I
guess my husband had an agenda I didn't know about, since
three months after graduation he left me for a blond nurse he
had met at the hospital.

I was numb with shock and just sort of moved through the
days like a sleepwalker. He hadn't been gone more than ten
days when I woke up to a constant nausea. I knew that feeling
all too well from my pregnancy two years earlier. I was pregnant! Oh, my God! The once-longed-for event had turned—
overnight, it seemed—into a disaster. I couldn't stand it. I was
barely coping with the collapsed marriage and being a single
parent to my little boy. There was no way I could cope with
pregnancy—the painful reminder of happier times. I needed a
job, not another baby.

I knew in that first hour of that first day, as I lay in bed fighting the nausea and wondering how I would find the courage to
go on, that I would have an abortion. There was not any doubt
in my mind. I was absolutely certain.

But how to do it? That was not easy. You would think, after
his four years of medical school, that I would have some special

connections. Not so. I might as well have put him through plumbing school for all the good it did me. I was on my own on this one—as I suddenly was with everything else in my life.

I tried hot showers, cold baths, jumping up and down, taking laxatives. I took quinine, which I got from a friend who was in pharmacy school while my husband was in medical school. It didn't do anything. It didn't even make me sick, which I thought it might, since I didn't have malaria.

My pharmacy school friend had learned about Ergotrate, and he got me these big black pills. I don't remember the exact dosage, but my instructions were to take a fairly high dose over about a six-hour period, two pills every hour or so. Maybe I took them wrong, maybe his directions were wrong, or maybe he got the wrong thing from the pharmacy lab, but they did scary things to my legs. It was like my legs were congested with blood or something. They were all tingling, and I couldn't walk right. I was really frightened, but I stayed in bed and kept taking the pills like I had been told. After about twenty-four hours, my legs felt better, almost normal, but nothing else happened. I was still nauseated and still pregnant.

My pharmacist friend was scared when I couldn't walk, and he told me there weren't any other drugs I could try. I would have to find a real abortionist. I was too afraid to ask my friends. Besides, suddenly it seemed I didn't have any. They were all fellow medical students and their wives, who couldn't comfortably see both of us, and it was much easier and cleaner to stop seeing me.

After what seemed like an eternity but was probably no more than two weeks, my pharmacist friend called me and said that a guy who had flunked out of pharmacy school was just kind of bumming around, but that he still lived in the same little college town and was getting by doing abortions on college girls. What luck! I had about given up ever finding anyone to help me. I don't know how pregnant I was. I felt like I couldn't even remember a time when I wasn't nauseated and that I had been looking for an abortionist forever, but I was probably no more than eight weeks pregnant.

The pharmacist had no desire to be involved in any way. By getting me the quinine and the Ergotrate, I'm sure that he was already more involved than he wanted to be. But he felt sorry for me. I guess he could tell how desperate I was after the Ergotrate failed, so he asked around and called me with this name and phone number. He had no idea whether the guy was good or bad. He just gave me the name because he knew I was desperate.

I called the guy, whose name was George. He told me he would come to my house at night, after Jeff was in bed and asleep, and do the abortion there. That was good. I wouldn't have to get a babysitter and then drive myself home. However, I had to have a hundred and fifty dollars in cash, which wasn't easy.

George came about three days later—it took me a few days to scrape up that much money. I remember that he brought a bag of equipment. I had no idea what was in the bag, but it comforted me, since it seemed to suggest that he knew what he was doing. He had me turn on the television so it would drown out any noise I might make, since he didn't have any novocaine or anything like that.

Do you know what was on TV as I lay there having my abortion? The Miss America Pageant. When they sang, "Here she comes ... Miss America," I felt a flash of red-hot anger. Who were they kidding? Being a young female in America in those days wasn't white dresses, red roses, and crowns. It was quinine and illegal abortions, and something was horribly wrong somewhere! That was almost thirty years ago, and I still get mad every time I hear the Miss America theme song. What hypocrisy!

George was efficient and quick and relatively painless. He sort of poked around with a catheter. I think it took about twenty minutes, maybe not that long. There wasn't any blood or anything. He told me to go to bed and the next day I would have some cramps and some bleeding and I would abort. He also told me that if I passed any clots or pieces of tissue, to save them in my freezer so he would be able to tell if he got everything. He didn't give me any antibiotics or anything like that. He just left, telling me he would be in touch in a day or two. I went to bed, relieved that it was over. I could hardly wait for something to happen.

The next morning, when I woke up, I knew something was different. Although no bleeding or cramping had started, for the first time in sixty or seventy days I wasn't nauseated. It was going to happen. I knew it. I'd be all right, and I'd still be around to take care of Jeff. I knew Jeff felt like he had lost his daddy, and for a while, I thought he was going to lose his mother as well.

I've never been as elated as I was that morning. It was a beautiful fall day. Feeling good for the first time in weeks, I jumped out of bed, got Jeff and myself dressed, and went out in the backyard to rake leaves. Jeff laughed and cooed, happy to be outside. For the past few weeks, I had spent most of my time in bed, so he had been forced to spend too much time in a crib or playpen, since I had no one to take care of him.

Suddenly I felt this wet sensation on my legs. I looked down. The leaves and I were covered with blood. Remembering George's instructions about any tissue, I dropped the rake, grabbed Jeff, and ran into the house to take off my blood-soaked clothes. I picked through the clothes for tissue. Finding nothing, I filled the tub with cold water to soak my clothes. This wasn't so bad, I thought. Dramatic, but short. Pulling on clean clothes and grabbing Jeff, I went back out in the yard to finish raking.

Well, my body wasn't yet finished, it seemed. The backyard hemorrhage happened three more times. Each time I picked through my clothes and the leaves looking for tissue. The last two times, there was some. I put the pieces in an ashtray and put them in the freezer. Most of it looked like pieces of dark red liver, but there was one part of it that was different—sort of white and yellow and firmer than the liverlike stuff. That different tissue was less than two inches long. I studied it very closely, because I figured it was fetal tissue and was what George would be concerned about. Well, it didn't have arms or legs or toes or anything like the posters and billboards the anti-abortionists seem so fond of displaying. When George saw it, he said that was all of it and I would be fine. I was. The bleeding tapered off and stopped in about a week.

After George left that second time, when he came to check the tissue, I went and looked at Jeff sleeping in his crib. He was real. He needed a mother, and now, again, he had one. I knew we would make it, and we did.

I still have that ashtray, and sometimes I look at it when the anti-abortionists are blocking clinics and telling people that fetuses are more important than living women and children. I disagree. Do they really believe that the contents of that ashtray are the same as Jeff asleep in his crib? To my mind, they're as hypocritical as the Miss America myth. Or maybe they've never really seen a fetus. I have, and I've never had a moment's regret.

It has been twenty-eight years since that backyard hemorrhage. During that time, there have been twenty-eight more Miss Americas chosen, with their high heels and bathing suits—so few women really dress that way—and twenty-eight more seasons of raking leaves. But happily for me, there have been no more backyard hemorrhages. Jeff and I did survive, as I knew we would. I remarried and had two more children, Jack and Maggie.

It is Maggie, my only "woman-child," whose story shows me how much things can change. When Maggie was twenty-five, married, working full-time, and attending graduate school at night, she became unwillingly pregnant. So like her mother: feeling, for her own personal reasons, that this pregnancy was impossible. So like her mother: instantly and constantly nauseated. So unlike her mother in the options available to her.

Do you know what Maggie did? No Ergotrate for Maggie. No pharmacy school dropouts coming to her home during the Miss America Pageant. No backyard hemorrhages. Maggie had her abortion in 1991. She called a clinic and made an appointment. Her health insurance paid for her abortion. She did share her decision with me—not to change it or veto it, simply to share it.

Her husband was to take her to the clinic, but she asked me to meet her there. I arrived at the clinic at eight a.m. Maggie had already been called. She was having counseling. How strange, how incongruous. Women hemorrhaging in the backyard have little need for, or interest in, counseling. They are concerned with more fundamental problems, like survival. Curious, I later asked her what there was to "counsel" about. "My choice," she answered. "Was it freely made? Was I being coerced? Contraception. We had obviously been unsuccessful. What were we doing wrong? How could we be more successful?" How incredibly luxurious, I marveled.

I sat there in the clinic waiting room, curled up in an introspective ball, worrying about my woman-child. I looked around me. The waiting room was full of people—husbands, parents, sisters, friends—all seemingly more composed than I was. They weren't unduly worried about the women in their lives. I didn't even think to wonder about the difference between us.

I mused about how nice it would be to be a grandmother, but almost before the thought was formed, I knew I could never say that to Maggie. However much I might desire a grandchild to bounce upon my knee, that was not a reason to coerce my daughter, even subtly, to continue an unwanted pregnancy.

As I sat there, suffering my illogical anxiety, I realized what was wrong. My Maggie was going to hemorrhage in the backyard. Maybe she would die. If she didn't die, she would certainly be destroyed if anyone found out, as I would have been twenty-eight years earlier. I couldn't tell the difference between Maggie and myself. I was reliving the fear of that backyard hemorrhage. It was almost worse than the original.

Lost in my frightening memories, I jumped when I felt a hand on my shoulder. A kindly gray-haired doctor said, "Are you Maggie's mother? She's fine. She's in the recovery room." I demanded—maybe "begged" is a better word—to see her. When I was ushered into the recovery room by the doctor— who couldn't know what baggage I dragged from twenty-eight years earlier, but who knew I was inappropriately anxious—do you know what I saw?

My little girl was in an overstuffed reclining chair, with a warm, white blanket tucked around her, a steaming cup of tea in her hand, a radiant smile on her face, and not one but two uniformed nurse-practitioners, with blood pressure cuffs and stethoscopes, attending to her. One was taking her blood pressure. The other was talking to her about contraception and post-abortion care.

Different? I can't even articulate it. She was, in a very literal sense, surrounded by competent medical care. Frightened? Not a bit. She appeared relaxed and secure—quite unlike her mother in the backyard. Her relief, like mine twenty-eight years earlier, was no big surprise. But there was also an unexpected similarity. Before this day, every blood pressure cuff I had ever seen had been gray. These blood pressure cuffs were different, each an incredibly vibrant plaid, in the most radiant colors— orange, brown, red, and gold. I had seen those same colors earlier—twenty-eight years ago—during the leaf-raking backyard hemorrhage. How powerful color can be as a memory enhancer!

I kissed her and left to go to work. Blinking back tears of relief and remembered pain, I exited the building and bumped into a man carrying a sign: "Abortion kills. Choose life." My God! Have they walked in my shoes or Maggie's? No. Abortion—even illegal abortion—saves lives. It saved mine, and Jeff's, and, now, Maggie's. Now the tears I blinked back were those of rage. I went home that night and called Jeff, thirty years old and six feet tall.

"Hi, Mom. What's up?"

"Nothing special. I just want you to know life is hard and I love you."

Puzzled: "Sure, Mom. Love ya. Bye."

"Bye."

And thank you, clinic, for making it easier and safer twenty-eight years later for my Maggie.

NORMA

I HAD AN ILLEGAL ABORTION IN 1966. I was twenty-one years old, married, with a year-old daughter. My husband was an extremely abusive man. I guess I was the classic "battered wife," but we didn't call it that in those days. I was not only beaten and battered—I was burned. Anyway, I had just left him about a week before. I had taken my daughter and gone home to my parents. I had managed to find a job and had started work, but with only a few days of employment under my belt, I hadn't gotten a paycheck and I had no money.

No more than a week after the separation, I realized I was pregnant. I didn't even suspect it when I left him, because I'm one of these women who actually has a period or even two during pregnancy. It was a complete and most unwelcome surprise!

I come from a kind of emotionally repressed white middle-class family. There was no experience with illegal abortion that I knew of. The women in my family just had illegitimate children. They all did! My aunt, my grandmother, and my grandmother's sister had illegitimate children, and none of them knew who the father was. I just find that very interesting! Part of what's interesting, as far as I'm concerned, in addition to how they handled the problem, is how very widespread the problem was.

My family training and upbringing had all been that abortion was wrong. I wasn't exactly taught that it was murder, but it was a very serious and very bad thing. In spite of some twenty-one years of hearing this, I knew immediately that I wanted an abortion. With an abusive husband, an infant daughter, and an unwanted pregnancy, my choice was easy. My mother was not keen on me moving in with a baby, but she let me do it because I had no place else to go. She sure would not have wanted me there with two babies. She would have wanted me to go back to my husband if she'd known I was pregnant.

I tried different things to make me abort. A man I knew told me he heard that drinking witch hazel would cause an abortion. I don't know what witch hazel is made of or how dangerous it is to drink it, but I actually went out and bought two bottles and drank them both. That didn't make me abort, and it didn't even make me sick, which is pretty amazing. Then someone told me to take laxatives, so I did. Because laxatives didn't seem as frightening as witch hazel, which hadn't made me sick at all, I took a *lot* of laxatives! I don't know if there's such a thing as a lethal dose of laxatives, but if there is, I came close. I got really bad diarrhea, but nothing else happened. Absolutely nothing!

Hal, a family friend, led me to the abortionist. Hal was an ex-felon who had spent twenty years in jail for killing a policeman but was out on parole. Whenever you needed anything shady, questionable, or downright illegal, you called Hal. He could get it for you—maybe not wholesale, but hey, he could get it! Hal owned several apartment buildings that were the legal source of his income. He had other, extralegal sources of income, but I never knew what they were, and with Hal, you just didn't ask.

I had spent over a month on the laxatives and witch hazel. After I decided that I couldn't afford to waste any more time and that none of these methods could possibly work, I called Hal and told him my problem. He was a lot easier to talk to than my mother. As I suspected, what was an overwhelming problem for me was no problem at all for Hal. He listened and told me he would get back to me. About a week went by, and then he called. He told me I would need three hundred dollars in cash. Now, that was a great deal of money in 1966. It was probably like a thousand dollars today. Because I had no money, I had to borrow from friends. I even borrowed money from my grandmother, but she had no idea what it was for. Hal didn't offer to loan me any of the money, but I was hardly in a position to complain.

As soon as I had collected the money, I called Hal to arrange an appointment. Because I was working, I could only do this on a weekend. Hal told me to meet him the following Saturday morning at his apartment with the cash. When I got to his place, we got into his car, and then he put something over my head so I couldn't see where we were going. I don't know how far we went or exactly where we went, but it seemed like a short drive, no more than ten blocks at the most. Hal stopped the car and uncovered my eyes. He told me to get into a different car that was parked and waiting for us. There was another man driving that second car. Hal didn't go with me. He told me he would wait there for me. I remember him just standing at the curb by his car, waving at me as we drove away.

I was absolutely paralyzed with fear. I had never seen this driver, and I had no idea what was going to happen to me. The driver didn't cover my eyes, which seemed strange after Hal's behavior. We drove a few more blocks, and then he stopped in front of a private home, a small brick house on a residential street. I remember thinking how quiet and deserted the street was. It was a hot, sunny morning in July. Birds were singing, but no one was out working in the yard or washing the car anywhere on the block. Maybe it was too early in the morning, or maybe it was too hot.

The driver motioned to the house and told me to go up and knock on the door. He waited in the car. A little old lady came to the door. She was probably in her early sixties, but because I was only twenty-one, she seemed old. She was short and stout, with white hair. She didn't say a word, just motioned me to follow her upstairs. We went to the third floor, her attic. The room was totally empty and brutally hot. I'm sure the temperature up there was well over a hundred degrees.

There was no furniture in that room. No bed, no table, no nothing. There was newspaper on the floor, nothing else. She told me to take off my clothes from the waist down and lie on the floor. She gave me a piece of newspaper to cover myself. Then she reached into her apron pocket and pulled out a piece of clear plastic tubing. It wasn't in a sterile package or anything. It was just loose in her apron pocket. She inserted the tubing in my vagina and said, "Okay, that's it. You're done." The whole thing took less than ten minutes.

Now, I had paid Hal the money, so whoever got the money from him must have paid her. She didn't mention money to me. She simply said to leave the catheter—that's what she called the tubing—in place. In three or four days, she said, I would begin to abort, and I could take the catheter out then. She didn't tell me anything else, like what to expect or what to do. Of course she didn't give me any antibiotics. She didn't seem to have any equipment of any kind. Remember, the room was totally empty. The catheter seemed to be all she needed.

I walked out, and the man who drove me there drove me back to Hal. Hal drove me back to my car, this time without any covering over my eyes, and I drove myself home. My mother had no idea what I'd been doing, and I hadn't been gone very long. At that point I felt fine—no cramping or bleeding or anything. On Monday I went to work and watched and waited for something to happen. By Wednesday I was beginning to have fairly uncomfortable cramping, and I took the catheter out, as I had been told to do. By Friday the bleeding was getting very heavy and I felt like I was hemorrhaging. On Friday morning I was on my way to work on the bus when I fainted. There hadn't been any seats, so I was standing, holding on to a pole. I just blacked out. My head hit the floor. I remember I had dirt on my forehead. What was amazing is that no one helped me or paid any attention to me. Maybe they thought I just lost my balance, but still …

By that time I was all the way downtown, so I stopped and

told my employer I was sick and wouldn't be at work that day. I went back home and spent the weekend in bed. The bleeding was really heavy, and I was passing big clots. I was frightened, but I didn't want to admit how bad I felt. I was passing it off as a touch of the flu so my mother wouldn't find out what was wrong with me. I figured that if I spent the weekend in bed, it would be better by Monday. I certainly wasn't about to risk going to the doctor. I'm not sure what my mother thought.

Finally, Tuesday or Wednesday of the next week—I had been home in bed all that time with this really heavy bleeding—I woke up during the middle of the night in intense pain. It was different than anything I had felt before. I woke my mother up, and I can still remember the first thing she said: "For heaven's sake! Go stand in the kitchen before you ruin the rug!"

When I look back on it, it was kind of funny in a horrible sort of way. I'm lying on the kitchen floor moaning in pain and bleeding all over. My mother woke my father up, not because of me, but because it was time for him to get ready for work. In my family, no one talked about menstruation or periods or anything like that in front of my father. I'm sure he never bought a box of sanitary napkins in his life. I don't know what my mother said to him, but it sure wasn't that this was any sort of medical emergency, because what she told me was that my father would drop me off at the hospital on his way to work. He was in the bathroom shaving and whistling and getting dressed. My mother was in the kitchen getting his breakfast and stepping over me as she moved around making coffee and oatmeal. It was the most ordinary behavior on both their parts, as if having their daughter lying bleeding on the kitchen floor was a completely normal occurrence.

Finally, doubled up in pain, I told her I couldn't wait until my father finished shaving and ate his breakfast, and would she please call an ambulance. She did, and I went to the hospital. Neither of them came with me. By the time I got there I was convinced I was dying. The bleeding was now just these giant clots, more solid than liquid, and I really felt like all of my insides were coming out. Funny things were happening to my vision. It was all dark around the edges, and I seemed to be looking through a bright pinhole in the center. I couldn't seem to see anything unless it was right in front of me. I couldn't seem to hear, either. People around me were talking and waving their arms, and they seemed to be talking about me, but it was just a faint buzzing noise. There weren't any words, and people disappeared when they moved out of the pinhole.

That's the last thing I remember for quite a while. When I came to—and I don't know if it was an hour later or a day later—they told me they had done a D and C. What was written on my chart, I later learned, was "aborted ten-week fetus." I was really upset that the doctor wrote that on my chart. I was afraid the insurance company wouldn't pay, since abortion was illegal, or that the police would come and arrest me. The doctor assured me that I was worrying unnecessarily, because it was just a medical term that could describe what I would have called a "spontaneous miscarriage." Of course I lied and professed to be stunned to learn that I had been pregnant. Everyone seemed to believe me. At least, no one asked me any tough questions.

My parents never asked me a single question about the whole episode. They seemed to believe it was some sort of spontaneous hemorrhage, unrelated to anything. They seemed not to even know I had been pregnant.

I saw Hal, the ex-con, many times after that. He used to get invited to my parents' home for Christmas every year. I don't think he ever told them what had happened. About a year before Hal died, he asked me to do something illegal for him. I refused. I guess that was my expected payback, because when I wouldn't do it, he quit speaking to me and even quit spending Christmas with my parents. They probably wondered why he suddenly dropped them after all those years.

I had mixed feelings about the woman in the attic. Although it was horrible in many ways, I would have willingly done things much worse if I thought they would work. I would have done anything. As far as I'm concerned, that woman was clearly providing a much-needed service. I never even tried to find a doctor to help me. I was too afraid that the doctor would report me to the police. I never had any illusions about this woman's "medical qualifications," if I thought about them at all, and I'm not sure I did. I didn't think she was a nurse or anything like that. I just thought she was a little white-haired grandmother.

Years later, I went back to see if I could find the house. I wanted to know what it really looked like. I probably thought that if I saw it again with a little distance between me and the events, it wouldn't be as frightening as it was in my mind. I found it fairly easily—a testimonial to the ineffectiveness of Hal's efforts to conceal the location. I stood there staring at the house. It looked very much as I remembered it, a little brick house in an older neighborhood. But you know what I noticed that I hadn't noticed earlier? Her house was actually within sight of and no more than ten blocks from not one but two hospitals. Isn't that crazy? Those hospitals weren't available to me. Just the little old lady in the apron.

JIM

I WAS BORN IN 1958. In 1962, when I was four, my mother died from an illegal abortion. She was only twenty-four.

My father drove a truck. We didn't have much money. My mother worked nights as a cocktail waitress. During the day she was a housewife. I have one sister, Beverly, who is three years older than I am.

My dad met my mother when he was stationed in England. She was English. Her name was Louise. She had dark brown hair and brown eyes. She was very dainty and petite. I thought she was beautiful. My mother was only sixteen and my dad was seventeen when they met and got married. My sister was born in England. When my dad's tour of duty was up, he got out of the army and brought his family back to western Pennsylvania, where he had grown up.

I remember once—I must have been about three—we were playing in the backyard. It was me, my sister, and a bunch of neighborhood kids. We had woods right behind our house, and I sort of wandered off into them. I didn't think I was lost, but I guess I was gone for a couple of hours and no one knew where I was. I was fine, but I guess my mother didn't know that. She had the police out looking for me. When I was found, not far from home, I couldn't understand what all the commotion was about. My mother was crying. When she saw me, she gave me a big hug and a spanking! I guess the hug was because she was glad to see me and the spanking was so I wouldn't do that again. It was a dramatic but somewhat confusing reunion, since I couldn't decide whether I was bad or good.

My mom was sick a lot. She had a history of ulcers. I don't know if it was the ulcer or other stuff, but I can remember being told that I couldn't play in the house or that I had to be quiet because she was "lying down" or was sick.

I don't remember the abortion, and I am pretty sure I never knew about it. I don't have any specific memories of any illness associated with that time. I don't know if she died in the hospital or at home, but I guess I think it must have been in a hospital. If she had been at home, that would have been pretty hard to hide, even from two little kids. No one really told me she died. My dad just told me that she wasn't going to be "around" anymore. I don't think I ever put that together with the idea of death, or whether my childish mind could even understand a concept like "death." I had never even had a pet die.

Neither my sister nor I were allowed to go to the funeral. I had no idea what a funeral was, but I remember Beverly crying and begging to be allowed to go. She was seven, so she had a better idea of what was happening. My mother's mother came from England for the funeral. She was nice, but she was a stranger. The next thing I knew, Beverly and I were shipped off to England with my grandmother.

We had certainly been far from rich in America, with my dad driving a truck and my mom waitressing at night, but I thought my grandmother's apartment was a slum. It looked like it had been bombed, and I couldn't believe that people lived there. It had an outhouse. Nothing I had ever encountered before prepared me for that experience. We lived there for five or six months, and then she moved to a better place with an indoor toilet.

I kept thinking that my new life was a bad dream or a bad joke. Nothing made any sense to me. I think I was sort of in shock. I was suddenly with a total stranger in a strange country. The kids laughed at me because I "talked funny" and I didn't know how to play the games they played in England. They used to sing "Yankee Doodle Dandy" at me, and it had a different, sort of jeering meaning, compared to what we are used to. Listen to the words sometime—a "Yank," or "Yankee Doodle Dandy," who sticks a feather in his cap and calls it "macaroni." He sure doesn't sound too smart. Anyway, I quickly caught on that to be a Yank was to be kind of stupid. They made fun of me a lot, as I remember, and that only made me feel more forlorn and homesick for the life I had lost. I cried and begged my grandmother to let me go home. She cried a little and said I couldn't go home.

I think I spent most of the two years in England crying and saying I wanted my mom or my dad. I sort of understood that I wasn't ever going to see my mom again, although I didn't really understand why, but I didn't understand why I couldn't at least be with my dad.

After we had been in England for about two years, my dad remarried and we were allowed to go home. I mostly lost touch with my English relatives after that. They all came to the United States once to visit us, my grandmother and my uncles. My mom had several brothers, but I don't think she had any sisters.

I never understood why, because I didn't know what had happened to my mom and no one would talk to me about it, but things were always strained between my mom's family and my dad. Now that I know what I know, it's easy to see why. I'm sure that they felt that my dad was somehow responsible for her death, either because he made her pregnant or let her get an abortion.

Coming home turned out not to be the wonderful thing I had dreamed. By now, it had been two years since I had seen my dad, and when you are only six, that's like forever. Besides, here was another stranger—a stepmother. She was nice enough to us until she and my dad had children of their own, and then my sister and I were sort of like outsiders. We were different and we knew it. Maybe we reminded my dad of things he would rather forget.

I desperately wanted a mother. I called her Mom right from

the beginning, and I thought of her as Mom. It was getting hard for me to even remember my real mother. Because I thought of my stepmother as my mom, it really hurt when she would treat me differently from her own kids.

My sister and I, being older, had to help a lot with all the little kids, so we kind of grew up fast, and that caretaker role probably distanced us even more from our half-brothers and half-sisters. My stepmother was so busy with the little kids that she didn't have much time for us. My dad had to work all the time to support six kids and a wife, so I never saw him.

I grew up sort of estranged and lonely. I very much wanted someone to love me and think I was special, but I didn't know how to get close to people. Every time I tried I got hurt, so maybe, on a subconscious level at least, I just quit trying. I guess I'm still not very good at relationships. I was married, but now I am divorced.

I was eighteen when I first found out that my mom died from a back-alley abortion. I've had lots of problems with ulcers. I always thought—I was probably told—that our mom died from the complications of ulcers. When I would tell doctors treating my ulcer that my mother died in her early twenties from an ulcer, they would keep me in the hospital a lot longer and do a lot more tests.

When I was eighteen, I was hospitalized for my ulcers. My sister, who lived in Oregon, was worried about my health. I remember it vividly. We were talking on the telephone, and I was telling Beverly what I had told the doctors—what I think I had always been told about our mom's death. There was a funny kind of awkwardness—a long silence—and then my sister said, "It wasn't an ulcer." She had gotten a copy of my mother's death certificate. The certificate said that the cause of death was "uremic poisoning." To me that didn't mean anything. It certainly could have resulted from an ulcer. My sister must have had more to work from than just a death certificate, because she told me, flat out, that it was an abortion. She must have done some detective work after she grew up, because as a kid, I don't think she knew any more than I did. I wanted to ask my dad about it, but I was afraid to. Besides, we were so alienated at that point that we weren't even speaking. My dad could be very abusive verbally. When I would get sick with my ulcer, he would say, "You're just like your mother!" I was pretty sure from his tone of voice that it was not intended as a compliment, so the last thing I was going to try to talk to him about was my mom. I asked my stepmother if it was true that my mom died from an illegal abortion and not from an ulcer, and she told me it was true.

My sister, who was the only constant in my life after my mom died, has long been estranged from the family. She never got along with my stepmother. There was friction from the day they met. When she was sixteen, she left home and she never came back. She lives two thousand miles away. I haven't seen her in years. We talk on the telephone occasionally. She's polite and everything, but that's what's wrong. There is no closeness between us anymore, just politeness.

It seems like after my mom died my life fell apart and never got back on track. It even carries over into the next generation. When I was younger, I tried to resist seeing how very differently my stepmother treated her own children, because I didn't want to see it. Now that we all have our own children, the differences are too painful to be ignored. I have a little boy. He is six. My stepmother is the only grandmother he's got. Once, for Easter or Valentine's Day, she sent all the grandchildren but him a card. When I confronted her with it, she said, "But I'm not his real grandmother." She's the only one he has. How much more "real" does it need to be?

I'm what you would call anti-abortion or pro-life. I've been taught that abortion is wrong, and I guess I believe it, but part of me says that what happened to my mother wasn't right. She shouldn't have died. I guess I don't mind the abortion. I mind losing her. I've never gotten over it and I never will.

KATE

I WAS BORN IN 1940 and grew up in Florida. I had two illegal abortions, one in 1963 and one in 1967. The attitudes I learned about sex and abortion growing up can be boiled down to two phrases that my mother drilled into my head over and over: "Nice girls don't do it" and "What will the neighbors say?" It wasn't a religious thing. My father was a Quaker and my mother was an Episcopalian and we were raised Episcopalian, but it wasn't that abortion was a sin or anything. It was more like, "Don't do anything that will cause the neighbors to talk."

Meanwhile, my best girlfriend had an abortion when she was fourteen. Her mother arranged it. My mother would never admit what was happening. She kept insisting that Sally had jaundice. I knew better, because like any fourteen-year-old best friends, Sally and I talked about everything. But I humored my mother and pretended that I didn't know.

When I was fifteen, my first true love and my first big crush was a guy who was twenty-one. His name was Danny, and he had just come back from Korea. Now, my mother wouldn't even allow me to date—especially someone who was that much older—so I just worshiped him from afar. It was strictly platonic, but I was madly in love, as only a fifteen-year-old can be. He went overseas or moved away or something. In any event, I lost touch with him.

Nice girls simply didn't have sex, and I listened to that message until I was eighteen or nineteen, when passion got the better of me, as it has a way of doing with young people. As a sexually active teenager still living at home, I had little access to or knowledge of birth control. My boyfriend would buy condoms at the drugstore, but there was no way I could get anything or go to a doctor, because my all-knowing, all-seeing mother would find out.

My mother is an intensely critical person. I tried hard to please her, but I felt like I always disappointed her, even with the things she knew about. Think how much more displeased and disappointed she'd have been if she knew about the things I hid from her. I'm fifty-one now, and I feel like I've waited all my life for my mother to tell me she approves of me, or of something I did. It's not just me. My sister, Julie, who is three years older, feels the same way.

When Julie was nineteen, she thought she was pregnant. My mother didn't have her examined by the doctor, because what would the neighbors think? She made her get married. About two days after the wedding my sister got her period, so she wasn't even pregnant at that point. The marriage was horrible and didn't last. He drank and beat her up. Julie escaped one night with her son and the clothes on her back, so I had a pretty negative opinion of shotgun marriages, and I had no intention of ever making that mistake.

My mother had worked before she got married—as an "aquamaid" at Cypress Gardens, as a matter of fact. When she was young, she was very pretty and a good swimmer. But she had strong ideas about the proper role of women, and after she married Daddy it was all white picket fence and apple pie and all that. She went back to work part-time when I was about fifteen, but her main job was as a wife and mother. That was the way my sister and I were raised too. Mother was by far the dominant parent. Daddy, a wonderful, sweet man, was almost a shadow figure in our lives.

Mother raised us to think that men were no good and that they were only after one thing. You know, that isn't a very healthy message to give your daughters. It kind of impairs their ability to have good relationships with men. I discussed that with Mother once, after I was grown up, and she said it was her way of keeping us from getting pregnant. Hey, there has to be a safer, healthier, and maybe even more effective way! I've had a lifetime of bad relationships with men. I don't know if it's because I have bad judgment or if I deliberately choose them as some kind of self-fulfilling prophecy of my mother's.

When I was only thirteen, I decided I was never going to have children, because I never wanted to do to them what my mother had done to us. I always felt like I wasn't wanted. One of my worst childhood fears was that I would come home from school one day and I would round the corner only to find that the house and everything else was gone—that they all just moved away without telling me. That haunted me for years!

In 1963 I was twenty-three years old and living in Orlando. I finally had a fairly decent job as a fashion illustrator for a department store. And then who happened into my life again but Danny. This time it wasn't platonic. He had gotten out of the army and had a job in Orlando as a radio announcer. He had a wonderful speaking voice. That was one of the things I always found so entrancing about him.

We had condoms, which we used from time to time. I suppose that if I had gone to a doctor, I could have gotten the pill, but I was still so much under the emotional control of my mother—even though I lived alone, in a different town, and was economically independent—that there is no way I could have done that.

After three or four months of an intense relationship with Danny, I realized that I had grown apart from him or beyond him, or maybe, at twenty-three, I was a different person than I had been at fifteen. I wasn't in love with him, and I wasn't ever going to be in love with him. It was as simple as that.

Just about when I was getting up the nerve to tell Danny that the relationship between us wasn't going to work, I discovered that I was pregnant. I missed my period. I didn't even bother to go to a doctor, because I didn't need confirmation of my diagnosis. I could guess what was wrong with me. I was nauseated all the time. I felt awful. When I told Danny I was pregnant, he offered to marry me, but I thought that was a bad idea, since I already knew I didn't want to marry him. He said, "Okay, I'll see if I can find someone to do an abortion."

It was very illegal, but he found a doctor in Tampa. I believe his name was Martinez. He was from Cuba, and he was a real doctor. It probably took Danny a month or more to find him, and I really have no idea how he did it. I suppose he just kept asking around until someone gave him a name. Because Danny was so supportive—good to me and paying for the abortion and everything—the waiting period wasn't as bad as it could have been, although I continued to feel horrible. I was nauseated all the time, not just in the morning like the books tell you.

I'm not sure how pregnant I was when I finally got to the doctor. At least two months, maybe three. Danny and I went to his office. It was on Buffalo Avenue, which was one of the main streets in Tampa. He examined me and confirmed that I was pregnant. He was very businesslike and appeared to know, without asking, exactly why I was there. There was a whole office full of regular patients, but there were three or four other women also there for abortions.

We were told that they didn't do abortions there in the office and that we were to be taken somewhere else. We had all been examined individually, and we were each told to go out and get into a van parked behind the office. There was a waiting room full of older people and a van full of young women. Pretty obvious to anyone who looked.

Danny was not permitted to get into the van with me. He was told to wait for me at the office. I went out and got into the van with the other women, none of whom I had ever seen before that day. No one spoke. I think we were all terrified. I know I was. Then they blindfolded us. The doctor's nurse explained that the blindfold was so that we would be unable to answer if anyone asked where we had been taken. The doctor didn't go in the van with us. I suppose he had to get rid of any regular patients and lock up the office.

I don't know where we went, but I kind of think it might have been his home. The room where the abortion was done was very clean. It was all white tile and looked like a clinic or a hospital, but I remember that as I lay there, children peeked around the corner at me, and I think that was his family. I remember three rooms. There was a living-room-type situation, where we waited until it was our turn. Then there was the white tile room, and then there was a room with cots.

The doctor gave me something, because I was only semiconscious. It was something in a vein in my arm. Years later, when I had my tubes tied, I had the same kind of thing. They gave you just enough to keep you real groggy but not actually going under. I don't remember much about the actual abortion, but it seemed brief and painless. He had a nurse helping him. I remember that. I noticed that there was blood on the floor and that he acted like a man in a hurry.

Afterward, I was so groggy I had to be helped to a cot. I and all the other women lay on cots for a couple of hours before we left. I don't know if that was so we could "sober up" or to make sure we were all right. He gave each of us a shot of Ergotrate and a shot of penicillin, told us to take it easy and not to have sex for two weeks. He also gave us a phone number to call if we had any bleeding or other problems. Then we were put into the van, blindfolded, and driven back to the office. All this in broad daylight. Wouldn't you think a bunch of blindfolded women would have attracted attention?

Danny was there to meet me. I didn't have any complications, but two or three days later I had a brief hemorrhage type of thing. I called the telephone number I had been given and talked to the nurse. By that time, the bleeding had pretty much stopped. She told me it was probably just a blood clot and that there would probably not be any more bleeding. She was right. The bleeding stopped, and I was fine. I didn't even miss any work, and no one ever found out about it. I kept this doctor's card in case I ever needed him again, although I sure hoped I didn't.

In 1967 I was twenty-seven. I was still in Orlando and still working as a fashion illustrator for the same store. I was just about to be promoted to art director. I had moved several times but was still living alone. By then I was dating the guy I was going to get married to. His name was Jim. My life was really pretty good on all fronts.

I was still psychologically under my mother's influence, and because I was unmarried, there was no way I could have gone to a doctor and admitted that I needed birth control. As a result, we got by on condoms and foam. I was good about using it, since I sure didn't want to ever have another abortion experience. In spite of our faithful use of condoms and foam, however, one morning I woke up nauseated. I knew what that meant. Then I missed my period. Jim and I had talked about marriage before I got pregnant, but neither of us was absolutely sure that's what we wanted to do. Besides, the timing was all wrong. So we started asking around among our friends to see if any of them knew a good abortionist. I had never told Jim about the earlier abortion, so I wasn't about to volunteer the full extent of my knowledge on these matters.

One of our friends was a nurse, and she told us about pills and things that I hadn't known about before. She didn't *do* anything, you understand. She just told me about stuff she had heard of. One of the things she mentioned was quinine, so I tried that. We just bought it at the drugstore without a prescription. It made me sick. I was dizzy, and it did something to my hearing and my eyesight. I think I'd rather have malaria than ever have to take that stuff again.

Jim and I actually even tried to insert something into my uterus. I used a mirror so I could see what I was doing, and I inserted an empty toilet paper cylinder so I could have a better view of my cervix. First we tried plastic tubing—you know, the kind you buy at a pet store to clean the fish tank. We put soap on the end and tried to insert it, but it was too limp. It would just bend. Then we got a knitting needle. It was stiff enough, but it hurt too much, so we gave up on that approach. Jim tried to help, but he was even more squeamish than I was.

Finally I admitted to myself that none of these things were

going to work and that I had to try to reach the doctor in Tampa. I just told Jim that I had heard of this doctor in Tampa and had gotten his telephone number from a friend. In a way, that was certainly true.

I called, and Dr. Martinez was still there. The up-front fee was six hundred dollars in cash. Jim and I had to go to Beneficial Finance to get the money. I told the man at the finance company that I was applying for a vacation loan—a "vacation" to Tampa, Florida, on a Saturday afternoon. Some vacation, as it turned out. The guy at the finance company kept saying, "Listen, you don't have to tell me what this is for." It was almost as if he knew. It took me years to pay off that loan.

Jim and I went to Tampa. My appointment was for eleven o'clock on a Saturday morning. I thought it would be like it had been four years earlier, but it wasn't, and that really threw me. I was totally unprepared for what happened to me.

Dr. Martinez had a different office on a different part of Buffalo Avenue. The nurse was different too. I found out later that the other nurse had turned him in to the authorities. He had had more than a little trouble with the police in the intervening four years since my earlier abortion.

When I got there, he gave me a physical, told me I was pregnant, and asked for the six hundred dollars. Then things began to get different and crazy. Instead of going to the van in back of the office, he told me I had to go into town and stand on a certain street corner. He explained that a white station wagon would come by and the driver would ask if I was "Frances Langsdale." That was the fictitious name I had given the doctor when I made my appointment. "You tell him that you are Frances Langsdale and then you get in the car," he instructed me. We're really talking a grade C movie here. I mean, this whole thing was real cloak-and-dagger.

Jim wasn't permitted to go with me in the station wagon. Because he thought the operation would take place at the office and I thought the van would be waiting out back to take us to the doctor's house, Jim and I had agreed that he would take the car and go to a movie or something, meeting me at the office at five p.m. So he was gone. I had no idea how to get into downtown Tampa, and I only had a few dollars. When I somewhat timidly complained to the doctor, he curtly told me to take a cab. I did, and the cab took me to the designated corner. It was not a great part of town, and I felt conspicuous standing there.

After ten or fifteen minutes, a white station wagon pulled up. The driver said, "Are you Frances Langsdale?" I said, "Yes, I am." She said, "Get in," and I did. There were two women already in the car, and we drove around and picked up three more women at three different corners. The driver turned out to also be the nurse-assistant.

Then we drove way out in the middle of nowhere, in the woods somewhere outside of Tampa, to a trailer! Apparently, the doctor had been so harassed that he had decided to go somewhere other than his home to do this. It was a horrible, primitive trailer, with hot and cold running roaches and not much else. It had an abandoned look about it. There was an old stove, and they were trying to boil instruments in a roasting pan on top of it.

Here we were, all jammed into this little trailer: six women, the doctor, and his nurse. There was a living room area and a kitchen area, but they were not real rooms. At one end of the trailer was a bedroom area, and that is where he did the abortions. That wasn't a room either. It just had a curtain over the doorway. Of course, everyone could hear everything that went on behind the curtain. This was a whole lot different than the white-tiled procedure room of four years earlier!

He got us all inside and said, "Okay, who wants to be first?" I knew there was no way I could sit there and let someone else go first while I got more and more terrified, so I volunteered.

There were no obstetrical stirrups or anything. Behind the curtain was a table with two iron rods along each side. He strapped my knees to those rods with wide pieces of rubber. There was no sedation this time, so he was going to try to make absolutely sure that I didn't do any moving. I remember him telling me not to move, no matter what. The nurse was there, holding my hands.

Then he dilated my cervix with the instruments that had been boiling on the stove. That was terribly painful and seemed to take forever. I was determined not to cry or scream. I'm sure I moaned a time or two, but I was very aware of the five frightened women on the other side of the curtain, and I didn't want to make it any worse than it already was for them. He dug me out, and that took about fifteen minutes. Then he gave me two different shots—Ergotrate and penicillin, I suppose—and told me I was done. He gave me a Kotex—no belt or anything—and told me to walk, and to keep walking, for at least forty-five minutes, without stopping or sitting down. No nice white cots this time.

Remember how tiny this living room area was. Well, it's real hard to walk around with four or five people sitting there. Later, as the other women were done, it was even more of a madhouse, with more of us marching around in that tiny area. Of course, the Ergotrate gave you major cramps, so it was really hard to keep walking. You just wanted to curl up in a ball. Some of the women couldn't deal with it, and they just sat down. I kept marching around, because I figured it would make the recovery faster and better.

Finally we were done and the last woman had finished her forty-five-minute forced march. We got back in the station wagon and were driven back to town and the doctor's office. There were several cars in the office parking lot. Jim and other husbands and boyfriends who were also waiting were visibly relieved to see us. Jim was really anxious. It had been five or six hours, and he couldn't imagine what took so long. He was surprised to see that there were so many of us, since he had thought I was the only one.

The hours in the trailer had been among the scariest of my life, I think, and I was awfully glad to get it behind me. I laid around on the couch for two days, but I really had no trouble. I felt terrific! Even if I had been in pain, my sense of euphoria was so overwhelming that I felt wonderful.

The last words the doctor said to me were, "You'll be back!" Well, I determined that no matter what, I would never go through anything like that again, so I did overcome my mother's influence and went to the doctor and got the pill. Later I got an IUD, and when I was forty-two, I got a hysterectomy, so I never had the problem again. I will say that I still can't go into a trailer, even a nice trailer, without feeling frightened. That was a terrifying experience.

You know, Jim thought the trailer abortion took a long time, but look at it this way: if we each paid six hundred dollars, that doctor made thirty-six hundred dollars for six hours of work. The overhead was pretty low too. No fancy office. No malpractice insurance. Not bad money for 1967, and I bet he didn't pay taxes on it either!

RACHEL

I HAD AN ABORTION IN 1968 OR 1969. I was nineteen years old. I can't remember the occupation of my abortionist. He was either a policeman or a barber. I think he was a policeman.

In retrospect, the sleaziest aspect of dealing with the medical community, in my efforts to secure the abortion, was that I first went to a legitimate doctor who *knew* my age. He gave me a pelvic exam to confirm that I was pregnant, and then, knowing my age in advance, he told me he couldn't do an abortion because I was "too young." Why did he do the pelvic exam? What was the point? I can't think of any legitimate reason.

The person who ultimately did the abortion was a black guy who seemed middle-aged—actually in his mid-forties, but when you're nineteen, that's middle-aged. His girlfriend was a nurse. As I said, I think he was a cop. The one thing I absolutely know is that he was not a doctor. The nurse-girlfriend was as close as we got to real medical expertise. However, they were both very nice, and they treated me very well.

My boyfriend's friend's sister had had five abortions with this guy. Now, that isn't a broad-based sample, but it is an in-depth sample. The friend's sister was fine and she had survived five abortions, so he had to be pretty good. He really came highly recommended, so I was pretty confident and not as scared as you'd imagine, given that he wasn't a doctor.

The sleaziest part of my dealings with illegal abortionists was probably the woman who acted as a liaison. The abortion cost two hundred and fifty dollars. The cop got two hundred dollars. The liaison got fifty dollars just for bringing me there. This intermediary wasn't the nurse, she was just another woman. I figured she was probably a friend of my boyfriend's friend's sister. Now, don't misunderstand me. I thought it would cost about seven hundred dollars. I was in college at the time, so money was real tight, but I would have paid anything and done anything. I'm not complaining about the price. It was a bargain. I am complaining about the intermediary exploiting another woman. She had to know what it was like. How could she do it?

There was no conflict in my mind about the abortion decision. The decision was immediate as soon as I realized I was pregnant. It was a time of raging anxiety for me. It was exam time. I remember going to a history professor and asking to be allowed to take the exam later. He said, "Is this a matter of life and death?" I said, "As a matter of fact, it is." He didn't really catch on to what was going on, but he recognized that I thought so, and he respected my feelings.

My gynecologist at the time was a born-again Catholic, and he was pretty horrible. He didn't say much, but he knew what I was going to do. He strongly disapproved, and he let me know it. I take that back. Given who he was and what he believed, he did offer some help. He kept his mouth shut. He didn't come down on me, which is what I expected—even though I wasn't concerned about whether he would tell my parents. They couldn't have stopped me. I would have done a lot—anything, in fact—to terminate this pregnancy. What this Catholic doctor could have done and didn't do was to use his position of authority to criticize or demean me. I would have been very vulnerable to that at the time. He didn't help me, but he didn't do that, and that's important. For the person he was, he did very well.

My relationship with my mother is not too good. We never discussed anything like this. Years later, I asked her what she would have done if I'd told her I was pregnant. Without a moment's hesitation she said, "I would have told you to leave." Wow! Actually, she did tell me to leave when she found out I was having a sexual relationship. I'd say my estimation of her reaction was right on the money. I didn't misjudge her. I knew what I had to do and I did it, without any help from my family.

I was taken to the abortionist by the intermediary. After all, she had to do something to earn her fifty dollars. I wasn't blindfolded, but I was taken on a circuitous route so I wouldn't know where I was. I never thought to insist that my boyfriend come along. It was just me, the fifty-dollar woman, and the driver.

When we got there, the policeman asked if my boyfriend was going to be coming and told me that would be okay. Now, remember, none of my friends or the real doctor are offering that kind of support or any awareness that it might be important to me. This policeman-abortionist was the only one who seemed to care about me and what I might be feeling. I am with two people, the driver and the intermediary, neither of whom I have ever seen before. They don't care what I'm feeling. They don't ask. He cares. He asks. I've got no horror stories to tell. That cop in Newark was probably a better "doctor," particularly in terms of "people skills," than any real doctor I've had before or since.

The driver and the intermediary went into the abortionist's apartment with me because they had to drive me back. I guess it was part of the fifty dollars. It was all very congenial, and they had obviously been there many times before. Jake—that was the cop—and his girlfriend took me into a bedroom. The intermediary and the driver waited out in the living room. I lay down on the bed, and Jake did the abortion, with the nurse-girlfriend assisting. All things considered, it was very well done. I tend not to be an alarmist, and that helps a lot. It could have been pretty gruesome and I still would have done it. I was very fortunate.

I was told, and I don't know if it is true or not, that the procedure was the method used in Scandinavian countries. A catheter was inserted. It stayed with me for three or four days, until it induced labor. The actual insertion of the catheter felt like having an IUD inserted. It hurt. It felt like a hard labor contraction. The conditions weren't sterile, but they obviously took care and did the best they could under the circumstances. For example, the catheter was kept in the freezer. Neither of them wanted to have any repercussions from a botched abortion. Afterward, they were very nice to me. It wasn't like, "Okay, you're done, get out." They told me to take my time until I felt able to leave. Jake had better bedside manners than some doctors I've met.

I felt nauseated from the procedure. I broke into a cold sweat. I ended up staying about an hour. When I left, I still had the catheter in place. Jake told me to leave it there until the pain got really intense. The end of the catheter stuck out about as much as the string on a Tampax so I would be able to pull it out when I thought it was time. Then I was driven back, by the same circuitous route, to where my boyfriend was waiting for me.

Even though I was in college, I was living with my non-understanding mother and my father. I sure couldn't go home. We drove down the Jersey shore and stayed at a motel that was well known among unmarried college students. I began to get cramps, which became more intense and more frequent as the hours went by. I kept pacing back and forth in that tiny motel room, waiting to abort. I was afraid to take the catheter out in case it was too soon, but the pain was really getting pretty bad. We spent the whole weekend there waiting for something to happen. Nothing did. Finally, by Sunday afternoon, we had to check out and go to our respective homes.

I still had the catheter in place, and I was in a lot of pain. On the drive home, we stopped at a restaurant for something to eat. I felt really sick. I made it to the restaurant bathroom and aborted right there. First I passed some tissue that looked like a piece of liver. Then the catheter came out. I was so relieved. The pain pretty much stopped, and I felt wonderful, but even if I had been in terrible pain, I would have felt terrific. It was over. Finally!

I never had any complications or problems, and my parents never found out. My mother was pretty hostile when I got home, because I had stayed out all night for two nights. What was worse, I was obviously with my boyfriend, so it was pretty apparent to her that I had been doing something she didn't approve of. She just never knew what.

After it was all over, I went to my born-again Catholic gynecologist to make sure I was all right. He confirmed that I was fine. I was emotionally and psychologically very relieved and was physically intact.

I had another abortion in 1973. I was twenty-four and had graduated from college. I was living in the Virgin Islands. I flew to Saint Thomas and had a suction abortion at a clinic. It was legal there. Maybe it was also legal in the United States by then, but in Saint Thomas I think it had been legal for a long time, so medical abortion services were widely available and easy to find. My own doctor referred me to the clinic. I didn't have to find three psychiatrists or say I was going to kill myself or any of that business, but I would have if necessary. I'd have done whatever it took. I did before and I would have again.

DISTRICT ATTORNEY
COLVILLE

I AM NOW THE DISTRICT ATTORNEY of Allegheny County, but back in the sixties I was a young beat cop and detective, and in that capacity I had some experiences with illegal abortion.

I joined the police department in 1964. I was a little different because I was a college graduate, and in that day and age it was unusual for a police officer to be a college graduate. That first year on the job, I didn't even let anyone know I was a college graduate, because I was afraid I would be shunned. I was also a law student. That combination led to some special advancement opportunities for me. In 1966 I got an opportunity to transfer to the detective bureau, which I did.

In the sixties the detective bureau didn't aggressively seek out complaints about abortionists, but we actively went after them when we did get complaints. Sometimes informants would lead us to abortionists, but the reverse was also true. We would use the abortionists to lead us to other people. Even though abortion cases weren't sought out, when one came in, you didn't divert it or downplay it, no matter who or what. We dealt with all of them.

I remember one occasion very vividly because it was almost a real disaster. An abortion case arose in the Hill District on Whiteside Road, which was the site of a giant housing project.

As I recall, it was in 1966. At the time I was a young and fairly inexperienced homicide detective. I had worked the Northside as a patrol officer, so they might have recognized me there, but I had never worked the Hill District, and there I was an unknown. Precisely because I was young and unknown, I was right for this particular case.

It seems that a young woman had died in Johnstown, Pennsylvania, from an illegal abortion. The information the Allegheny County Detective Bureau received was that this young woman had gotten the abortion from a woman in McKeesport but that the woman had now moved her operation to the Hill District. The abortionist had no medical background that I was aware of.

Someone other than me had made the telephone contact with the abortionist and scheduled the appointment. A young female police officer was to masquerade as the pregnant woman who wanted the abortion. My assignment was to pass as the boyfriend who had gotten her into trouble. Now, this abortionist had a husband who had a substantial record of aggravated assaults on police officers, as well as assaults on other people. My supervisors showed me a mug shot of this guy and said, "If he's there, be very careful. He is dangerous."

I left all my police equipment—gun, blackjack, handcuffs, identification, everything—at home, because I was supposed to be a boyfriend, not a cop. The young female officer and I—her name was Angela—were to go together in my car. Behind us, in an unmarked police car, were to be two backup detectives. As we were ready to walk out the door, one of the backup detectives asked me if I had any kind of weapon at all. When I told him I didn't, he insisted that I take his blackjack so I would at least have a weapon of some sort, in case I needed it. So I stuck the blackjack down the front of my pants, hanging by the strap. I also had some marked money that I was to use to pay for the abortion.

The abortionist had instructed Angela and me to meet her on a particular street corner at ten a.m. on the day of the appointment. However, we knew nothing about our ultimate destination. The two backup officers were to follow us wherever the abortionist ended up taking us. They had to be hidden but close enough that they could hear us yell if we needed help.

Angela and I got into my car and started on our way. By happenstance, an accident occurred behind us and the backup car couldn't get past it. They lost us! I hadn't seen the accident happen, so I didn't even know there was a problem.

We pulled into Whiteside. It was an all-black community, and here we were, two whites—very conspicuous. The woman met us on the street corner as arranged. She was black and looked to be in her late forties but could have been younger. She took us to her apartment. She was on the second or third floor, and we went up a spiral staircase made of cement and steel. Hers was a typical housing project apartment. First you went through a metal door. They all have metal doors. As we walked into the apartment, on our left was the kitchen. Sitting at the kitchen table were four guys playing cards, and one of them was the guy in the mug shot—you know, the one who was always assaulting police officers.

The apartment was clean—no dirty dishes stacked up or anything like that. To the right was a living room. We went into the living room, and off that room were two doors leading into bedrooms. I didn't yet know that they were bedrooms, but I was pretty sure they were. It was a typical efficiency apartment in the projects, and I had been in hundreds of them as a beat patrolman. Some were cleaner than others or in better condition, but basically those apartments all looked pretty much alike.

I explained that I was the boyfriend and that I was paying for the abortion. I showed her the money—three hundred dollars, as I recall. I didn't give her the money at that point, I just flashed it. I told her that I wanted an explanation of what was going to happen, because I felt a responsibility toward the young woman I had "gotten into trouble."

She went into one of the bedrooms and came out with some things to show me. First she had a little metal box, the kind that throat lozenges come in, but there weren't any throat lozenges in it then. She opened it up, and inside were white tablets, which she told me were penicillin tablets. She said that she would use a catheter, and she had four different types which she showed to me. These were of different thicknesses, which she said went from ten to fourteen centimeters. They all had thin metal wires running up inside them. She also showed me a straightened-out coat hanger that had been filed so that it had a sharp point on one end. Although she explained to me what all these different things were for, I don't recall now under which circumstances she used what instrument.

She told us that the procedure would take a very short period of time and that Angela would be able to leave with me as soon as it was over. She motioned toward the bedroom, and both of us got up and started over to the door. Then the abortionist indicated that only Angela was to follow her and that I was to wait in the living room. Well, I was not about to allow this young policewoman out of my sight, especially with those four men in the kitchen, so I yelled, "Stop! I'm a police officer and you are under arrest." I tried to grab the abortionist, who got very agitated as soon as I revealed who I was. She put up quite a struggle, and the two of us were actually down on the floor wrestling. I had no handcuffs and no way of containing her except by holding her.

The very second the four guys at the table heard me say I was a police officer, they leapt up and fell all over each other trying to get out the front door at the same time. Thank God they did! At that point we didn't know that we had no backup. Unarmed, we would have been no match for those five people, plus whatever friends they had in the neighborhood who felt like getting involved.

When the backup officers realized that they had lost us, they really panicked, knowing we were unarmed. They knew we were somewhere in Whiteside, but that place was a real maze. It was a very complex housing project, and it would be impossible to figure out where we were if you hadn't watched us go. They knew what corner we were to meet the abortionist on, but once we had been picked up, they had no idea where the abortionist would take us. All the backup officers knew was what my car looked like. They had called the police station and reported that there were two unarmed officers lost somewhere in White-side and that we were with an abortionist whose husband had a propensity for violence.

So here we were in the apartment, not yet knowing that we had no backup. The four men had left, and I was still trying to contain this struggling, angry abortionist. To try to hold some-one who doesn't want to be held, for any protracted period, without doing serious injury to them, is a very difficult thing to do. I yelled for Angela to go get our backup to help us subdue this woman and control the situation. I figured that they were right outside somewhere, and I wondered why they didn't burst in when they heard all the commotion.

Well, on the off chance that they weren't already long gone, Angela decided to actually chase the four guys out into the street and—she thought—into the arms of the waiting backup. The four men were nowhere in sight, which was lucky for her, since neither was the backup. When she discovered there was no backup, she began to yell at the top of her lungs. By that time the station had police officers all through Whiteside try-ing to find us. As soon as they heard her, they all came run-ning. There were cops all over the place, and these were uni-formed guys, not just the plainclothes backup, who were also looking for us.

We went to trial on this case. Before the trial, the abortion-ist's lawyer asked me if I was going to testify that his client actu-ally touched Angela—that is, actually started to do the abor-tion. I said, "No. That didn't happen, because I arrested her before she could start." The law in those days was that they had to touch you and begin to do something to cause the abortion, so what she ended up being convicted of was solicitation to do an abortion. On the attempted abortion charge, she was found not guilty.

In 1967 or 1968 I had another case with an abortionist, and this one was a white male doctor. We went after him with the same vigor that we had used on that black female non-doctor abortionist. This doctor was an osteopath, and I remember that his mother kept his books for him. In addition to abortions, he fixed a lot of bullet wounds that he didn't bother to report—stuff like that.

This particular time he did an abortion on a young girl and she died. He had injected some solution into her uterus, and it killed her. The problem was that he hit a vein, and this solution, whatever it was, got into her heart or brain or whatever, and she died instantly. I remember standing there when the autopsy was being done. It was a heartbreaker. She was a young woman in her early twenties. To me she looked young and attractive—the flower of American womanhood. There was just one problem. She was dead.

The doctor just had this woman sort of dumped into a hospital after she went into shock. At that point we didn't know that this doctor had done it, and since she was dead, she couldn't tell us. I was given a tip that she had had a prescription filled at a certain drugstore and that the prescription was written on blue paper, which was odd and memorable since most were on white paper. When we went through the pharmacist's prescriptions, there it was—a script from the osteopath, for the dead girl, on the telltale blue paper. So we were able to arrest him.

At the trial his mother testified that she was his receptionist at the office and that on the day in question this woman had not been there. The jury believed her, and this guy walked. That was a bad thing. This young woman should not have died, and this guy should not have beaten the rap.

In an earlier era there was a much greater police tolerance toward abortion. Because my father was a police officer, I had the opportunity to talk to him and his friends about what police work was like a generation earlier. Back in the forties, it was not unheard-of for the police officer to act as a sort of intermediary, if you will, and to actually arrange the abortion. That was perceived as the way to go, and in some ways it made sense. The police would know who in the community was doing abortions and who was good and who was not so good. This difference in abortion attitudes had a lot to do with what police were like in the sixties versus the forties. During that twenty-year period, police departments underwent major changes in attitudes and in professionalization. As they became more professional, they lost a lot of their political nature—and there is both good and bad to that.

In the sixties, you got hired as a police officer because of *what* you knew. You had to take a test. But in the forties, you got hired because of *who* you knew. If you were a police officer under the political system, you had probably been hired by the ward or precinct political leader, the political power broker in that neighborhood. Your chief responsibility in those days was to be aware of the community's needs and see that those needs were met in the best possible way. If prostitution or gambling or abortion was a need, you looked the other way, even though they were all crimes. But you only looked the other way for the cleanest and safest operators, because you wanted to meet those community needs in the cleanest and safest way. The police officer appointed by the political boss was very much a part of the community. It isn't like that today.

In the 1960s, all over the nation, police departments began to standardize their operations and to use testing as a means of deciding who got hired. The police officer didn't come out of a particular neighborhood and didn't have loyalty to anyone in the neighborhood. Those changes in police hiring and training affected how police responded to the presence of an abortionist in the neighborhood. Under the new order, if you received complaints about abortionists, you went after them, no matter who they were or where they lived.

I'm not sure that this professionalization I'm talking about is necessarily the best thing that we could be doing for our communities, because in a sense we have become "isolationists." For example, I am not as willing to give a particular community what they think they need as I might have been if I had been part of the old system.

Almost never was the woman the one who contacted the police. When she went to the hospital, she was interested in solving her own fairly serious medical problems. That's all she cared about. She didn't see herself as the victim of a crime. If anything, she saw herself as a criminal. So usually the hospital or the doctor, rather than the woman, would be the one calling us. It was unusual for someone to call us if she didn't die, but that did happen sometimes. Knowing that a woman had just had an abortion, a Catholic hospital might be more likely to call the police than a secular hospital that tended to view it solely as a medical problem. Her family wasn't about to call us either, unless she died. They were usually trying to cover up the real reason she was in the hospital, and sometimes even the real reason she died.

Some district attorneys think that their function is to investigate certain types of crime—really to conduct a "war" on this or that. For example, one of my predecessors saw it as his role to rid the county of pornography. I don't see it that way. I see our office's function as prosecuting alleged crimes brought to us, not ferreting them out. I believe that we are not the "moral police" and we shouldn't be. To the extent that district attorneys have different philosophies, that difference is going to influence the types of matters they are using their resources on, and that affects how law enforcement agencies will respond to illegal abortionists. What causes crime to go up and down is not a function of any law enforcement agency. It's a function of society and the resources that are out there for people—schools, health care, things like that.

Since abortion became legal in 1973, I don't recall a single prosecution of an illegal non-doctor abortionist. Now all of our involvement is with cases arising out of the protesters. I can't imagine that there are any illegal abortionists in Allegheny County now, for the simple reason that they couldn't make a living. No woman is going to choose one of those people if she has any other choice.

ATTORNEY SAM

I HAVE BEEN AN ATTORNEY FOR MANY YEARS. In the late sixties I represented a doctor accused of abortion. I got him off and that's good, because I'm sure he didn't do it. I had known this doctor for about five years at the time he was arrested. As I recall, I had originally met him through clients of mine who were patients of his. His reputation was that he was sort of a man-about-town.

At the trial, the woman's boyfriend testified that she had called the doctor, my client, and made an appointment for six in the evening. The appointment was duly recorded in the doctor's appointment book. The boyfriend said that he drove her to my client's office. Shortly after she went in, she came out. Then, according to him, she complained that she was not feeling well and that she wanted to go home to the apartment they shared. He testified that about two hours later, saying that she still didn't feel well, she asked him to take her to the hospital, which he did. He said that they got to the hospital about eight-fifteen or eight-thirty that night and that she was dead when they arrived.

On cross-examination, I established that the boyfriend didn't know what had taken place in the doctor's office, that they left the doctor's office no later than six-fifteen that night, and that they stayed at their apartment until about eight-fifteen, when he took her to the hospital. He was alone with her for that two-hour period. The boyfriend also admitted—and this was important—that during that two-hour period she was talking coherently to him and was lucid. He said that she was talking right up to the time they got to the hospital parking lot.

The next witness for the prosecution was the coroner, who testified that the cause of death was the injection of tincture of green soap. Now, my client had tincture of green soap in his office, but so do most doctors and many individuals as part of a household first-aid kit. Tincture of green soap is cheap and readily available at any drugstore. The soap solution had been forced up into the uterus in such a manner that the instrument used to inject it had perforated the uterine wall and entered a major vein. When the soap got into the bloodstream, it was carried to her heart. The cause of death was a massive soap embolism in her heart.

My medical expert looked at the autopsy report and explained to the jury how swiftly the soap embolus would have been carried to her heart once it entered the bloodstream. Death would result very quickly, in a matter of minutes, certainly no more than fifteen minutes at the outside. If it had happened as the prosecution maintained, this young woman would have died in my client's office or in the boyfriend's car before they ever got back home. She never could have lived and talked for two hours. The autopsy report showed that her heart was literally filled with soapsuds.

Then my client testified in his own behalf. He said yes, that the woman had an appointment at six p.m. and that her boyfriend brought her. The boyfriend waited in the waiting room while she went into his office. He examined her and determined that she was pregnant. When he told her that, she asked him to do an abortion. He said no, that he didn't do things like that. Besides, he said, it was against the law. She and her boyfriend left, and he never saw her again.

All the prosecution had was the doctor's bottle of green soap that any household might have had, an appointment book, a dead woman who couldn't tell what happened, and an autopsy report that told how she died but not who did it. My client was acquitted. A few years later he did get arrested and convicted for illegal drug sales. He actually went to jail for that. When he got out, he left town, so I'm not sure what happened to him. I think he ultimately got his license back and is practicing medicine today.

But let me tell you who I think did the abortion that killed this young woman. Both the coroner and my medical expert testified that it was a very amateurish job, not professional. I think you can conclude that it was not what you would expect from a doctor or any person with that much medical training. Although he was never charged with it, I believe the boyfriend did it. All the facts fit. They went to the doctor, he turned them down. In two hours they probably couldn't have found anyone else. Besides, he testified that they were alone. I think they bought the soap and a syringe or enema bag or something readily available at a drugstore, and then he did it. Oh, maybe she asked him all right, but he did it. Who spent the last two hours of her life with her? Given the way she died, who spent the last critical fifteen minutes with her? He did.

Some people would look at this and say, "What a good defense." That it was. But I think what this case illustrates is that desperate people do desperate things, sometimes with tragic results. It all fits. When they couldn't get medical help, they just did what they desperately thought was the next-best thing.

COMMONWEALTH V. PAGE

CENTRE COUNTY, IN THE MOUNTAINS of central Pennsylvania, has a population of 112,760 people. It was established in 1800 and named for its location in the state. The county seat, with a population of approximately 6,000, is Bellefonte—French for "beautiful spring"—a name said to have been suggested by the French statesman Talleyrand. It is in Bellefonte that trials are held.

Centre County's main "industry" is Penn State University, located in State College. Founded in 1855, and now with a student population in excess of 30,000, it is the oldest and largest of the campuses in the state university system. The presence of thousands of college students changes the entire demographic makeup of the county in some highly relevant ways. There are also some surprising demographic inconsistencies.

It is perhaps not surprising that Centre County is the most highly educated county in the state. Between 24.0 percent and 27.5 percent of the people in the county age twenty-five or older have four years or more of college. The statewide average is only 13.6 percent. Also not surprising is the fact that the median age in Centre County is the youngest in the state—less than twenty-five. Similarly, the county has the fewest people age sixty-five and older, and the highest percentage—39.4—of single women age fifteen and older. Yet in spite of its plethora of presumably fertile young people, it has the lowest fertility rate—number of births per 1,000 women in their fertile years—of any county in the state.

It is true that unmarried females who choose to continue their pregnancies may well leave college. However, if we concede the probability that college students have a higher than average incidence of sexual activity, the disproportionately low fertility rate suggests the effective use of contraception—and also of abortion, if we find no reason to believe that college students are more skilled than the general population in using contraceptives.

Into this environment came Barry Graham Page, a man with two occupations—motorcycle mechanic and abortionist. It was the second that was to bring him notoriety and trouble.

Some say that an abortionist in a university town is like a gambler in Atlantic City, a pig in mud, a fox in the hen house, that there is more business than one person can handle. In any event, it was for doing abortions on college students that Barry Graham Page was arrested. The story first made the headlines on June 13, 1968. Two Penn State University students were involved, and although neither of the young women died, one was hospitalized for several days as a result of a septic abortion. At the trial, Janet H. described her encounter with Mr. Page.

> I am eighteen years old and a student at Penn State. A friend, another college student, called him for me. Then she put me on the phone. In that first phone conversation, I didn't really tell him anything. He asked if I had a problem and I said I did. He said he could take care of it and I gave him my dorm phone number.
>
> Well, he called me at my dorm and asked me how pregnant I was. I told him I thought about two months. We set up a date for me to go to his house and have the operation. He told me how much it would cost—$225—and asked if I could get that much money. We agreed that I would pay $100 when he did the abortion and $125 when he brought me back to the dorm. As it turned out, I paid $100 at the time and only $120 later.
>
> I was at his house on two separate occasions in 1968—June

3rd and June 8th. The first time was a Monday around 10 at night and the second time was the next Saturday afternoon. At the first meeting on Monday night, my friend Marilee E. was with me. Mr. Page picked us up and took us to his house. We just talked. We had a few drinks, because he thought it would relax me. He kissed me. I didn't resist when he kissed me.

The second meeting, on Saturday afternoon, is when he did the abortion. No girlfriend was with me that time. Again, he talked to me for a while to relax me. Then we went into his bathroom and I took off my clothes from the waist down. He had me lie on the floor on my back. My heels were on the floor and my ankles were pulled up close to my body.

He had this red bowl that was filled with a soapy solution. He said it was 75% soapy water, but he wouldn't tell me what the rest of it was. Then he took this long rubber tube which had a bulb on one end, so that, when it was filled with a solution, it could be forced out. Then, on the other end was a syringe-type thing, about as thick as my arm. He inserted the long rubber thing into my vagina. The liquid went inside me and that's all there was to it.

He took me back to the dorm and I paid him all but $5 of the money I owed him. He told me that, if this was going to work, in about 24 hours I would have some cramps and then I would miscarry. He guaranteed that his method would work, but cautioned me that it might take more than one treatment.

I went out with my boyfriend that night and came home quite late. Then I started getting cramps and bleeding. One of my friends in the dorm called an ambulance, which took me first to the university dispensary and then to the hospital.

Marilee E. described her experiences with Barry Graham Page in similar fashion.

I am 21 years old and I am a nursing student at Penn State. I heard about Mr. Page from one of my girlfriends at school. She heard about him from another girl named Yvonne, who worked in a downtown movie theater. I called Yvonne. She took my name and telephone number and told me she would have Mr. Page call me. He did and that is when we talked about money and about how pregnant I was. The charge was $150 and I was to pay him $75 now and the other half after the operation. He asked me how pregnant I was and I told him ten or twelve weeks.

I had made arrangements for him to come to the dorm and pick me up and take me to his house to do the abortion. When I got to his house, we went immediately to the kitchen. We sat at the kitchen table. I was very nervous and he got me a cigarette and a drink to help relax me. He thought that, if we sat and talked for a while first, I would relax. It's true. I was really tense and needed to try to relax.

We sat and drank and smoked and talked for a total of about three hours. It is true that I had sex with Mr. Page. When he did the abortion procedure, he was dressed only in his underwear. When we were sitting in the kitchen drinking and talking, after about an hour Mr. Page said he felt very uncomfortable with his clothes on and that he wanted to take them off. Then he took his trousers and his shirt off, but he did leave his underwear on. We sat there for another two hours talking. Then I gave him the money I had brought with me. He explained what he was going to do and what I should expect afterward.

Then he took me into the bathroom and told me to undress from the waist down and to lie down on my back on the bathroom floor. Next, he showed me the equipment, which was a red bowl and a bulb-type syringe with tubing and a sort of nozzle attached to the tubing. Then he did the procedure. It took about 15 or 20 minutes. It was not really painful, but it was mildly uncomfortable because it caused a certain amount of pressure. After that, he took me home.

Nothing happened that weekend. He called me on Sunday afternoon to see what was going on. When I told him that I was still waiting for something to happen, he explained that it would take a second treatment. We arranged that I would go back on Monday night at 10 p.m. Janet went with me just to keep me company. He redid the procedure exactly like he had done it three days earlier. This time it worked, and, on Tuesday night at about 10:30, I aborted.

Next, State Police Officer Smith testified. He was the one who arrested Barry Graham Page and searched his house for abortion paraphernalia.

The date was June 12, 1968. We received a call from the Centre County Hospital medical staff. It seems that one of their patients, Janet, had told them that Mr. Page did her abortion. We went to Mid-State Motors where Mr. Page worked as a mechanic. He was there and we arrested him.

Immediately after his arrest, we took him to his house and served him with the search warrant. He looked at the warrant and just said, "What you are looking for is in the bathroom." When we looked in the bathroom, there was the red bowl, the tubing, and the syringe, just as the witnesses described.

Dr. Clair, who treated Janet at Centre County Hospital, also testified about her medical condition.

I saw Janet in May of 1968. Her last menstrual period was March 28, 1968. Her pregnancy test was positive. She was not seen again in our office.

On June 9, 1968, I got a call from the university dispensary that they had a patient up there who was very ill with what we call a "septic abortion." That is an infected miscarriage.

She had peritonitis. Her abdomen was tender and she jumped when even gentle pressure was applied. There was still tissue in the uterus and she was infected. She had a temperature of 100 degrees at that point. The official diagnosis was "incomplete septic abortion."

Unfortunately, this is a condition I have seen many times. It is typical for a patient to have an infected incomplete abortion if she was aborted by someone who didn't use sterile techniques. The pelvis can withstand some infection. However, in her case, there must have been a lot of contamination when the procedure was done to create such a massive infection.

On October 21, 1968, Barry Graham Page pleaded guilty to the charge of performing abortions. On December 9, 1968, he was fined one thousand dollars and sentenced to the state penitentiary for not less than two or more than five years. Having pleaded guilty, he did not appeal his conviction based on anything that happened at his trial. While he was in jail, however, he became aware of other court cases around the country in which people were making the argument that their state's abortion law was constitutionally defective and unenforceable. On March 4, 1970, from jail, Mr. Page filed a petition for postconviction relief, alleging that the existing Pennsylvania abortion law, which essentially dated from 1860, violated the constitutions of both Pennsylvania and the United States. The arguments he used were similar to those eventually upheld by the Supreme Court in *Roe v. Wade*.

On July 23, 1970, the trial judge, who made no secret of his displeasure over mechanics performing abortions in his county, reluctantly agreed with Mr. Page. The judge held that Pennsylvania's abortion law was an unconstitutional invasion of the right of individual and marital privacy guaranteed by the Bill of Rights and the Fourteenth Amendment to the United States Constitution. He also found it "so broad, unlimited and indiscriminate that it invades areas which the state has no compelling interest in or right to regulate and is therefore unconstitutional." That made the law unenforceable in Centre County, with the anomalous result that abortion was now illegal in only sixty-six of Pennsylvania's sixty-seven counties. In Centre County there was no longer a law against it. It seemed that the county was to be a leader of sorts. And as it turned out, Barry Graham Page had done something special for the women of Centre County. He was later to do something special for the women of the other sixty-six counties, when the Pennsylvania Supreme Court found for him.

BARRY GRAHAM PAGE

I AM FIFTY-SEVEN YEARS OLD NOW. I was in my late twenties and early thirties when I was doing abortions. I gave all that up when I got arrested, and I have never done another one since. It was over twenty years ago, but my memories are still very vivid even though I try never to think about those days, which were not a good time in my life. And there is no need to think about it now, not anymore. It seems very far away, that time when we did abortions like that.

I grew up in England and Wales and didn't come to this country until I was an adult. Medicine was always a part of my family background. My mother was the director of nurses in a Birmingham hospital. During my early childhood days, as a toddler and up, my "playground" was the hospital. My mother was what they called a theater nurse, so she was in the operating room a lot. I was around there a lot myself—not really inside, of course, but around. She was also the district nurse for the town, and the midwife as well, so I just got constant exposure to medical things.

My mother was very much against abortion. We weren't Catholic, she just thought it was morally wrong. I was raised to believe the same thing, but I guess with me it didn't take. I never did buy my mother's values on abortion. It's not that I once thought it was wrong and then changed my mind, it's that I never felt the way she did, not really.

In 1952, when I turned seventeen, I went into the merchant navy, as it's called in England. On some of the smaller ships I would be the only one on board who knew anything at all about medicine or even about first aid. If anyone got hurt, I was always the one bandaging him up. My formal education is high school, merchant navy training school, and many schools and classes in motorcycles, cars, auto mechanics—anything having to do with cars.

I came to the United States in October of 1958. I was twenty-three, and I was married to an American woman. We settled in New York City. I found a job working as a motorcycle messenger. What I did was to pick up film from all the famous New York photographers and take it to the lab to be developed. Then I brought it back. A motorcycle was quite a quick way to do it. My wife and I got divorced in 1960, and by then I was living in Philadelphia. I was a mechanic for a Harley-Davidson motorcycle dealership, taking care of all of their European bikes. I also raced for them.

Philadelphia is where I did my first abortion. It was in 1961. I did it for married friends of mine who had three children and just didn't want any more. In those days it was not easy to get sterilized if your only reason was that you didn't want more kids. My friend in Philadelphia said, "Barry, my wife's pregnant again, and all the abortionists around here use knitting needles and coat hangers, and I don't know what to do." I said, "Hey, there's a lot easier way of doing it, and it's a lot safer too. All you need is a Higginson's syringe and some soap and water." I didn't get paid for that first abortion. I did it for nothing, as a favor.

At the time I had never watched anyone do an abortion or read anything about how to do an abortion. Even so, I wasn't particularly scared. Although it was the first time, I felt pretty confident, what with the fact that I'd been around doctors all my life. I'd been planning to go to medical school in England, but my math wasn't good enough and I couldn't get in, so I had to give it up. But I always read a lot of medical stuff, and I was a male nurse in Capetown, South Africa, for a while. I never had any gynecology experience during any of this, because males weren't even allowed in the operating room when the patient was a woman. Only the doctor got in. I just used common sense, I guess. I sort of put two and two together and figured it out. Somehow, I just did it.

I always used the same technique in every abortion I did. I used a Higginson's syringe, which can't even be found anymore. It's an old-fashioned enema syringe with a bulb in the center that you squeeze and let go of, like on a blood pressure cuff. There's a one-way valve on each end of the bulb. When you pressed, it would blow out, and when you let go, it would suck in from the other end, very much like a siphoning thing that you can get for cars. I used a solution of Ivory soap and water, and I boiled it for twenty minutes. I also boiled the syringe for twenty minutes to sterilize it. I don't know how good that was, but it was the best I could do under the circumstances. I would just barely touch the end of the cervix and then insert the tiniest bit of this lukewarm soapy water. I knew that any foreign object entering the womb would cause an abortion, *if* it was done early enough in pregnancy. It can only be done up through nine or maybe ten weeks of pregnancy, no more. It doesn't work after that point, but it doesn't do any damage either.

I did a few more abortions in Philadelphia, probably no more than five, and all for married couples I knew. Originally I did it strictly to help someone. Later I did it for the money, which was too good to resist.

I moved to State College in 1964. At first I didn't do any abortions. Instead I bought a motorcycle dealership. I stayed in and around that area until 1972. Then I moved to New York, where I still live.

I got started doing abortions in State College after I had a bad motorcycle accident and lost my business because I was laid up so long and couldn't work. By 1967 I was working for

Grand Prix Motors in State College. This man came into the shop one day and asked for me by name. That sort of surprised me. He was a graduate student at Penn State. It seems that he or friends of his knew someone in Philadelphia that I had done an abortion for. He explained that his cousin—she really was his cousin—was a freshman at Penn State. She had only been there about three months, I think. She was pregnant and didn't want to be. He said that he knew I had helped people in Philadelphia and asked if I would be willing to help his cousin. I had no problem trusting this guy even though he was a total stranger. When he mentioned my friends in Philadelphia, I knew it was what I would call a direct connection, and I just assumed he was on the up-and-up. He said, "I'll give you three hundred dollars if you'll do this for me."

I talked to the girl and asked her how far along she thought she was. She said, "I'm coming up to missing my second period." I figured it was just the trials and tribulations of being away from home and being in a big school and all that, so I suggested that maybe it was just stress-related and she ought to wait and see if she was really pregnant. Well, she wasn't going to have any part of that. She wasn't waiting, and she insisted that she was pregnant. She said she'd never missed her period before. She'd had her first one at age twelve, and one every twenty-eight days after that, just like clockwork until last month. Oh, she was sure, all right, real sure! So I said, "Okay, I'll help you out." I figured this was pretty nice. The money was good, and the work was easy and quick. I had remarried by then, so being unemployed was hurting more than just me. I had a family to support, so I went ahead and did it and never had any problems.

In State College I got busier and busier with abortions as more and more people called. Soon I had to start turning some people down. But I began to worry. With this many people, I reasoned, something had to go wrong. It just had to. As it happened, my "career" as a campus abortionist turned out to be fairly short. The cousin was in 1967, and I was arrested in 1968. I had probably done another eight to ten abortions during that period.

With those next eight or ten women, I tried to be pretty careful about screening them so I wouldn't be set up. But you know, they were all so desperate and would tell such a sad story that I never really thought about being set up. My rule was that the girls had to be referred by someone I knew. It was a sort of word-of-mouth thing. If Sally Smith said that Mary Jones sent her, and if I thought Mary Jones had been trustworthy, I'd agree to do Sally Smith. Of course, that necessarily meant also trusting Sally Smith. A lot of it would be from one dorm, because a girl would refer her roommate or the girl across the hall or her best friend, that kind of thing. It wasn't like they just came to me cold. My name wasn't all over town or anything like that. It was very discreet. I charged three hundred to five hundred dollars, depending on who it was, but five hundred was the top. I got that if I could. None of these women but the last one ever got infections, or any other complication either. And until the last two, none of them ever reported me.

The technique I used was pretty good. I only remember one time when I had to repeat the abortion because it didn't work the first time. That was for one of the two girls who took me to court, and the reason that happened is this. Usually when I was using the syringe, the woman would start to get a cramp when the fluid went in. As soon as she got a cramp I'd stop instantly, because that was enough. In twenty-four or forty-eight hours, she would just abort. This girl who went to the hospital— Janet—had asked me how much pain was involved. I said, "You get cramps like your period. Just think of your worst period, and that's what it will be like." Little did I know that this young woman had never had menstrual cramps in her whole life, not once! Well, when she got the abortion cramps in the dorm, she got real scared. She was sure that something terrible had to be wrong because it was nothing like she'd expected and nothing like she thought I'd told her to expect. She panicked, and then her friends panicked and took her to the hospital. The hospital said it was an "incomplete abortion." Maybe it was only incomplete because she panicked too soon.

Janet went to the hospital on a Saturday night or Sunday,

and they arrested me on a Monday. I learned from a friend of mine that she was actually questioned under sodium pentothal—you know, "truth serum"—because they gave her that when they did the D and C. She only knew my first name, so I'm not sure how they put it together. Maybe she described where I lived, or maybe there just weren't too many Barrys around at the time. I'll never know.

My wife knew I was doing abortions because I was doing them at the house. It wasn't like some of the newspapers said— that I was doing them in the back of a motorcycle shop. Some of the news stories were really awful, a lot of sensational, untrue stuff. My wife didn't approve or disapprove. It didn't make any difference to her. She just liked to spend the money.

I have no idea who this Yvonne at the movie theater was— the one who's supposed to have given my name to Marilee. I never heard of her, but I suppose more people had heard of me than I realized.

I'm almost glad I got arrested when I did. I got to thinking, "Good God! What'll I do if something happens?" If anything had happened during the abortion, I'd have brought the girl right to the hospital and taken the consequences, I really would have. But what if someone lied to me? What if I got a girl who was a hemophiliac? If she didn't tell me I would never know, and she might just go back to the dorm and bleed to death. Abortion is a simple procedure, and things like that shouldn't happen, but under those conditions something was just bound to happen.

The police came to where I was working. It was still in the same building, but it was called Mid-State Harley-Davidson. They arrested me right there. I was stunned. I had no idea it was coming. They took me to my house, showed me the search warrant, and started looking for evidence. The state trooper was a young fellow I knew really well. In the car on the way to my house he said, "Boy, they really got you cold on this one, Barry!" I didn't say anything like they do on TV—"I want to talk to my lawyer"—I just said something like, "What's going on?" I still believed that nobody had ever been put in jail in Pennsylvania for doing abortions, so I wasn't as worried as I should have been. The police said, "We want to search the house." I said, "Fine, no problem," since I thought no one ever went to jail for this.

The police had a list of stuff they were looking for, like a red bowl. They said, "This stuff, where do you keep it? Do you want to tell us, or do we have to find it?" I said, "No, I'll tell you. It's in the bathroom." Unfortunately, I had left the bowl—and it was a very distinctive bright red ceramic bowl—in the bathroom cupboard, and I hadn't dumped it out. That was so stupid! The Higginson's syringe was still in it. It wasn't at all hard for the police to figure out. What's worse, the solution had jelled. You know how soap jells? Well, there it was, with the syringe still partially filled, still in the bowl, and the whole thing looked like it had been cast in bronze or cement or something, just waiting for the police to arrive! A clean, empty bowl in the kitchen, or even in the bathroom, might have had some legitimate non-abortion purpose, but not this thing! I had never left stuff dirty before, and to this day, I can't figure out how that happened.

They took the bowl, and then they started rummaging through the basement. That was really awful. We had had some problems with the sump pump in the basement. It hadn't worked right, and stuff had gotten on all kinds of newspapers and magazines that were stored down there. It was a really gloppy mess, because all the wet paper that needed to be thrown out had started to disintegrate. The police didn't know what this mess was. They thought it was some horrible thing related to abortion. They were so stupid about it—couldn't even recognize wet newspaper! I'd bet that some of them had a broken sump pump somewhere in their own lives, but they were busy bagging all this wet newspaper as "evidence." Oh, well. That was one way to get it out of my basement! Unfortunately, they didn't take it all, and they sure did leave an awful mess behind. They even pumped the septic tank and all kinds of crazy stuff, but that was dumb too, because no one ever actually aborted at my house. That wasn't how my method worked.

I didn't lose my job, even with all the bad publicity, because I'd become a partner in the business, so that wasn't a problem. Several of my close friends, including my business partner, knew about the abortions before I got arrested and it didn't bother them. My wife knew, but once I got arrested that was the end of the marriage. We separated, and I got an apartment in State College.

About the woman who said I had sex with her—well, that's true, but it's not at all like it sounded at the trial. I started to go out with her *after* I was arrested and *after* my wife and I were separated, when I had my apartment. I was out on bond, working at my same job and waiting for my trial. Marilee and I dated a few times then. I told you I didn't understand why she ever got involved at the trial, since she never had any problems. Maybe the police made her do it. I still don't understand.

After the arrest I was out on bail, and life went on pretty much as it had before. A few people were up in arms, but most people were supportive. When I was in jail in Pittsburgh, waiting for them to decide which state correctional institution was appropriate, one of the prison people pointed to a whole stack of letters they'd received on my behalf and said, "Barry Page, are you really as good as all these people say?" I just said, "Yes, sir!"

The reason the trial was sort of short and the reason I pleaded guilty was because when they had Janet on the stand, they really started to badger her and she broke down and cried. I was pleading not guilty at this point, but I couldn't stand it. It was awful, and I just jumped up and yelled, "Stop it right here! I'll plead guilty, but stop badgering her."

Well, I pleaded guilty, I got fined, and I actually went to prison. So much for my "information." My sentence was two to five years in the state penitentiary. I was really shook when I went to jail. I never expected that. My daughter was just a little girl then, and I thought how much of her childhood I was going to miss. Would she even know who I was when I got out? Worrying about that was the worst part.

My fellow inmates seemed to like and respect me. There

were people there from State College who hadn't been out of jail for maybe fifteen years. They had read about all my racing and thought it was great to be able to talk to me about it. Of course, I liked that too. I probably had as good a time in prison as anyone could have. Don't misunderstand me. Prison time is "hard time." It is never good time. But it could have been a whole lot worse.

I never did another abortion, but every time the police got wind of an abortion—and of course they kept happening—they accused me of doing it. I couldn't have done one even if I'd wanted to, because I couldn't have gotten another Higginson's syringe. They had quit making them by then. The one the police took I'd bought at a small neighborhood drugstore in Philadelphia, and at that point the druggist had already had the thing for fifteen years! It was an antique when he sold it to me.

My daughter was too little to know what was happening when I was sent to jail. All she knew was that her daddy went away. When she was a teenager, she asked me about it and I told her. She didn't like what I told her because of what people would say. You know how teenagers are. They hate anything that makes them different.

My mother and my brother in England never knew why I was in prison because I would never tell them. All I said was that I had "goofed," that it was more complicated than I could explain in a letter, and that I would tell them all about it when I got out. Well, my brother called the prison and they told him. Now the secret was out, and my family in England knew the story. My mother, who all my life had been so opposed to abortion, was pretty good about it. Right away she wrote to me in prison. She accepted the fact that what was done was done. I was her child and she would love me forever, but there was a thread of "How could *my* son do something like this?" I hadn't seen my mother since 1958, when I left England, but I think she had mellowed as she got older. She was much less opposed to abortion than she had been in the 1950s, but she certainly felt that abortions ought to be done by doctors and not by her son. I had to agree with her on that!

Things were tough after I got out of prison. The district attorney of Centre County tried to get the judge to sign an order saying I couldn't ever come back to the county after I was released, but the judge refused. I was afraid I might be deported. After all, I was a registered alien, and a conviction could have gotten me deported. When I was released from jail on the judge's order—he said that the law under which I was convicted was unconstitutional—I had to go immediately to Philadelphia to meet with authorities in the immigration department. They were fine about it. They just didn't consider it the kind of thing for which people ought to get deported. They treated it more like white-collar crime. Now, don't get me wrong. I'm not trying to minimize what I did. It was serious and I sure wouldn't want to see those days come back. That was bad stuff. I've got granddaughters now, and I wouldn't want them to have that kind of stuff as their only choice.

My case got to the Pennsylvania Supreme Court, and they agreed with the Centre County judge that the law was unconstitutional. That made the abortion law unenforceable everywhere in Pennsylvania, not just in Centre County! I was the first one to make that happen in Pennsylvania. I changed the law, and I'll always feel good about that. I paid a high price, though—both emotionally and financially—but it was a good thing I did, and I'm glad. I hope it never changes.

DR. FRANCIS

I GREW UP IN THE NORTHERN HILLS of New Jersey, where a jeep is nice in the wintertime. I'm a Roman Catholic, and growing up, I certainly absorbed and accepted my church's teachings, although abortion wasn't something that was discussed at our house. I went to an all-boys high school and an all-boys college, and I didn't have a lot of money to do much dating, so I didn't have any real experience with girls.

There were two boys and two girls in my family. The girls were so much younger that I'd never heard any discussions about female chastity or fertility by the time I left home for college at age seventeen. Nor did I have any particular interest in it. I was a male, so abortion wasn't a problem for me.

I went to medical school at Georgetown University and graduated in 1968. Now, Georgetown is a Jesuit institution, and in our first year we took a class in medical ethics, so I know we were taught then that abortion was wrong. I don't remember much about whether this message was repeated in other classes in medical school, because I was still a male whose life had not been touched by abortion. It had nothing to do with me, nor I with it.

In medical school I got more than enough training to enable me to do a D and C, and therefore, to do an abortion. And at D.C. General Hospital, where I was during my senior year, I could have done a D and C if I had wanted to, because there were plenty of them being done.

D.C. General is, and was then, the classic big inner-city slum hospital. It was the hospital of the "Friday Night Rod and Gun Club." Every Friday and Saturday night, you were sure to have a bunch of shootings and stabbings. One part of the hospital had a four-hundred-bed acute psychiatric wing. We aren't talking about chronic stuff. These were acutely psychotic patients. The regular hospital was divided into three sections, for Georgetown, George Washington, and Howard—the three medical schools in the area. Each medical school assumed responsibility for one-third of the hospital and did one-third of the work, providing physicians to staff the hospital. In exchange, the medical schools got a great training ground for their students and interns.

Now, this was not a nice, orderly hospital setting. For example, in obstetrics, the women had never had any prenatal care. They just walked in off the street and had their babies. They did it without any anesthetic, too, unless it was a cesarean or a high forceps delivery. Often the doctor or medical student, as the case might be, did little more than catch the baby, and sometimes we didn't even do that. When we got there, the woman would laugh and say, "You weren't fast enough, Doc. I did it myself."

Now, this big inner-city slum hospital also had a representative share of women suffering from abortion complications. A "representative share"? We had a ton of them! There was a septic abortion ward. That was back in the days when there were still twenty- and thirty-bed wards. The septic abortion ward was sort of a separate unit off in a corner of the hospital. It was dingy and dark, and there were always a bunch of women in there, typically fifteen to twenty, and they had all had septic abortions. They were real sick!

At night, as a medical student, I had to mix up and dispense their antibiotics because there was no RN on the unit. There were no nurses at night because there wasn't enough money. The law said nurses could dispense antibiotics. So could doctors. But nurses' aides couldn't. The law was silent about medical students, but because there was no available RN or doctor, we did it. Otherwise the patients wouldn't have been able to have their medicine. This gave me more contact with the abortion patients than might otherwise have been the case.

These women were sicker than hell! They were among the sickest people I have ever seen—before or since. They had high fevers. They were vomiting. Most of them had bad infections in their bellies, and some of them died. Some responded well to the antibiotic therapy and survived. A high percentage of those who survived must have been sterile because the infection had been so bad. They were very, very sick—as sick as people can get and still survive.

Sometimes it took them only hours to die if they were pretty far gone when they came to the hospital, but sometimes they hung on for days. The only real treatment was antibiotics and IV fluids. Our ability to sustain critically ill people was not as good in 1968 as it is now. We've got better antibiotics than we had twenty years ago, too. It would take them longer to die today, and probably fewer of them would die.

These abortion patients were from the slums of D.C. They were desperately poor. Many had recently arrived from the South. They may have even come to D.C. for their abortions, seeking the greater anonymity of a large city. Many were older women who already had several children. The septic abortion death rate at D.C. General was probably higher than in the rest of the country. These women were not well nourished. Their general health care had been poor. That's why they were there. The nice middle-class ladies had their nice middle-class abortions elsewhere and didn't get into trouble—at least not into as much trouble as these women did. It is always the poor that suffer the most from laws like the anti-abortion laws.

When one of the abortion patients died, the police would try to investigate it, but that was kind of like trying to stamp dandelions out of your grass. You stamp out one, and two more take its place. And don't forget, much of it—a significant amount—was self-done, so when they died, there was nothing for the police to do. The self-help methods I saw were douches with irritating solutions and "instruments"—a knitting needle, a straightened-out coat hanger, or literally any kind of implement that they could force up into the cervix.

This was the first time I saw abortion as a social problem. I was madder than hell about the hypocrisy of the whole situation. These women were being murdered, basically because they were poor and didn't have the sophistication and the knowledge to do what more affluent women did—either not get pregnant in the first place or be able to get a safe abortion. Remember, this was 1968, not 1958, so it had become possible to get a safe abortion. It was not like it would be after 1973, but if you were in New York or certain other states and had some resources, you could get a legal abortion.

If abortion becomes illegal again, doctors are not going to do them. Why should they? Who wants to put their license on the line? The only doctors who would be able to do abortions are those who have picked some island retreat they want to retire to, a place where abortion is legal. You would have to have charter jet flights so that you could keep the booming business going. Then you could just sit back and say, "Thank you, U.S. legislators, for making me a rich man!" Think about it. Always summertime and the living is always easy. Not bad.

What is happening with RU486 has never happened in our country before, to my knowledge. Here is an important, useful, valuable drug that we are keeping out of the country solely because some people find its use "immoral." Tobacco and alcohol are both drugs, and they cause more illness and probably more immorality than any other drug in this country. Yet these same people are silent about that.

When I graduated from medical school, I got into surgery and then urology. I never had any further experience with gynecology or abortion, but I never forgot the experience I did have at that hospital. I'm married to a woman. I have two sisters who are women. A few of my patients are women. Half the population is female, and to make abortion illegal again would have a very adverse medical impact on women generally.

I'm still a practicing Catholic, and yes, I think abortion should be legal. I suppose that on some level I do think abortion is wrong, but if I had a pregnant thirteen-year-old daughter, I'd want her to have an abortion, because I think it is even more wrong for children to have children. It is an area of morality about which there is debate, and given that fact, it is imperative that people have a choice, in my view. Those women on the abortion ward really didn't.

LAURA

I WAS RAISED CATHOLIC and conditioned from childhood on—
at home, at school, everywhere—to believe that abortion is
wrong, birth control is wrong, sex without marriage is
wrong.

In 1970 I was nineteen years old. I had been away at college
for one year and was very unhappy at the college my father had
chosen for me, Wheeling College in West Virginia. I had
wanted to go to Duquesne University in Pittsburgh, but he
wanted me in Wheeling, so that was where I was sent for my
first year.

My father was a very dominant figure. My mother was an
alcoholic. I didn't want to be around my mother; I didn't want
to disappoint my father; but more than anything, I didn't want
to be in Wheeling. It was a real power struggle between my
father and me, one that I had no chance of winning. To punish
me for my rebellious and ungrateful manner, he made me
drop out of school for a year and live at home. I was working as
a salesclerk at Penney's during my year of punishment. I was
very unhappy.

I was dating an "older man." He was twenty-three and had
just gotten out of the Marine Corps. I had been involved with
him the year before, but I got more involved with him during
the year of punishment. Since he lived in Pittsburgh, I saw him

much more frequently than I had when I was in Wheeling.

Knowledge and access to birth control for nineteen-year-olds really didn't exist in 1969 and 1970. Young unmarried females certainly didn't go to gynecologists once a year. I bet our mothers didn't even go to gynecologists as regularly as women do today. I might have had more access than I realized, but I was very naive, and my naiveté probably further impaired my access.

We didn't use any birth control. Of course I got pregnant. My denial was total. It is incomprehensible to me, looking back, how I could deny so much for so long. In the back of my mind, I think I knew I was pregnant. I remember digging through my class notes—in high school I had taken a "family living" class. In that class they discussed pregnancy, and I remembered taking notes about the signs and symptoms. Well, I found my notes, and as I read them, I just got sicker and sicker. I mean, I had them all: no periods, nausea, sore breasts, the whole nine yards. There was nothing else it could be. But I still wasn't ready to accept it.

I was raised in a very strict Catholic family. There were three girls and one boy. I was the youngest by many years. I am sixteen years younger than my brother and nine years younger than my older sister. Because they were all so much older, I ended up being the only child living at home for quite a few years. My family procreated like rabbits. One of my sisters had five children in six years. But the destiny of a woman was to get married and have babies, *not* to have babies and then get married! And never mind the babies. Even if you might be lucky enough not to get pregnant, you certainly did not have sex. This was not the kind of family environment where I could go to my mother and say, "Hey, Mom, I think I have a problem." That just wasn't done. In my family, people were so "private" they brushed their teeth behind closed doors.

Back then I thought that no one else in my family or among my friends had ever had an unwanted pregnancy. I probably thought that no one but me *ever* had this problem. In hindsight, my sister probably wanted an abortion for each of the rapid pregnancies that followed her first. I suspect that my mother was frantic when she got pregnant with me. I had to be a crisis in her life. I know I was an unwanted pregnancy, but understand, if the women in my family didn't want to be pregnant, they sure didn't talk about it.

As I said, I was raised to believe that abortion was terribly wrong. Birth control was terribly wrong. I remember the priest telling us over and over, "You can't use birth control. It is a mortal sin. If you do, you will go to hell and you will burn in hell." Powerful stuff! I saw my sister and my brother's wife have baby after baby because you just didn't use birth control. It was wrong. I saw my mother distressed because my sister continued to get pregnant, but it was never talked about. No one said, "Why isn't she more careful?" It was just accepted.

My other sister got pregnant when she was not married. I remember that "shame" and "disgrace" seemed to be the dominant themes. I was nine years old, and it made a big impression on me. My sister, who was eighteen, ran away from home when she found out she was pregnant. My father called the police. My brother even came home from college. It was a big family crisis. For years after that, my sister was the black sheep of the family, and no one seemed to forget it or to forgive her. She was a bad girl, or at least, she had done a very bad thing. I remember that my father sat me down and told me my unmarried sister was pregnant. There were tears in his eyes. He told me that if I got pregnant like that, he *never* wanted to know about it. I should just get married—no matter how old or young I was or what the man was like.

At nine, I knew nothing about sex, so much of what was going on was over my head. But I got the message loud and clear. My sister had done a terrible thing, and if I found myself in the same predicament, I better make sure my parents never knew it! I remember thinking, even then, that it was such a horrible thing for him to say, but I had no doubt that he felt that way.

My sister married the guy and had the baby. They had three children altogether before the marriage broke up. That lesson was not lost on me either. Pregnancy did not seem to guarantee a happy marriage.

You know, my father always treated that child differently. Of his twelve grandchildren, the one he knew was conceived out of wedlock was the thorn in his side. He never really liked that granddaughter. Poor kid.

All of this stuff from the past had a big impact when I became pregnant nine or ten years later. I absolutely denied that I was pregnant for at least eight weeks, if not longer. It's like I knew I was pregnant but as long as I never said it out loud it wasn't real. The denial phase ended not because of an event but because I just couldn't keep that awful secret any longer. When I finally acknowledged my problem, I *never* considered abortion. That was the most heinous crime imaginable, and it never entered my mind.

I finally told my boyfriend that I was pregnant. His response was classic: "Are you sure?" Of course I was sure, although I really had no idea how to go about getting the official confirmation he seemed to want. He didn't react at all like I wanted him to react. I wanted him to be strong and to tell me not to worry. I certainly didn't want him to freak out worse than I was freaking out.

He decided to take me to his family doctor. There was no way I could go to my own family doctor. He had taken care of me since I was a little girl, and I was more than slightly afraid that he would tell my parents. Going to Art's family doctor seemed to be a good idea, and it was better than any idea I had.

It was terrible. That doctor treated me like dirt. I wasn't used to that. I came from an upper-middle class family where there was always plenty of money. I was used to being treated with respect and with class. He treated me like I was a slut! I felt bad enough to begin with, and he made it much worse. When I first went in, before he knew what was wrong with me, he had a big smile. He was very friendly, shook my hand, and asked what he could do for me. As soon as I told him I thought I was pregnant, his whole body language changed. He snapped away from me, folded his arms, and was very gruff and brisk. He said—belligerently, I thought—"What do you expect me to do about it?" He was so hostile. Maybe he thought I wanted an abortion. That was the furthest thing from my mind at that moment, and I wondered later, if he had been more supportive, whether things might have turned out differently. Anyway, I answered by starting to cry and saying that all I wanted was to know whether or not I was pregnant.

He ordered a pregnancy test. I was so shy and naive that I was embarrassed by the fact that I had to produce a urine sample for the test. Today's pregnancy tests can tell you in three minutes whether or not you are pregnant. I had to wait three days for the results, and they were the longest three days in my life. I remember sneaking down to the corner drugstore to call his office for the results of my pregnancy test. I will never forget the nurse's words when I called: "It's positive."

I hung up the telephone and sat there. I remember thinking that my world had come to an end. I had no idea how I was going to work my way out of the problem or even what I wanted to do about it. I did know I didn't love Art enough to marry him.

I couldn't tell my mother or father. I certainly couldn't go to my sisters or my brother. Here they all were, having babies right and left, and all properly married. I couldn't go to a home for unwed mothers, because to do that would have meant telling my parents. Even the idea of telling my father was unthinkable! I never even thought about abortion. I remember Art saying to me, "Well, we'll get married." But it wasn't, "I love you. Let's get married." It was more pragmatic: "Oh, damn! You're pregnant. I'll do the right thing."

Even though I didn't really want to marry Art, I wanted to tell my parents that we were getting married—remember what I had been taught when I was nine. When I mentioned telling my parents to Art, he quickly said, "Oh no, don't do that!" It was pretty clear that he didn't really want to run away and get married. The whole thing didn't set right with me, and a lot of red flags started to go up in my mind.

It was obvious that I wasn't going to get married, even if I had wanted to. I was miserable. My mother was drinking, and we were fighting a lot. I was moody and irritable. My sister came home from Ohio. She could sense that something was going on. I'm sure it never occurred to her that I was pregnant. She knew our mother was an alcoholic, and that's what she thought was causing the stress, so she took me home with her for a while.

One night, while I was at my sister's, my mother called. She was loaded. She might have been drunk, but she wasn't dumb. In my review of my old class notes, I had found information about the total number of days a pregnancy lasted—from the last period to the birth of the baby—and I had marked it off on a calendar. Well, my mother found this calendar. All I had marked were these two dates, nothing else. I think she just studied them, and in spite of her alcoholic fog, she had been pregnant often enough that she figured it out.

She called me at my sister's and told me that if I was pregnant, I should just not bother coming home. So here I am. Art doesn't particularly want me. I can't go home. My sister doesn't know, but at some point she too is going to figure it out, maybe just by looking at me.

My sister didn't know yet, though. Because she was my big sister and our mother was such a mess, she wanted very much to do the right thing, whatever that might be. She even went to her doctor and got some birth control pills for me, because she thought I might be sexually active. She handed them to me and said, "Here, Laura, just in case. Don't be stupid and get pregnant like I did." Stupid? Pregnant? Oh, God! How could I tell her I was already stupid and pregnant? I couldn't. She would want me to get married, and I knew I couldn't marry Art.

I left my sister's house because I couldn't stay there forever. Since I couldn't go home, I decided to stay with Art. That caused a major scene when I went home to pick up my clothes, but it wasn't as "major" as the scene I remembered from my childhood when my sister had gotten pregnant.

Art met me at the Pittsburgh airport when I came home from Ohio. He said, "I think I found a solution to our problem. I think you can have an abortion." I remember standing there in the crowded airport. I was feeling nauseated from the pregnancy, but when he said that, I had a very strong urge to throw up right there in the airport. I didn't want to have an abortion, but I didn't really feel that I had any other choice. Art had an abortionist all lined up by the time he first mentioned it to me. I don't know how long it took him or how difficult it was, but the moment I reluctantly agreed, things happened very quickly.

To get me to say yes, Art dangled every dream I'd ever had in front of my eyes. If I would just have this abortion, I could finish school. He would get a better job. We would save our money, get married, buy a nice little house, have a nice life and everything else he knew I wanted. He just convinced me that this was the only way. He was a very manipulative man, and I was easy to manipulate. Being a twenty-three-year-old ex-marine, he was much more worldly than I was. But if he was so worldly, how come he didn't know anything about birth control?

The abortionist he took me to was a real doctor. He had an office in the kind of neighborhood where, when we rode through when I was a child, my father would say, "Laura, lock the door." The neighborhood was run-down, and the office itself was very seedy-looking. The doctor was black. Even though the civil rights movement was going on and there was much less racial prejudice than there had been, white women simply didn't go to black male doctors, let alone doctors who had run-down offices over seedy grocery stores in a bad part of town.

When Art pulled up in front of the place, my heart sank. I had no idea what to expect. At that point, I had never even had an internal exam. The closer we got, the worse it got. The stairwell leading up to the office was filthy, and the paint was peeling off the walls. It was a very hot day in early September, and the place had a smell about it. We climbed the stairs and opened the door to the waiting room. The room was packed. Everyone turned and stared at us, but no one uttered a sound. It was eerie—like a silent movie. Here I was, a young white girl with a white guy, and everyone else in the waiting room was black. But that wasn't all. Everyone else in the waiting room was visibly poor—with missing teeth, tattered clothing, and newspaper stuffed into their shoes. No wonder there was silence when we arrived. Everyone there seemed to have clothes from Goodwill, but mine were from Saks. I couldn't have been more conspicuous if I had been naked. I sat down and tried to fight off the waves of nausea. I wanted to bolt and run, but where would I run to? Art didn't want me. My parents didn't want me. What else was there? I stayed seated.

Somehow Art knew that this abortion was going to cost about six hundred dollars. When the doctor opened the door to the waiting room and saw this little white girl sitting there with her diamond earrings and her silk blouse, his eyes lit up. I know he thought, "Whoopee! Six hundred dollars just walked in the door." He had to make more money from one patient like me than from everyone else in the waiting room combined.

It was a Friday night. We waited and waited. Finally, when it was about midnight and there was no one else in the waiting room, the doctor called me into his office. There was no nurse or anything, just him and me. I was so scared. He told me to get undressed. I was used to my family doctor, where there were nurses and other people around, where everything was clean and new, and where I knew the people and they knew me. Here I was in this dirty office, with this stranger, late at night.

He did an internal exam and told me I really had to take care of things quickly because in another week I would start to show. "Oh, my God!" I thought. If I didn't act now, my father would find out for sure. The doctor told me the cost would be six hundred dollars and asked if we could afford it. I told him we didn't have that much money, and he said that since I had to have a follow-up visit, if I brought three hundred and fifty dollars in cash the day of the abortion, I could bring the balance when I came for the follow-up. Meanwhile, I didn't have a dime to my name. I wasn't working at Penney's anymore, and the little pocket money my parents gave me before I went to my sister's was long gone. We had virtually no time to raise the money, because my abortion was set for the next morning.

I guess I was a little bit disappointed. Having gotten this far, I wanted it all to be over. I hadn't thought about how the doctor would do the abortion. I hoped he would just wave a magic wand and take my problem away. Art didn't have any money either, but his parents had a friend who ran a small and rather sleazy neighborhood bar not far from the doctor's office. We went to the bar. Art talked briefly with the bartender—I have no idea what he said—and the bartender gave him the money. Then we went to Art's apartment and I went to bed, but I was so keyed up it was impossible for me to sleep.

We got up the next morning and went back to the doctor's office. This time the waiting room was empty. Art didn't want to go in with me, so I went in by myself. Again I was told to undress and climb up on the examining table. I don't remember the doctor washing his hands or anything like that, but I was so frightened I might not have noticed. I don't remember there being a sink in the room. I just remember how dirty it was. Out of the corner of my eye, I caught a glimpse of a piece of red plastic tubing. I didn't know what it was then, but being a nurse, I know now. It was a Foley catheter. He inserted the catheter in my vagina, and it hurt like hell. When I caught a glimpse of it, I only saw the tip, so I had no idea it was eighteen inches long. I didn't know then that he was inserting it into my uterus. To this day, whenever I have to use a Foley catheter on a patient, I get weak in the knees, remembering the pain I felt.

As soon as the catheter was inserted, the doctor told me to go home because I was done—no waiting around until I felt better or the pain subsided. He told me something would happen sooner or later, probably within a few hours. The pain was intense, and I could hardly stand up. I couldn't believe he expected me to leave when I could hardly stand upright, let alone walk.

It was funny. As soon as the job was done, the doctor seemed not to want anything to do with me either. He just wanted me out of there. He was sort of a black version of the white doctor who didn't want anything to do with me. This turn of events kind of surprised me, because originally the white doctor had treated me like dirt but the black doctor was going to be my savior. Now, in my eyes, there wasn't much difference between the two of them, at least in terms of their attitudes toward me.

I could barely get down the steps and out to Art's car. There was a searing pain in my pelvis. It was probably a combination of the pain and still being so nervous. I'll never forget the relief on Art's face when I came out of the office and he knew that the abortion would definitely happen. He was on a real high, laughing and talking. As far as he was concerned, it was over. But I didn't know what was going to happen. As far as I knew, it could be a long way from over.

Art took me back to his place. I crawled into bed and began having these terrible chills. My whole body was twitching and vibrating. The pain was still severe. Then I felt like I had to get to the bathroom because I was going to throw up. Once I got in there, I felt more like I had to have a bowel movement. The doctor hadn't told me anything about what to expect, so I had no idea what was going on. Now I know that my uterus was contracting and my cervix was dilating. The contractions were bad. I was screaming, and the sweat was pouring off my body. Art never came near me!

I can still see the design in the linoleum on the bathroom floor. I remember thinking, "At nineteen, this linoleum is the last thing I'm ever going to see, because I'm dying. I'm going to die because I was stupid. I got pregnant and then I went to a doctor with a dirty office." It was the worst pain I've ever had in my life.

There was this strong sensation of pressure, and I felt like I needed to get back on the toilet. I did, and right in the middle of the worst pain, I heard this splish, splash, plop, and everything just came right out into the toilet. Buckets of stuff were flying out of me into the toilet. I felt this new, really strange sensation and struggled to my feet. That's when I realized, for the first time, that the catheter was still in me. It was now hanging partway out. I was afraid to pull on it because I didn't know what would happen. I must have stayed in the bathroom for two hours waiting for the catheter to come out. I was bleeding profusely. Finally the catheter did come out, and I managed to stand up and drag myself back to bed. I just lay there crying. I didn't know what was going to happen next, and I didn't know what I was supposed to do.

Art came nowhere near me. I think that if he had thought I was dying, he would have cut out and just left me there.

The bleeding lasted for four months. I had lots of symptoms, like dizziness and feeling I was going to faint. I was probably severely anemic from loss of blood. I never got an infection or anything, though.

I had been supposed to go back for a follow-up visit, but the doctor didn't even know my name, so there is no way he could have contacted me. Because we didn't have the money for the follow-up, I never did go back. I never went to any other doctor either. Remember how hostile the white doctor had been when I hadn't even mentioned abortion? How much worse would a doctor act now, when it was obvious what I had done?

I had a lot of guilt. Guilt about the abortion and about the way it was done. Art and I were still living together, but it wasn't going well at all. We were fighting a lot. I couldn't stand to be around him, and I absolutely couldn't stand to be in the bathroom where all that terrible stuff had happened to me. I ended up calling my father, who came and got me. I went back home. My mother had to think there was something wrong with me. I'd used more tampons and pads in a month than I used in a year. She probably knew but didn't want to face it. I never told her, and we never talked about it.

I know several other women who went to that same doctor around the same time I did. One was a girlfriend of mine who was a student at Indiana University of Pennsylvania. I found out that I had been unusual because Art had a car. The way it worked for other young college students is that you stood under a clock on a street corner in front of one of Pittsburgh's leading department stores. A car came by and honked, and you got in. You had never seen the driver—usually a black man—but you just got in. Think of all the conditioning little girls get about never getting into a car with a stranger. That had to be a very scary thing to do. Well, the driver took you to the doctor, where you paid cash up front and had the catheter inserted, and then the driver took you back and let you out under the clock. How you got home was your problem, and if they felt as bad as I felt after the catheter was inserted, it must have been a big problem.

I did end up marrying Art later. In my eyes, with my Catholic upbringing, I had killed a baby, and the only way I could atone for my sin was to marry Art and have babies with him. I never did have any children, though. About ten years after the abortion I had to have a hysterectomy because I'd had serious gynecological problems all my adult life. The guilt was still so bad that even then, when I was having the hysterectomy, I couldn't tell the doctor about the abortion I had when I was nineteen. He just thought I had a lot of inexplicable gynecological problems.

I never felt the relief a lot of women feel after an abortion. There might have been some relief of sorts that I managed to keep my secret, but my overwhelming emotion was one of guilt—a terrible, Catholic, sin-and-damnation kind of guilt. I have guilt to this day over that abortion. I will never get over it, I guess. I had another abortion—a legal abortion—in 1976, and I feel absolutely no guilt over that. I guess it isn't abortion itself that makes me feel guilty. I no longer buy my church's teachings on this topic. It is the terrible way I had the first one done.

Art and I were only married two years. We got married in 1971 and divorced in 1973. The divorce was Art's idea. I knew there was nothing in the relationship, but I never would have gotten a divorce, because my church taught that divorce, too, was wrong. I'd have stayed in a bad marriage forever as some kind of further atonement for my sins, but I was really relieved when the marriage ended.

My 1976 legal abortion was a very different experience. It was done in a hospital. The man I was involved with went with me. We had counseling, individually and together, so I was very sure in my decision and very comfortable with it. There was a thorough explanation given to me about the abortion procedure, what they were going to do and what I could expect. The procedure room was spotless. A young resident did the abortion. He was very clean-cut, competent, and nice to me. Everyone was nice to me. They treated me with respect—not like I was some kind of slut, but like I was a woman who had made a decision to terminate a pregnancy for a reason she thought was a good one.

After the abortion, they gave me a book about follow-up care, gave me an antibiotic, gave me a telephone number I could call night or day if I had any problems, made the follow-up appointment for me, and gave me birth control. It was as different as apples and oranges, night and day. It was so unlike my earlier experience that it was hard to believe it was basically the same surgical procedure. The difference was phenomenal.

Birth control became much easier to get after the sixties and early seventies. Access to birth control is the real "sexual revolution," not the casual, unprotected sex of the sixties. I think it's great, but it still startles me. But even if contraception is readily available, we still need abortion because no contraception is foolproof. Until you have actually walked in the shoes of an unwillingly pregnant woman, you can't understand how desperate she is.

CONCLUSION

What has this look at what used to be shown us about what might be? What has it shown us about our future if we recriminalize abortion? Would we go back to what these women and men saw and experienced twenty to sixty years ago? Or might illegal abortion be less dangerous thanks to medical advances that have made virtually every medical procedure safer? There is both a medical answer and a political answer to these questions.

MEDICAL CONSIDERATIONS

It is true that doctors have now learned safer abortion techniques, many of them developed in the last twenty-five years. However, if abortion goes underground again, that safety record is not likely to follow. Nor are doctors. Indeed, we have already begun to see a decline in the number of doctors willing to perform legal abortions, because they are unwilling to deal with harassment and intimidation by abortion foes. And some medical schools and hospitals are no longer training doctors in modern, safe abortion techniques.

Common sense suggests that even a minor surgical procedure is likely to be safer if done by a physician rather than a beauty operator or motorcycle mechanic. Many women who have come of age since *Roe v. Wade* naively believe that the same doctors who have been providing them with abortion care would continue to do so if abortion were recriminalized. But the doctor-observers tell us why that is not going to happen. Why would physicians risk fines, imprisonment, and—perhaps the ultimate sanction—loss of license? The answer is that they won't. There is no reason why they should, since most can earn an extremely good living doing medical procedures permitted by law. Just as before, very few physicians will be willing to take the risk. Abortion care will be provided, as before, by non-physicians with varying degrees of competence.

The most significant safety improvements have been brought about by the development of the D and E—the dilation and evacuation, or suction method of abortion, which greatly reduces the likelihood of perforation, and by antibiotics, which greatly reduce the likelihood of infection.

The experiences of Audrey and Estelle suggest that antibiotics were fairly easily available in the underground and would continue to be—if the abortionist, like Audrey's colleague, Flo, insisted on using them. However, there is no guarantee that all underground practitioners would be so motivated. Indeed, most of the underground abortionists we have met here did not routinely use antibiotics.

We can expect that underground use of vacuum curettage or suction to perform D and E's would be much more unusual than the use of antibiotics. The average suction machine costs at least fifteen hundred dollars. Is it likely that the Flos, Barrys, and Fays of this world would make that kind of financial investment when catheters and coat hangers are so much more readily available at so little cost? Such an investment seems all the more unsound in view of the fact that the police would probably confiscate the machine if the abortionist was arrested. Moreover, a suction machine, unlike a coat hanger or a bicycle spoke or an umbrella rib, does not blend in as an ordinary household item. When the police came to arrest Barry Graham Page, they were looking for a simple red ceramic bowl. Can we expect them to overlook a fifteen-hundred-dollar suction machine whose sole function is performing abortions? Hardly.

Another disadvantage of the suction machine, at least from the abortionists' point of view, is that their clients would actually abort at their place of business instead of several hours later in a restaurant bathroom on the New Jersey Turnpike, in the backyard, or at home in the bathroom—more incriminating evidence for them to deal with. What sensible, self-protective abortionist is going to choose that added risk? Not many.

It is true that some women are now teaching each other to perform abortions through the technique of menstrual extraction, using a mason jar, a syringe, and rubber tubing—a sort of homemade suction machine (see Appendix B). However, this technique is cumbersome, requires two people, and is not nearly as quick as a two-minute poke with a catheter or coat hanger. While home abortion techniques have always been with us, it is perhaps an index of current concern, and of women's determination to continue to be able to terminate an unwanted pregnancy as safely as posible, that the November 1991 issue of *In Health*, a consumer-oriented magazine, featured a major article on menstrual extraction.

Some believe that the "abortion problem" would be eliminated if RU486, the French "abortion pill" invented by Dr. Etienne Baulieu, were legal and widely available in the United States. RU486, a synthetic steroid, appears to function by mimicking an early miscarriage. It tricks the uterus into not manufacturing progesterone, which is necessary for a fertilized egg to be implanted. Without progesterone, the lining of the uterus breaks down, as in normal menstruation, and expels any fertilized egg. Thus, RU486 would make surgical abortions a thing of the past, many claim. Alas, that is not the case.

In September 1988, RU486 was approved for use in France, in combination with a prostaglandin agent, for terminating pregnancies of less than seven weeks. In France, women take three tablets of RU486 under the medical supervision of a clinic or hospital licensed to perform abortions. The shedding of the uterine lining usually starts in a day or two, lasting an average of ten days. Two or three days after the first visit, the women return to receive either an injection or a vaginal suppository of prostaglandin, which causes mild uterine contractions. In most cases, the tissue is expelled within a few hours. Eight to twelve days after taking the RU486, the women return for a checkup to make sure that the abortion is complete.

Unfortunately, RU486 is only effective early in pregnancy. For this reason, according to Dr. Ted (pp. 71–75), it would be of limited use, whether it was legal or illegal. Women would have to decide to abort and get access to the drug very quickly, because it is most effective when taken five weeks after the last menstrual period—a point at which many women don't even know they're pregnant. As Dr. Ted says, "At seven weeks from the last period, which might be about five weeks of pregnancy, there is a ten percent failure rate. After that, it just doesn't work. Many women with irregular periods, denial, lack of knowledge, lack of money, or a host of other common problems will be beyond the point where RU486 could do anything for them."

By September 1989, RU486 had been used, with an effectiveness rate of 96 percent, by 30,000 French women. By the end of 1989, RU486 accounted for approximately one in three abortions in France. According to French health officials, between 2 and 5 percent of the women experienced adverse but generally mild side effects.

A drug cannot be distributed commercially in the United States unless the manufacturer applies for and receives approval from the Food and Drug Administration. Roussel Uclaf, the pharmaceutical company that developed RU486 and currently markets it in France, has not sought FDA approval. Roussel and its parent company, Hoechst AG, which had sales totalling $6.4 million in North America in 1989, are concerned about a possible boycott of their other products by American anti-abortionists.

Early research indicates that RU486 may be an effective treatment for Cushing's syndrome, ovarian and breast cancer, hypertension, brain cancer, diabetes, and AIDS. However, in June 1989, pressure from anti-abortion forces in the United

States led to a federal import ban on the drug and the virtual cessation of such medical research in this country. In July 1992, when Laura Benten arrived in New York on a flight from London, U.S. customs officials confiscated the RU486 she had brought with her for the purpose of terminating her pregnancy. She sued the FDA, arguing that the rule prohibiting an individual from bringing RU486 into the country was illegal. While a lower court agreed with her, a federal appeals court and later the Supreme Court upheld the rule. Laura Benten then terminated her six-week pregnancy by means of a surgical abortion.

It seems highly unlikely that if abortion were recriminalized, RU486 would ever be approved for distribution in the United States, despite its non-abortion medical potential. We would have to smuggle it past customs officials, as Margaret Sanger and others did with diaphragms in the 1930s. If smugglers can do a brisk business in heroin, cocaine, and other illegal substances, there is no reason to believe that they will not do the same with RU486, particularly if they can realize the same gargantuan profits that other illegal drugs generate. Of course, if abortion is illegal, an enormous price markup might force women to choose catheters and coat hangers anyway. And even if RU486 is affordable, women would be exposed to the same dangers inherent in dealing with any contraband substance.

From a medical perspective, it appears unlikely that the factors that make abortion safe—qualified personnel, suction machines, and other improved abortion techniques—would survive the recriminalization of abortion, at least in accessible, affordable form. If *Roe v. Wade* is overturned, American women can probably expect little if any improvement over "the worst of times."

POLITICAL CONSIDERATIONS

Politically, the period that would follow a reversal of *Roe v. Wade* might accurately be called the Fourth Great Abortion War, or— so we can hope—the Last Great Abortion War.

The First Great Abortion War was the medical community's struggle, in the nineteenth century, to make abortion illegal and drive out the openly flourishing non-doctor abortionists. The Second Great Abortion War was the fight, from approximately 1965 to 1973, to legalize abortion. The Third Great Abortion War continues today. It has been waged throughout the *Roe* period, during which abortion became both safe and legal for the first time. The Fourth Great Abortion War will begin if policymakers try to force American women back to the shadowy world of the underground. What will happen? Will women go quietly?

It is nothing if not apt to compare the recriminalization of abortion with Prohibition, an exercise in mass hypocrisy or mass delusion. Although substantial numbers of Americans drank, we ignored reality and made the sale or consumption of alcoholic beverages illegal. The end result was to turn criminals into millionaires and law-abiding citizens into criminals. In many ways, the original criminalization of abortion had the same impact, and so would its recriminalization. Abortion would regain its former status as the third-largest illegal enterprise in the United States, and ordinary American women would become criminals as they attempted to control their reproductive lives.

But the Fourth Great Abortion War would be different from Prohibition's blind hypocrisy in one major way. With Prohibition, it might be argued that people couldn't foresee the rise in crime and the other undesirable consequences of that "noble experiment." Not so here. In this case, we know *exactly* what will happen to American women and their families. We know because we have already experienced it once.

There are now millions of women—more than twenty-four million in the twenty years since the Supreme Court's decision—who have had firsthand experience with safe, legal abortion, in clinics and doctors' offices rather than back seats and back alleys. Moreover, at least one other person cared about what happened to most of these women and therefore had, if not direct experience with, a direct investment in legal abortion. By the same token, there is now a whole generation of women who may have an intellectual grasp of what underground abortion was like but never had to live through the worst of times. In this sense, the politics of the post-*Roe* era are vastly different from those of the underground period.

When abortion was illegal, women had no access to medically safe abortions. Like black Americans during the civil rights struggles of the fifties and sixties, or participants in the gay rights movement that began in 1969, activists who were fighting to legalize abortion had not experienced what they were trying to achieve; it was a wish, a hope, a dream of what might and should be. What post-*Roe* women have experienced for the last twenty years is no mere wish or hope. It is a right—a right and an expectation. There is a big difference between a hope and a right. There is a big difference between trying to crush a hope and trying to take away a right.

Policymakers should brace themselves, because today's women are likely to be far less docile than their pre-*Roe* counterparts. If *Roe v. Wade* is overturned, women may simply refuse to go back. And if they do, the Fourth Great Abortion War will be far different from the first three, and perhaps from any social and political struggle this country has ever seen.

APPENDIX A

A BRIEF HISTORY OF U.S. ABORTION LAWS

bortion in the United States has made a number of journeys from legality to criminalization and back again. In 1800 there were no abortion statutes at all in the United States. By 1900 every state in the union had laws prohibiting abortion for virtually any reason.

In colonial times and in the first quarter of the nineteenth century, Americans simply followed English common law in this matter, as in many others. Common law drew a distinction based on "quickening," the point during pregnancy when the woman can actually feel fetal movement. Although it varies from woman to woman, and even for the same woman from pregnancy to pregnancy, quickening generally occurs at about twenty weeks, the midpoint of pregnancy. Under common law, there were no prohibitions against abortion prior to quickening, and women could and did terminate their pregnancies if they chose to do so. Abortion after quickening was a crime, but it was a lesser crime than manslaughter or murder, and the penalties were much less severe.

Home medical manuals of the day routinely provided abortion information. Buchan's *Domestic Medicine* (1816) suggested several courses of action to restore menses following a missed period, among them bloodletting and taking quinine or tincture of hellebore, a violent gastrointestinal poison. Later in the book, the author warned the reader about certain common "causes" of abortion, including vigorous exercise, jumping, falling, and blows to the belly, as well as severe vomiting.

In 1803 the British Parliament passed a law that made abortion before quickening a criminal offense. However, in 1812, in *Commonwealth v. Bangs*, the Massachusetts Supreme Court declined to adopt the British change and continued to make the pre- and post-quickening distinction. Mr. Bangs, who was alleged to have given a woman an abortifacient, was acquitted because the indictment against him failed to assert that the woman was "quick with child." The *Bangs* precedent was widely followed by other states, at least until mid-century. Such indictments as there were occurred only in situations where the woman was deemed to be "quick" or somewhere beyond the first twenty weeks of her pregnancy.

The first American abortion statute preserved the quickening distinction. Enacted in Connecticut in 1821 and limited in scope, it made abortion a crime if it was done by administering a "deadly poison" or "noxious substance" after quickening. Since hellebore and other herbs and plants then used to induce abortion could be fatal in large doses, it can be argued that the Connecticut statute, like some later anti-abortion laws, sought to protect women. It did not prohibit abortion by use of an instrument, even after quickening. In Connecticut in 1821, abortion by noxious substances before quickening was permissible, and so was abortion by any other method, at any point.

Two more states followed Connecticut—Missouri in 1825 and Illinois in 1827. The Missouri and Illinois statutes, like the Connecticut model, aimed only at punishing abortion by poisonous substances. Again there was no mention of abortion by other means. However, unlike the Connecticut act, these laws made no reference to quickening. For the first time, abortion prior to quickening became a crime if poisonous substances were used.

In 1828 New York passed a more comprehensive law with separate provisions based on when in the pregnancy the abortion was performed. The first section preserved the legality of abortion before quickening. The second section made the abortion of an "unborn quick child" second-degree manslaughter and subjected the abortionist to criminal penalties. The woman herself could not be charged with the offense; rather, she was considered a victim. The third section was strangely inconsistent, since it was silent on quickening and said that abortion by any means, medicinal or otherwise, was illegal unless necessary to save the woman's life. Thus, arguably, abortion by any method, at any time, was illegal in New York after 1828. However, the life-saving or "therapeutic" exception, which had not appeared in earlier laws, suggests that the motivation of the New York legislature may have been to protect women.

In the nineteenth century, many observers maintained that only single women desperate to hide the "shame" of nonmarital sex were having abortions, but this argument crumbled in the 1840s. The growing number of abortion providers and the proliferation of abortion home remedies and patent medicines made it abundantly clear—in an era of poor to nonexistent contraception—that white, married, upper-middle-class, native-born Protestant American women were resorting to abortions to delay childbearing or limit the number of children they had.

By the 1840s, because of increased demand, abortion—the only existing birth control measure known to be effective—had become an American medical specialty, a service publicly traded in the free market by recognized practitioners, most of whom were not doctors. As had been the case during the preceding forty years with other medical services, there was intense competition between "real doctors" and these lay practitioners, or "irregular doctors." At the time, there was great variation in the training and competence of medical practitioners. In 1800 two-thirds of the "doctors" in Philadelphia were not graduates of any medical school. In rural areas faith healers, midwives, and folk doctors took care of the medical needs of the community, including uncomplicated surgery. And even medical school graduates were not necessarily qualified physicians. Before 1860 most American medical schools competed aggressively for paying students, without regard to their intelligence or abilities. Few applicants were denied admission, since in a very real sense their tuition kept the doors open. Some of these schools were nothing more than diploma mills. If you paid your money, you got one.

One of the most prominent nineteenth-century abortionists was Madame Restell, of 148 Greenwich Street in New York City. She was so successful that she had branch offices at 7 Essex Street in Boston and 7 South Seventh Street in Philadelphia, as well as an army of door-to-door salesmen who peddled her "female monthly pills."

At a time when there was no federal regulation of medicines, patent medicines promising miracle cures for an assortment of human ailments were openly advertised in the classified sections of newspapers, through handbills and flyers, and by word of mouth. "Female monthly pills," "renovating pills," and "lunar pills" were vague but popular remedies for such conditions as "irregular" menses, or, in a somewhat more accurate description, "obstructed" or "suppressed" menses. In case the potential user still had not caught on, the small print on the label contained a "warning" that married women who might be pregnant should not take the pills, since they were "sure to produce a miscarriage."

How effective these home remedies and patent medicines were is not known. Indeed, it's difficult even to speculate, since the patent medicines were not required to describe their contents. What we do know is that there was a lively interest in, and market for, products believed capable of correcting "suppressed" menses.

Madame Restell's pills were guaranteed to cure the "suppression problem." To accommodate those not within reach of her door-to-door salesmen, she advertised that the pills could be mailed anywhere in the country. The reader was cautioned to beware of imitation monthly pills—the genuine article bore Madame's signature on each box. Madame Restell, whose real name was Ann Lohman, also had facilities to "board ladies overnight," should their condition require it.

Many abortion practitioners billed themselves as doctors, but their actual medical training is not known. In January 1845, the *Boston Times* carried the ad of one Dr. Carswell, who treated such female complaints as "suppressions." A Dr. Dow advertised "good accommodations for ladies," and a Dr. Kurtz treated "private diseases." Female abortionists tended to prefer the title "Madame"—Madame Drunette, Madame Costello, Madame Carson, and Madame Moor gave Madame Restell plenty of competition—though they often added "ladies' physician" or "ladies' doctress" in advertising their services.

Abortion was a highly visible and profitable industry by the middle of the nineteenth century, although the earnings of individual abortionists, whether medical doctors or lay practitioners, probably varied greatly. The demand for abortion was also substantial enough to sustain several supporting industries. For example, by 1850 the manufacture of abortifacients had become a significant part of the drug industry. In 1871 it was estimated that sales of abortifacients surpassed the million-dollar mark. The profits were sufficient to convince Parke Davis and Company to engage in the wholesale manufacture of abortifacients called Emmenagogue and Emmenagogue Improved. In 1871 Madame Restell was reported to have been spending sixty thousand dollars a year on advertising alone.

By mid-century the medical community had begun a concerted effort to improve, professionalize, and ultimately control the practice of medicine in the United States. In line with that goal, doctors increasingly took the view that abortion at any time was to be avoided. Some doctors may have objected to the profits being enjoyed by the "irregulars," but the primary motivation of the medical establishment was probably the undisputed fact that in this era, some twenty years before Joseph Lister introduced modern antiseptic surgery—abortion, childbirth, and surgical procedures of any sort were hazardous undertakings. Thus, discouraging or even outlawing what could be considered "elective surgery" would surely save lives.

If doctors were to succeed in stamping out abortion, they had to convince women to reject it. Though health concerns provided the most compelling argument, some doctors began to denounce abortion as "morally reprehensible" as well as medically unsafe. It was a short step from "reprehensible" and "disreputable" to "damnable," "evil," "abominable," and finally "unnatural." It mattered little whether women rejected abortion because they thought it was dangerous or because they thought it was wrong, just so long as they rejected it.

Doctors began to organize against the commercialization of abortion, which they called "Restellism" after their best-known irregular competitor, and to lobby state legislatures for new restrictive laws. Some of these laws were apparently designed to protect women, like the legislation common in the early part of the century, but more followed the "regular doctor" model intended to drive commercial abortionists out of business, along with pharmacists who prescribed their own abortifacients and any other non-physicians who might be involved in the abortion decision and implementation.

The medical community was successful in getting a stronger antiabortion law passed in New York in 1846. The law ignored the quickening distinction and made it a crime for anyone—doctor or not—to "administer" to or "prescribe" for a pregnant woman with regard to abortion, or even to "advise" her on the subject—a provision that implicated even family members and friends. New York's law went a step beyond any previous legislation in making the woman herself liable for prosecution. However, because women were still viewed as victims by society if not by the law, this provision was evidently not enforced.

In 1847, for the first time anywhere, Massachusetts made it a crime for an abortionist to advertise publicly. At around the same time, there was concern about the falling birth rate; the Massachusetts ban, it was hoped, would check the dissemination of information about abortion, still the only reliable form of contraception. Soon five more states (Virginia in 1848, California, New Hampshire, New Jersey, and Wisconsin in 1849) enacted anti-abortion laws that reflected the growing opposition—and power—of the medical community.

This major crusade by physicians to squelch their competitors lasted until 1880. Prior to the formation of the American Medical Association in 1847, opposition to abortion was scattered and largely ineffective. The "regulars" associated with the AMA quickly got their feet under them, and by the beginning of the Civil War, they had launched an aggressive anti-abortion campaign. Once the AMA came to speak for a large part of the "respectable" medical community, it became a force capable of controlling abortion policy in the United States.

The AMA was steadfastly committed to outlawing the "irregulars" and the pharmacists while saving the "therapeutic exception" for themselves. After all, who could tell better than a "real doctor" when the continuation of a pregnancy was life-threatening? Between 1860 and 1880 the AMA's campaign to criminalize abortion began to have measurable results. Home medical guides, which had once discussed abortion techniques openly, were now silent or mentioned them only to condemn them. In the end, the AMA's effort to outlaw virtually all abortions met with total success. Their effort to drive the non-doctor abortionists out of business, on the other hand, did not. The abortionists simply went underground—a result as ironic as it was unintended. Now, with abortion illegal, it was mainly the underground abortionists, not the doctors, who were performing the procedure. One hundred years later the AMA, speaking *amicus curiae* in the 1970s court challenges to these same restrictive laws, spoke eloquently and persuasively of the compelling medical need to legalize abortion so that it would be safe.

The AMA was not solely responsible for the first wave of laws outlawing abortion. Some segments of organized religion, Protestant as well as Catholic, began to speak out about the "evils" of abortion. In 1869 Bishop Spaulding of Baltimore set forth what was to remain the official Catholic position for the next hundred years: "No mother is allowed, under any circumstances, to permit the death of her unborn infant, not even for the sake of preserving her own life." More influential, because of their greater numbers, were the Protestant denominations opposing abortion. Many Protestants feared that they would not keep up with the reproductive rates of Catholic immigrants, who tended to be opposed to both contraception and abortion. A leading Congregationalist characterized abortion as "fashionable murder."

The Presbyterians adopted a national resolution calling abortion "murder" and "a crime against God and nature."

In the 1870s Anthony Comstock's anti-obscenity movement gave the foes of abortion the final boost they needed for complete success in criminalizing abortion. Comstock was head of the New York Society for the Suppression of Vice. In 1873 he was sufficiently powerful to persuade Congress to pass an "Act for the Suppression of Trade in and Circulation of Obscene Literature and Articles of Immoral Use," allegedly intended to suppress the traffic in pornography. Under that law, it became a federal offense to sell, offer to sell, give away, offer to give away, or even possess with the intent to give away, a book, pamphlet, paper, advertisement, or anything else of "indecent or immoral nature." A similar ban extended to contraceptive devices and to any article or medicine that would cause an abortion, unless prescribed by a "physician in good standing"—a provision that gave doctors a powerful boost in their efforts to suppress their lay competitors. The law also made it a federal crime to write or print or cause to be written *any* information about how to obtain "obscene or indecent" articles or how to get an abortion.

"Comstockery," as it came to be called, did more than anything else to drive abortion underground, where it was to remain for nearly one hundred years. Comstock himself became a special agent of the federal government, charged with enforcing the act's provisions. In the 1870s he was the leading abortionist-hunter in the United States, basing his prosecutions primarily on charges of illegal advertising. In 1878 he arrested Madame Restell after buying an abortifacient from her. She committed suicide before her trial, making Comstock a hero in the crusade against abortion.

Between 1860 and 1880 a burst of legislative activity produced at least forty new anti-abortion statutes, thirteen of them in states that had never had anti-abortion laws. Most fostered the medical establishment's goal of absolute prohibition, under virtually all circumstances, no matter what the method, at any stage of pregnancy. Pennsylvania's abortion law, passed in 1860, made attempted abortion a crime even if the woman wasn't really pregnant. These new statutes made the woman liable, along with the abortionist and any advertiser or other provider of information. During this period, married women who desired to limit family size were said to be avoiding the responsibilities of married life and even to be living in a state of "legalized prostitution."

States, often led by their medical societies, began enacting their own anti-pornography "Comstock laws" to prevent publication of "obscene" advertisements. Aimed at the commercial abortionist, most of these laws had an anti-abortifacient clause as well. By 1880 the quickening distinction had all but disappeared from state anti-abortion laws, women seeking abortions were no longer victims but criminals, and the dissemination of any kind of abortion information was a crime. A decade later every state had an anti-abortion law.

By the turn of the century, most traditional physicians had been taught Lister's antiseptic techniques, so surgery and childbirth were immeasurably safer. So too would abortion have been if it had not disappeared from the open market. The medical community and the larger society had fallen under the spell of their own illusions. It was commonly believed that most women had been "educated" to reject abortion; that married women, conspicuous consumers fifty years earlier, had seen the error of their ways; and that only the unwilling victims of seduction, impregnated and then abandoned, sought abortions.

Conveniently, it seemed that the demand for abortion had disappeared at about the same time as the abortionists themselves. But the demand was by no means gone. Abortionists and unwillingly pregnant women had simply been driven underground, where they would remain, hidden and silent, for the next seventy years.

Today, in the last decade of the twentieth century, abortion has come to dominate the American political arena to a far greater degree than at any time prior to its legalization on January 22, 1973. On that date the United States Supreme Court, in two cases—*Roe v. Wade* and its lesser-known companion case, *Doe v. Bolton*—effectively struck down laws regulating abortion in all fifty states.

At the time, abortion laws in this country were of two main types: absolute prohibition or, in thirteen states, "reform" statutes based on the one proposed by the American Law Institute, a prestigious body of legal scholars charged with drafting model legislation on various topics. The reform statutes generally legalized abortion if women had the "right reasons." Examples of acceptable reasons were the possible impairment of a woman's life or health due to pregnancy, the presence of a fetal abnormality, or a pregnancy resulting from rape or incest. A small minority of states—New York, Hawaii, Alaska, and Washington—had newly enacted statutes that permitted abortion through the first portion of pregnancy, typically the first twenty weeks, without regard to the woman's reasons.

In *Roe v. Wade,* a challenge to an absolute-prohibition statute in

Texas, the Supreme Court held that in the first trimester of pregnancy, a state could not restrict a woman's right to have an abortion for any reason; in the second trimester, a state could impose restrictions reasonably related to protecting the woman's health; and in the third trimester, a state could prohibit abortion unless it was necessary to save the woman's life. In *Doe v. Bolton*, a challenge to a Georgia reform statute permitting abortion in cases of rape, incest, and fetal abnormality, the Court held that the reform laws suffered from the same constitutional defects as the prohibition statutes.

The *Roe* decision, which gave women much greater control over their bodies as a matter of right, was based in large measure on the right of privacy implicit in the Constitution. Speaking for a majority of the Court, Justice Harry Blackmun stated, "We recognize the right of the individual, married or single, to be free from unwarranted governmental intrusion into matters so fundamentally affecting a person as the decision whether to bear or beget a child. That right necessarily includes the right of a woman to decide whether or not to terminate her pregnancy." Sharing his view were Chief Justice Warren Burger and Justices William O. Douglas, William Brennan, Thurgood Marshall, Lewis Powell, and Potter Stewart. Justices William Rehnquist and Byron White dissented.

Overnight, American women had a constitutional guarantee of safe medical care for abortions. A legislative pronouncement can be revoked within a month or even a week, but a Supreme Court decision is much more durable. This one told the states and Congress that they could enact no law that would impinge on the constitutional right of control and choice in reproductive matters, guaranteed by the federal Constitution.

The decade preceding *Roe* had seen the politicizing of abortion. State legislative battles raged as abortion bills were introduced and reluctant lawmakers were forced to take a stand on the issue. It is estimated that perhaps as many as 70 percent of elected public officials had no particular feelings about abortion. Most desperately hoped that they would not have to express an opinion on the issue, since whatever they said was guaranteed to alienate a substantial bloc of voters.

Roe brought a period of political insulation. Confronted by opponents of legal abortion, politicians could safely if not truthfully say, "I agree with you, but what can I do? The courts have spoken." But on July 3, 1989—more than sixteen years after the landmark *Roe* ruling—the United States Supreme Court put abortion back in the political spotlight with its decision in *Webster v. Reproductive Health Services, Inc.*

While declining to overturn *Roe*, the court held that the Missouri statute regulating abortion, including its preamble stating that life begins at conception, did not place an unconstitutional obstacle in the path of women seeking abortions. If the Missouri restriction was a "constitutionally sound obstacle," might there not be others? The search was on.

The goal of opponents of legal abortion is a revisiting and reversal of *Roe v. Wade* so that states can recriminalize abortion if they choose to do so. In the interim, however, finding those constitutionally permissible limits, impediments, and deterrents has become the order of the day in this last decade of the twentieth century. In upholding constitutionally valid roadblocks to abortion without specifying what they are, *Webster* presented an open invitation to test for the soft spots in *Roe*.

In the wake of *Webster*, dozens of new abortion bills were introduced in state legislatures. These proposed laws were largely based on the National Right-to-Life Committee's model measures and typically included such provisions as forbidding abortion as a means of birth control or sex selection. Some called for a return to the rape, incest, and other "socially correct" criteria of the late 1960s. Some mandated "informed consent." Quite unlike informed consent for other surgical procedures, this version would require women to view information about fetal development and alternatives to abortion, and to wait an additional twenty-four hours before having an abortion, over and above the days or weeks that have already gone by.

Bills to limit young women's access to abortion by requiring parental consent or notification became another popular tactic, along with proposals stipulating that a woman's husband or partner be notified and permitted to have a hearing before she can have an abortion. Since the Supreme Court has already ruled that the biological father cannot have veto power, it is unclear what purpose, other than harassment and delay, such hearings would serve.

A common theme of state legislation—and one upheld in *Webster*—is a provision preventing or limiting the use of public funds, facilities, or personnel in the performance of abortions. This drying up of access to medical care can be very effective in forcing women, especially poor women or women in rural areas, back to illegal abortionists. Bills to restrict the use of fetal tissue in medical treatment or research, and bills that criminalize certain behaviors of pregnant women, such as drug use or alcohol consumption, are not directly related to the central goal of limiting access to abortion, but they are frequently combined with other restrictive provisions.

By April 1990, less than a year after *Webster*, three restrictive abortion laws had been passed, in Pennsylvania, Guam, and South Carolina. By March 1991 there were three more, in North Dakota, Mississippi, and Utah. The first of these new restrictive laws to reach the Supreme Court was *Planned Parenthood v. Casey*. At issue in this challenge to the constitutionality of the Pennsylvania Abortion Control Act of 1982 were several of the restrictions promoted by abortion opponents after the *Webster* decision: "informed consent," a twenty-four hour waiting period, spousal notification, and consent of one parent or court approval for minors.

The Supreme Court that heard *Planned Parenthood v. Casey* was a very different body from the Supreme Court that heard *Roe v. Wade*. The composition of the Court has changed dramatically since 1973. Of the original *Roe* majority, only Justice Blackmun remains. The two *Roe* dissenters are still on the Court, and Mr. Rehnquist is now chief justice. There have been six post-*Roe* additions to the Court: John Paul Stevens, Sandra Day O'Connor, Antonin Scalia, Anthony Kennedy, David Souter, and Clarence Thomas—all but one appointees of Ronald Reagan or George Bush, both of whom seem to have made opposition to legal abortion a litmus test for the federal judiciary.

On June 29, 1992, the Supreme Court handed down its decision in *Casey*. Speaking for the Court, Justice O'Connor, joined by Justices Kennedy and Souter, insisted that the "central right" recognized by *Roe* was still the law of the land, but they rejected the *Roe* trimester standard. (Only two justices, Blackmun and Stevens, would have retained it.) Instead they established a new constitutional standard, the "undue burden" test, hinted at in *Webster* and now articulated: "An undue burden exists, and therefore a provision of law is invalid, if its purpose or effect is to place a substantial obstacle in the path of a woman seeking an abortion before the fetus attains viability." What constitutes a "substantial obstacle" remains to be answered by future legal challenges.

The fundamental right guaranteed by *Roe v. Wade* was seriously crippled by the *Casey* decision. Still more alarming, Chief Justice Rehnquist and Justices White, Scalia, and Thomas declared in their dissent that they believe *Roe v. Wade* should be overturned.

In his dissent in *Webster*, Justice Blackmun wrote, "I fear for the future. I fear for the liberty and equality of the millions of women who have lived and come of age in the sixteen years since *Roe* was decided. . . . For today, at least, the law of abortion stands undisturbed. . . but the signs are evident and very ominous, and a chill wind blows." Three years later, in *Casey*, his words were more urgent: "I am eighty-three years old. I cannot remain on this Court forever, and when I do step down, the confirmation process for my successor well may focus on the issue before us today. That, I regret, may be exactly where the choice between the two worlds will be made."

Whether the coming years will see a reversal of *Roe*, a slow erosion, or a standoff on the Court is not yet clear. But whichever it is, legislators can expect continued confrontation in the political arena over abortion issues. The majority of legislators who do not themselves have strong convictions on the issue long for a compromise position. They will not likely find one, for abortion is less amenable to compromise than any social issue in the last hundred years. If one believes that abortion is murder, then even rape, incest, or any other tragic circumstance cannot justify it. If one believes that just as an acorn is not an oak tree, a fetus is not a person, or that in a pluralistic society each woman is entitled to make this determination for herself, it is unconscionable to deprive her of access to safe medical care or to make such access dependent on the social correctness of her reasons. While one side says, "Abortion can never be justified," the other responds with equal vehemence, "State-enforced compulsory pregnancy can never be justified."

What *is* clear is that women will continue to have abortions, legally or otherwise.

APPENDIX B

UNDERGROUND ABORTION

No one knows how many women needlessly died from illegal abortions, but we do know to what desperate remedies they subjected their bodies. The abortion techniques of the underground must surely seem barbaric to a generation unfamiliar with abortions except as performed legally in hospitals and clinics since 1973. The complications resulting from illegal abortion, which seem more like battlefield injuries, are equally frightening. Perhaps even more startling to the modern observer is the frequency of underground abortion. It may comfort voters and policymakers to pretend that if we simply outlaw abortion, it will stop happening. That is not so. It will only become invisible again, and infinitely more dangerous.

FREQUENCY OF UNDERGROUND ABORTION

For one simple reason, the frequency of underground abortion cannot be accurately determined: like any illegal activity, it was carried out clandestinely. Income from illegal abortions was not reported on tax returns. "Abortionist" was not an occupational category in government statistical data, and if it had been, most people wouldn't have listed it, even if they did consider it their primary occupation. During the period of illegality, abortionists did not advertise themselves in the Yellow Pages or elsewhere. There were no colleges or trade schools teaching abortion techniques to a quantifiable number of future practitioners. Abortionists did not report to appropriate governmental agencies charged with monitoring their activities.

The best indications of the frequency of underground abortion are analyses of other phenomena that can be measured with some degree of reliability, such as contraceptive failure rates and hospital admissions for post-abortion complications. Unofficial reported levels of the profitability of various activities of organized crime provide further information. For example, in the decade immediately preceding legalization, the annual "take" for underground abortionists has been estimated at more than $350,000,000, the third-largest illegal money-maker in the United States, exceeded only by narcotics and gambling—not unlike our national experience with Prohibition.

Estimates of the annual incidence of illegal abortion in the United States during the underground period range from the hundreds of thousands to more than a million. In 1934 Dr. M. E. Kopp published a report on 10,000 women at the Margaret Sanger Birth Control Clinic in New York between 1925 and 1929. In that five-year period there were 38,985 pregnancies, resulting in 27,813 live births and 11,172 abortions, or one abortion for every 2.5 births. Further, 5,000 of the women—50 percent—admitted to having had prior abortions. In 1936 Dr. Frederick J. Taussig, professor of clinical obstetrics and gynecology at Washington University School of Medicine in St. Louis, estimated that there were 681,600 abortions per year in the United States.

In 1955 Planned Parenthood held a national conference on abortion attended by physicians and other health care professionals who had treated septic abortion or otherwise observed demographic evidence of illegal abortion, usually in the form of recorded hospital admissions for post-abortion complications. It was the consensus of the conference that there were 200,000 to 1,200,000 abortions a year in America at the time. Most of the participants believed the figure to be between 800,000 and 1,000,000. In each year since legalization, with accurate reporting possible, the annual average has been somewhat in excess of 1,000,000 abortions.

Perhaps the best check on pre-1973 abortion estimates is women's own after-the-fact testimony, at a time and for a purpose such that they would have little motive to lie. In his 1955 survey of the sexual behavior of the American female, Dr. Kinsey reported that 22 percent of all married women said they had had at least one abortion by age forty-five, and that the average number of abortions was not one but two over the course of the women's reproductive life.

UNDERGROUND ABORTION TECHNIQUES

The abortion techniques used during the American underground period of 1900 to 1973, and earlier, can essentially be grouped into three categories: (1) noninvasive "activity," such as hot baths or strenuous exercise; (2) ingestion of a chemical or herbal substance believed to have abortifacient (abortion-causing) properties; and (3) invasive mechanical or surgical techniques. The physician-abortionist was more likely to do a curettage, or surgical scraping, while the lay abortionist and the self-abortionist were more likely to introduce a foreign object or substance into the uterus or to use an oral medication or chemical.

The activity approach was attractive to women because it required no medication, surgery, or mechanical invasion. Better yet, it cost nothing and generally did not involve third parties. "Information" about various activities was widely repeated from one generation to another and one woman to another. There was one major drawback—the activities did not work.

Most of these commonly recommended "sure cures" reflected the biases or beliefs of the time. Ice cold showers and hot baths were popular in an era when daily bathing, so impractical, was believed unnecessary, even dangerous, and therefore capable of inducing abortion. What we might call the "violent movements" approach—jumping, falling, reaching too high, lifting heavy weights, doing somersaults, and even "joking and prolonged laughter"—was perhaps influenced by the Victorian belief in female delicacy. Although we may question the motives of the recommending source, "vigorous sex" was also deemed effective.

Then there was bloodletting, which doesn't really fit into any of the three categories. Long after it had fallen into disfavor as a treatment for a host of other human conditions, bloodletting remained a common abortion treatment, perhaps because it produced a sort of "surrogate" menstrual period.

Once a woman had exhausted the activity approach (or vice versa), she could choose from an astonishing array of chemical and herbal teas, nostrums, poultices, and pills touted as home remedies for abortion. Among the herbs rumored to cause abortions were angelica, snakeroot, savin, gentian, mayapple, jalup, tansy, hellebore, squaw vine, squaw root, squill, ash bark, cottonroot, biting smartweed, foxglove, hemlock, pennyroyal, and rue. Desperate women also resorted to ergot, quinine, opium, and belladonna. At best, these various home remedies were ineffective. At worst, they were dangerous or even fatal.

Some popular substances, like opium and belladonna, were simply mood-alterers or pain-killers that may have made women feel better but probably never caused an abortion. Some were true abortifacients that could end a pregnancy, usually by producing uterine contractions. In this category are pennyroyal, rue, quinine, and ergot. Ergot, the most powerful, is frequently used in more traditional medical settings to induce labor late in pregnancy. It is also a powerful hemostatic agent, meaning that it arrests or slows the flow of blood through the vessels. (Ergot was probably the cause of the peculiar sensations Paula experienced in her legs; see p. 224.) As the women who tried it discovered, however, ergot is generally ineffective when taken early in pregnancy.

Some herbs, among them angelica, savin, and tansy, are emmenagogues—substances capable of producing a menstrual discharge. These may have been effective abortifacients if the discharge was sufficiently powerful to carry the fetus along with it. More commonly, however, they produced a much-desired menstrual period without affecting the pregnancy at all. Some were nothing more than emetics capable of causing violent nausea or diarrhea.

It is now clear that many of these substances can be extremely toxic. Hemlock is a well-known poison. Angelica is a suspected carcinogen. In high doses tansy can cause convulsions and even death. If a woman was trying to abort herself with home-grown herbs, she would have no way of knowing the concentration or toxicity of what she was ingesting. Even if she knew, as in the case of ergot or quinine obtained from the drugstore in pill form, she may not have cared. A desperate woman might well reason, "If one pill doesn't work, five may."

Among the more hazardous underground abortion methods was the ingestion of substances known to be toxic to the fetus: lead, mercury, phosphorus, prussic acid, and strychnine. Alas, they were toxic to the woman as well, though if she was lucky, not fatally so. The fetus is particularly vulnerable to lead. Indeed, abortion is a known health hazard for pregnant female workers in the lead industry. Nostrums such as Mrs. Wardell's Pills were mainly lead.

All of the invasive mechanical or surgical abortion techniques involve the introduction of a foreign body or substance into the uterus. However, there is considerable variation in the degree of invasion: anything from a slight penetration into the cervix or neck of the uterus with the tip of a catheter to the scraping of the uterine wall. The more invasive and disruptive the procedure, the more likely it is to cause an abortion—and the greater the risk of perforation or other complications, including severe hemorrhage and infection.

Many lay abortionists used douches of Clorox, pine oil, turpentine, Lysol, or plain soapy water, a popular favorite. These solutions were inserted, by means of a catheter or syringe, through the cervix into the uterus, which contracts in the presence of a foreign and irritating substance. In an effort to expel the offending substance, the uterus, it was hoped, would expel the fetus as well.

Potassium permanganate, sometimes in crystalline or tablet form, sometimes dissolved in a solution, was also widely used to induce abortions. Like soapy water, potassium permanganate is an irritant that the uterus seeks to expel, but unlike soapy water, it is highly caustic and in its dry concentrated form can cause severe chemical burns and bleeding if it comes in contact with moist flesh. A woman who had the potassium permanganate solution inserted into her uterus might well have aborted. The unfortunate woman who inserted the dry tablet or crystal into her vagina would have experienced severe chemical burns while remaining pregnant.

Another invasive technique involves foreign material that draws moisture from surrounding body tissues. Inserted into the neck of the uterus, such material—slippery elm, a dehydrated tree bark, and laminaria, a dried seaweed, for example—enlarges as it absorbs fluid, causing the cervix to dilate, which in turn, in combination with the presence of the foreign object, causes the uterus to contract, evacuating its contents.

The mechanical methods can be ranked in terms of the level of sophistication and skill they require. The least sophisticated techniques were typically used by the least skilled—the self-abortionist, perhaps aided by her equally unskilled partner or best friend. Women who were too poor or too frightened to go to an abortionist, or didn't know how to find one, resorted to inserting common household objects into the uterus: crochet hooks, knitting needles, hatpins, curtain rods, screwdrivers, chopsticks, coat hangers, bicycle spokes, umbrella ribs. One farm woman is reported to have successfully aborted herself twenty-eight times with a goose quill dipped in kerosene.

The most commonly used foreign body was the catheter, readily available in drugstores without a prescription. Sometimes a metal stylet was threaded through the catheter so that the tip would be rigid enough to insert through the cervix. Often a coat hanger served the same purpose.

Underground abortionists used two main catheter techniques.

Sometimes they inserted the catheter and then removed it almost immediately. With this method, the foreign substance the uterus tries to expel is not the catheter but the infection it leaves behind, though in some cases the uterus contracts simply in response to the irritation caused by the introduction of the catheter. The other, more reliable technique was to insert the catheter and leave it in place until the woman actually aborted, hours or days later. This method is almost always effective, since a catheter is too large and too invasive an object to be ignored by a pregnant uterus. From the viewpoint of the abortionist, though, there was a slight disadvantage. The catheter could not be reused because the woman left with it.

In the early 1960s women began forming self-help groups to teach themselves how to do abortions through the technique of menstrual extraction—in some ways a throwback to an earlier time when women handled all such "female matters" among themselves, without the knowledge or involvement of men. Menstrual extraction is a low-budget variant of the aspiration syringe suction method, which was widely promoted in developing countries in the late 1960s as a cheap, easy procedure.

In this "home" abortion technique, a sterile cannula, about the length and circumference of a soda straw, is attached to plastic aquarium tubing, which is inserted into one hole of a two-hole rubber stopper in a mason jar. Plastic tubing in the second hole is attached to a syringe that provides the necessary suction when the plunger is pulled back. With the aid of a flashlight and a speculum, the cannula is inserted into the uterus until it reaches the uterine wall. Then one operator slowly moves the cannula back and forth across the uterine wall while the other operator gently pumps the syringe, creating a vacuum in the mason jar. The contents of the uterus are removed and pass through the cannula into the mason jar in a process that takes from ten to thirty minutes.

Menstrual extraction is possible only in the early stages—approximately the first eight weeks—of pregnancy. It is not really a do-it-yourself abortion technique, since it takes two people to operate the equipment. Further, because the procedure is painful and slow, it is highly unlikely that either of the operators will be the pregnant woman herself.

Today women are once again teaching each other how to perform menstrual extractions. Meanwhile, in a return to the united front of the 1800s, the anti-abortionists and the established medical community condemn menstrual extraction. Both Operation Rescue and the American College of Obstetricians and Gynecologists claim that it is highly dangerous in the hands of laypeople. They may well be right, but if medically safe abortions are not available, American women may have no alternative.

ABORTION COMPLICATIONS

Any medical procedure, even the simplest, involves a risk of mishap, including a possibly fatal mishap. Penicillin shots, routinely administered to millions of Americans, have a mortality rate of approximately 1.1 per 100,000. The mortality rate for normal childbirth is approximately 6.6 per 100,000. Legal abortion has a mortality rate of 0.5 per 100,000.

Before the introduction of antibiotics and more effective emergency medical treatments for acutely ill post-abortion patients, underground abortion had a mortality rate of 500 per 100,000, according to some estimates of both recorded and concealed abortion deaths. It is possible that during the earlier part of the underground period as many as 5,000 American women died each year as a direct result of illegal abortions.

By 1950, when antibiotics were widely available, the number of reported abortion-related deaths in the United States was 316. Starting in the mid to late 1960s, the figure dropped further as greater numbers of women had access to safe abortions performed by physicians in more appropriate medical settings.

Although illegal abortion poses many risks, the most serious are perforation of the uterus, hemorrhage, an air or chemical embolism, infection, septicemia, and septic shock. Moreover, a woman who survives a serious infection may be left sterile as a result of scarring.

Whenever a foreign body—catheter, coat hanger, knitting needle, or any similar rigid object—is inserted into the uterus, there is the risk of a life-threatening perforation of the uterine wall. Perforation can cause hemorrhaging and can lead to peritonitis if the object has also punctured the bowel, releasing fecal material into the body cavity.

The term "septic abortion" refers to an abortion complicated by an infection. Infections are caused by the presence of nonsterile foreign objects in the uterus. Soapy water or a finger can produce such infections as easily as a coat hanger can. Infections may be localized—in the fallopian tubes, ovaries, uterus, or vagina—or may have spread throughout the body, involving organs outside the reproductive tract. The more widespread the infection, the more dangerous it is.

Septicemia is a condition in which infection is so advanced that bacteria or their toxins have invaded the bloodstream and are circulating throughout the body. It is accompanied by chills, profuse sweating, intermittent fever, and severe weakness. Septic shock occurs when the body is so overwhelmed by infection that there is a general circulatory collapse. Blood pressure drops. The skin is pale and clammy. The pulse is rapid but feeble. Respiration slows, and the patient may lose consciousness. Often there is kidney or liver failure. Historically, families and doctors have used this massive shutdown of other systems to conceal abortion deaths by listing renal failure, for example, as the cause of death—true in a technical sense, but certainly misleading.

As I have said, the types of infection associated with abortion complications are startling in that they seem more like battlefield traumas than gynecological problems. Anaerobic bacteria, which flourish without air, often find that the uterus is an ideal new home. These organisms all produce highly toxic substances and catastrophic septicemia if they get into the bloodstream. One variant causes tetanus. Another causes gas gangrene. Here, the tissue becomes discolored and red. The bacteria produce a gas. As the tissue rots, a foul-smelling odor oozes from the area. Death usually results from the bacterial toxins in the bloodstream.

Sometimes the infecting organism is staphylococcus, the great pus-producer found in boils and cysts. If a staph infection goes untreated and gets into the bloodstream, overwhelming septic shock is a likely result.

An air bubble or embolism is a common complication of underground abortion. Generally, air is introduced accidentally when the abortionist is using a technique that involves squirting a solution into the uterus. Air trapped in tubing or a syringe may be forced into the uterus and into a blood vessel as the fluid is introduced. If the embolus is big enough and if it makes its way to the heart and lungs, instant death occurs. Sometimes the embolus is not air but fat or other oily substances from a soapy solution. It doesn't matter. The end result is the same: death.

When abortion is illegal, a woman who suffers complications is unlikely to give her doctor a complete and accurate medical history. Unless the evidence is blatant or the symptoms are classic or acute, the doctor may be hampered in his efforts to treat her. When abortion is illegal, a woman who suffers complications faces the impossible choice of risking serious legal consequences if she tells the truth or serious medical consequences if she doesn't. If she is lucky, the wrong choice is not fatal.

If we are determined and organized, no woman in America will ever have to face that choice again.